Cities for a small country

First published in 2000
by Faber and Faber Limited
3 Queen Square London
WC 1N 3AU

Typeset by Steven Gardiner Ltd,
Cambridge
Printed by the University Press,
Cambridge

A CIP record for this book is
available from the British Library

ISBN 0–571–20652–2

2 4 6 8 10 9 7 5 3 1

Cities for a small country

Richard Rogers
and Anne Power

ff

faber and faber

Contents

Foreword
by Will Hutton

Judge a civilisation by its cities. They are where most people live. They are where they work, associate, recreate, politic, scheme and love. Where parliaments meet and newspapers are written. Where theatres are watched and business deals done. Where life is lived. This is not to disparage or undervalue the countryside; just to acknowledge the reality that cities are the pulsating heart of modern life. If they function well, so does the civilisation they embody; if they do not, then the civilisation ails.

Yet the British, and the English especially, have rarely taken their cities seriously. Urban life is regarded as something that has to be suffered; the real McCoy is the country. When poets celebrate England, they celebrate its hedgerows, flowers and countryside. The tumult of the city is to be deplored and avoided. There is little expectation that its streets might be pleasurable and its public spaces appealing. It is the world beyond that reflects our real selves.

This book is predicated on a very different assumption. It believes that if we want to live better and richer lives in every sense – from the vitality of our democracy to the health of our society – then a crucial and indispensable precondition is well-functioning and well-designed cities that encourage the full panoply of human association rather than deter it. Whether it is the contemporary renaissance of Barcelona or the pride Victorian and Georgian Britain took in quality cities, the message is the same. The good life and quality urban design are intertwined.

You may think this almost a truism not worth stating, but in British terms it is almost revolutionary. I know at first hand the reaction of ministers and senior officials to the Urban Task Force's report on which this book is based. Apart from an honourable minority they regard it as largely misconceived. They don't understand how anyone could believe that the pace of wealth creation and degree of social inclusion are integrally related to the physical structure of cities. For example one of the key arguments in *Cities for a Small Country* – that sprawling green-field suburban development has direct and reciprocally poor consequences for the inner city and thus on its economic and social conditions – is a proposition that they just don't 'get'. What matters is good schools, cheap public transport and interventions to make the labour market work. The physical backdrop against which these efforts are mounted matter not one jot.

Of course, such initiatives are part of the story of redress. The minimum wage, the New

Deal and the new resources allocated to transport and schools, for example, are all welcome and important – but they will not solve Britain's urban crisis on their own. The problems besetting many inner city comprehensive schools are a case in point. The socially-balanced neighbourhood comprehensive is a noble idea and, where it works, probably the least-bad form of secondary education. But such comprehensives can only be constructed if their catchment areas are socially balanced. If the bulk of their pupils come from low-income, socially-distressed homes the schools become educational sinks with results that we all know.

Yet socially-balanced neighbourhoods do not naturally appear as a result of market forces; indeed markets tend to polarise unequal neighbourhoods rather as they polarise incomes. They have to be constructed and designed, and one of the best means of creating them is to require that living densities are higher in our cities, so the range of income groups is necessarily living more on top of one another and school catchment areas become less dependent on one income group. Yet argue that education, planning policy and city architecture are interconnected and the mainstream economic and political establishment will regard you as coming from Mars.

Yet the argument is not lost. The ideas in this book do have some champions in high places. Part of the task of the pages ahead is to offer some intellectual robustness to the arguments and to democratise them so they can be understood by the average citizen – and in so doing to stregthen the case of those who believe that an urban renaissance is the key not merely to more economic and social success, but to our individual fulfilment as citizens and human beings. I believe that arguments matter, that culture and policy are made in tens of thousands of conversations; and that books like this, informing those conversations, can really make a difference. I hope you read it; hope you agree; and hope you join the struggle for better.

Preface

The government set up the Urban Task Force in 1998 to work out how to tackle the challenge of providing around four million additional homes over the next twenty-five years in England. Re-using brown-field sites – land that has already been built on in some way – is central. This book is a follow-up to the Urban Task Force report and pushes the frontier of cities forward. Our work developed against a backdrop of urban fragmentation, growing abandonment of inner cities and erosion of the countryside.

As architect and community organiser we first met and worked together on council estates in the Isle of Dogs, seeing the interactive problems of design and community pressure through similar and yet very different eyes. We both searched for what we could do to help beleaguered low-income communities. This book results from sixteen years of working together in cities and communities, attempting to help people and make places better.

We use England as our main test-bed, but we draw on much wider examples and hope that our ideas will apply in many cities and communities both here and abroad. We could not cover everything in a short book. We have concentrated on the problems we are most familiar with and the solutions we believe are most do-able.

Many people have helped us, particularly the Urban Task Force. Some have played a special role: Andrew Wright, Peter Hall, Martin Crookston, Wendy Thomson, Phil Kirby, Alan Cherry, Lorna Walker and Jon Rouse. Staff at the London School of Economics helped in many ways. John Hills, Ruth Lupton, Katharine Mumford, Becky Tunstall and Maria Stasiak gave detailed comments, advice and suggestions; Michael Kennedy, Paula O'Brien, Nina Woods, Rebecca Morris and Jane Dickson gave endless help with the text, charts and references; Nicola Harrison, Ricky Burdett and Caroline Paskell provided exceptional editorial assistance, research and illustrations. The Joseph Rowntree Foundation generously supported the research. Sharmans and the National Park Office, Glenridding, helped transmit drafts. John Roberts of DETR, Jo Murtagh, Alex Blum and Julian Loose offered constant support. Maurice Brennan gave invaluable advice. Chris Holmes of Shelter and Alan Holmans of Cambridge University made helpful suggestions. Any mistakes are ours.

We must finally thank the hundreds of organisations that have willingly provided information on urban conditions. Without their practical co-operation our task would have been impossible.

1   Introduction – what is the future of cities?

1 Barcelona, an industrial city that has revived after decades of decay, did so by galvanising its citizens around the idea of an urban spaces project. In 1979, it elected its first local government for forty years, after two generations of the Franco dictatorship and bitter struggles over the suppression of the Catalan language and culture. The port – one of the largest and oldest in the Mediterranean – was in steep decline, the centre city was degraded and the newer suburbs were unintegrated. The city's urban renewal team, led by architect Oriol Bohigas from the University of Barcelona, wanted to restore the city's compact character by creating or renovating at least one open space in every neighbourhood. Between 1981 and 1987, a hundred public spaces emerged across Barcelona, from the centre to the fringes, from the poorest to the richest neighbourhoods. Throughout the entire city, local people were involved in the process.[1]

Barcelona is Spain's second city and has 1.7 million inhabitants. It is a city of extraordinary density – about four hundred dwellings to the hectare in the central areas, compared with one hundred to two hundred in central London and fifty to seventy in the inner city – with tall, six-storey apartments abutting on to the pavements and the narrow streets, some of which are too tiny for cars. Barcelona has an impressive architectural heritage, including the church of the Sagrada Familia, and other masterpieces by Gaudí, Foster and many more. The city has a medieval core and a closely woven nineteenth-century grid pattern, created by Cerda, the famous planner, that continues uninterrupted to the sea's edge. This has encouraged a mixture of activities at street level and above that, multiple apartments looking down into small courtyards. Only Glasgow adopted a similar grid pattern in Britain.[2]

With its long seafront and high mountainous backdrop, Barcelona has little room for manoeuvre, so the new plans could not demolish buildings or displace people and activities from the surrounding

▲ *page ix*

Constellation of cities at night in Europe
W T Sullivan III and *Hansen Planetarium/Science Photo Library*

▲ *previous page*

Cerda's tight nineteenth-century grid plan for Barcelona
Barcelona City Council

◄ High-quality public realm, Manchester
Manchester City Council

◄ A traditional, dense, urban
neighbourhood in Barceloneta
John Hills

streets. The aim was to minimise suburban expansion because it consumes energy and takes up land.[3] Resources were limited – unemployment was high and the Spanish economy weak – so care and conservation were central to success. Each open-space project worked within the confines of what was there already. This helped to minimise costs and to show visible improvements within a short time frame.

Around the tightly packed medieval core, a small *placeta* – a mini-square – might be carved out of the crowded streets with two or three benches and a small fountain to underline its public character. The car park outside the main station became a public pedestrian square. Most famously, the run-down old port became a magnet for the entire city's habit of strolling late into the evening, with new promontories, designer footbridges, restaurants and restored ancient paving intermingled along the seafront.

The socialist mayor Pasqual Maragall, elected in 1982, and his two successors put their weight behind the urban spaces project, encouraging an unusual level of experimentation and architectural investment. Maragall was able to advance Barcelona's successful bid for the 1992 Olympic Games because this re-instatement of city spaces rapidly led to city-wide regeneration, eventually involving the whole metropolitan area. The polluted and largely disused docks area was dramatically transformed into five kilometres of new beaches, marinas and promenades as well as the Olympic Village. The new housing, once uncomfortably stark, has become 'greened', and the seafront now truly belongs to the landscape and to the sunbathers and strollers. But as the new Barcelona wears in with the old, it continues to draw Olympic-size crowds, who come to be part of a vibrant, new and democratic city that is reclaiming its streets.

Barcelona has become an international showplace not because it is a typical tourist city – it is a regional capital facing the familiar

▲ Barcelona: aerial view of the waterfront before regeneration

▲ Barcelona: aerial view of the Olympic village after regeneration

◄ Barcelona: new beach and compact neighbourhood reclaimed from derelict shore (architects Elias Torres and JA Martinez Lapena)

problems of decay in both its physical environment and its economic base. Its revival has generated enthusiasm because participation is genuine and progress is visible. People want to be on the streets of the city because they feel safe; in the 1990s crime fell in every neighbourhood of Barcelona, including the poorest. A 1998 survey of residents found a much greater sense of belonging since the changes, particularly to their immediate neighbourhood.[4]

The secret of Barcelona's success lies in certain key ideas: going with the grain of the existing city, which is dense, compact, old and bounded by mountains and sea; using the development of public spaces as a way of involving citizens of all incomes and classes; delivering local projects in every neighbourhood within a much bigger strategic plan; making people feel involved and proud of their city; creating a powerful consensus across parties and sectors that would last beyond the next election; using the highest design talent. Barcelona has kept up the momentum by constantly creating new targets, by drawing in international advisers, and by asking an international panel of architects and artists to vet all new projects.[5]

Where Barcelona triumphed as a regional capital, Manchester lost out. Like Barcelona, it bid for the Olympics, but failed. Bad weather is against Manchester, but so too is a bad attitude towards city life. Manchester is the oldest industrial city in the world and centre of the largest industrial region in Europe. It is now being gradually transformed. But the earliest industrial buildings ever built, only a ten-minute walk from the reviving city centre, are literally falling down, helped by vandals, while the city amasses resources to go ahead with the next and most critical phase of recovery. It could be too late, for thousands of acres of Manchester's inner neighbourhoods are losing people and property. Confidence dissipates in a climate of such steep, continuing decline.[6]

Manchester lost out in other ways too: its weak metropolitan government was abolished in 1985, creating a group of competing local authorities. With its tightly drawn boundaries, Manchester has become one large, impoverished inner city, struggling to revive its core within a ring of decayed, disinvested and evacuated inner neighbourhoods, while the richer suburbs are governed separately.[7]

If you arrive at Manchester's main railway station in the evening, there is no visible information point or city guide to help you. Nor are there crowds in the streets. Walking through the largely deserted centre will feel slightly threatening to someone who does not know the city. The occasional bar, restaurant or club does not make up for the emptiness of many of the streets. This is the opposite of a reborn city. But if you are lucky, you may discover, buried away in the steep, dark streets leading down to the old docks, a new hotel in a restored warehouse. Sleeping in a gigantic converted Victorian building and waking up beside the slow, inky waters of the River Irwell turns out to be exciting and totally unexpected. It signals a reversal of decay.

There are other green shoots in Manchester. The terrorist bombing of the city's ugly modern shopping centre in 1996 gave new momentum to the plans already in train. The heavy, enclosed 1960s architecture was irreparably damaged. In its place, large squares have been opened up, surrounded by the monumental architecture of Manchester's public buildings. The shopping streets give pedestrians priority and are now competing strongly with nearby Trafford's giant shopping mall. Such developments had threatened to turn Manchester inside out, but major stores have now begun to opt for the city centre.

Manchester is the first city in Britain to relay tramlines across its centre, and there is an ambitious plan to link up with the surrounding cotton towns and wealthier suburbs. The universities, one of the biggest concentrations of higher education in the country, offer

▲ Manchester: the bomb that
wrecked the city centre, 1996
*Manchester City Council Special
Projects Office*

$\frac{1}{10}$

▲ Manchester: new public
squares, 1999
*Manchester City Council Special
Projects Office*

youthful talent and the potential for science parks. The introduction of super-fast *pendolino* rail links to the south and Scotland in the next five years may attract desperately needed inward investment and kill at last the prejudice that Manchester is 'too far and too decayed'.[8]

Like Barcelona, Manchester is an atmospheric place. The dense network of canals, warehouses and office buildings dating from the first industrial revolution give the central parts of the city a unique character. We cannot rebuild Barcelona in Britain – but can we rebuild confidence in dense, thriving, shared cities? Businesses and residents are moving back into Manchester's heart. For the first time in a century, the centre is growing in population and new apartments are selling before they are finished, even though the city overall is still losing people.[9]

Many argue that we cannot and should not try to make people's choices for them. If they vote with their feet and their wallets to build in the countryside, then that's life. We take a different view. People originally fled the city because of overcrowding, ill health and squalor. In response, cities improved. But we have now reached the point where they have become too physically dispersed, too traffic-bound and too socially polarised. People often leave cities today because they are too depleted – as Manchester certainly is. On the whole, it is the better-off who move out, leaving behind marginalised communities. Yet cities need a mixture of incomes and activities if they are to thrive. People will move back into well-planned, well-managed city neighbourhoods.

Some cities face the opposite problem: over-rapid growth. The new global high-tech and knowledge-based economy means that international cities are prospering. But their success generates serious environmental and social pressures, intense competition for space and a constant squeeze on poorer people. Again, richer people can buy their way out of these problems. But modern cities simply cannot work without people who will do the service jobs on which the new economy depends. New York, London, Paris, Amsterdam, Rome, Berlin, Shanghai, Tokyo, Jakarta and Mexico City all have third-world communities within first-world capitals.[10] Solving the problems of land, transport and social cohesion within such vast and rapidly changing cities has defeated local authorities and citizens world-wide. Yet we can learn some lessons from the international cities that do work. After decades of violence, decay and filth, New York has made its parks, streets and subways feel safe as the result of eight years of intense reforming effort. There is a new pride, and the streets are humming with people. London does not have New York's problems to start with, so New York's success in driving through change makes us more confident that we can succeed.

Smaller and more self-contained cities experiment more because they can be more participatory: for example, Copenhagen, Portland, San Francisco, Rotterdam, Lyon and Curitiba. These cities are pioneering new approaches to public space, public transport, compact mixed development, social integration, environmental care, density and constrained land use. Over the past twenty years Copenhagen has stopped the growth of cars, whereas traffic is strangling most other European cities.[11] By favouring buses, trams, bicycles, and pedestrians while incrementally reducing parking spaces, Denmark's capital has made its streets more inviting, more populated, more sociable.

Cities that succeed in meeting the transport needs of a modern economy and reducing traffic are the cities of the future. The same applies to housing. Cities that manage to provide affordable housing for low-income workers while continuing to attract higher-paid employees can grow. The social mixture helps to create secure, attractive environments with good services, which encourage professional workers to stay. Without this mixture, cities simply

polarise into a collection of ghettos. This is the biggest threat facing our cities. Manchester is now advertising its older, less-popular blocks of flats near the centre to attract new workers. We need to build on these ideas, not in the small pockets that we see today, but from city centre to city edge, including the semi-abandoned inner areas that we need to revitalise if we are to counter sprawl.

After Bangladesh and South Korea, England is the third most densely populated major country in the world.[12] As a result of our centuries-long clamour for wealth, our cities have been blighted by over-use. But too often it is bad modern design and the growth of traffic that make our cities seem inhospitable. We are afraid of our cities: more than two-thirds of the population say that urban crime is their greatest worry.[13] To escape this past, we have created a double problem: abandonment and sprawl. Can we recycle cities so that they feel safe enough for people to *choose* to live in them?

Architecture is about meeting human needs by introducing a sense of physical order and beauty, 'gluing together' the complex interactions of living communities. Yet the decayed physical fabric of our cities unglues communities, forcing some people to flee and leaving others trapped amid the dereliction. Unless we do something, we will jeopardise our increasingly urban future.

◄ East Manchester's fragmented streets, abandoned housing and derelict land
Jefferson Air Photography

A sustainable city bequeaths to future generations a better urban environment. We are far from doing this, for as our consumption accelerates and our individual wants grow we are edging ever closer to the limits of what our environment can stand. We need liveable cities that help us to contain our abuse of the natural world while at the same time countering social isolation. Liveable cities would pull more people in.

Cities need a critical mass of people and activities if they are to work properly. In spite of the explosion in information technology, face-to-face contact is still essential for human development. Cities provide the hub for this new communications network.[14] Only by ordering buildings and spaces to enable a dense network of access, interchange, contact, and innovation can cities stay alive. So we need to be constantly remaking our cities for the new needs they must meet. Successful design helps urban density to work. It pulls together the conflicting currents of urban life into a coherent pattern, creating compact, interdependent spaces within our built environment.

Cities go through cycles of prosperity and decline as their functions change. Sustainable design can help us to re-use and beautify what is there – brown land, redundant buildings, cracks and spaces in the urban fabric. We need to regenerate the decayed inner neighbourhoods that are bursting with under-exploited opportunities. It is far more rewarding to design attractive buildings and spaces within existing cities than to plonk a series of identikit structures on straggling roads and open land. 'Edge cities' may be new and dynamic, but they are ugly and wasteful as well.[15] They make little sense even to the people who use them. By contrast, city centres are rich in cultural assets, remarkable buildings and public spaces that can be economic as well as social magnets as long as people feel at ease within them.

The problem is that we do not think of cities as 'people-friendly' places. Many neighbourhoods are so poor and run down that no one with any choice is willing to move in or invest. Older cities have played out their traditional roles as makers and builders, and as they smarten up their poorer areas, so they evict the rejects onto the streets. We have many broken-down citizens as well as cities. Thus Glasgow is knocking down two thousand council flats a year, but has many destitute street sleepers. Manchester has homeless people but acres of boarded-up, unlettable property. Homelessness and empty property go hand in hand in throw-away cities.[16] Parents move home

▼ Newcastle: traditional, attractive town houses at popular densities – about 60 dwellings to the hectare
Professor Alan Simpson

to avoid sending their children to 'rough', under-achieving schools, thereby exacerbating the problems. Violent crime is still rising in most inner-urban areas. Employers go – so jobs go too.[17] There is a real risk that, as controls weaken in depleted neighbourhoods, people will no longer feel they have a stake in staying. Social conditions and community relations will then break down completely. US inner cities display these symptoms in extreme form.[18]

We have only one world and its land is finite. So we have to resolve the conflict over the use of green-field land or brown urban land. Environmental damage extends far further than the plots on which developers build detached houses. Sprawl creates the clutter of building, the congestion of traffic over ever wider areas. People pay nowhere near the true cost of environmental damage.[19] If we charged the real cost of new development on green-field sites, we might have the resources to make cities work. We do not have to live with this triple legacy: detached private estates around every country town and village; depopulating, decayed inner cities; broken-down social structures leaving the most vulnerable people to a new destitution.[20] Other countries do better.

Over half the world's population now lives in towns and cities. In England, the proportion is 90 per cent. We know that in this country alone we may have to accommodate nearly four million extra households over the next twenty years.[21] This gives us a chance to look again at cities. Proximity brings cities to life, but ordering such condensed space and activity in a harmonious, productive and humane way has often eluded city governments over centuries. How we make cities work for all their citizens, rich and poor, is a major challenge for the new millennium. We can sprawl further round the edges of existing suburbs in predominantly single-person households, or we can make our cities worth living in for those who like cities but do not like what we are doing to them.

We need to create 'a world of things held in common . . . which gathers us together but prevents us from falling over each other'.[22] Cities can be energising places where wealth is generated and shared. Or cities can overwhelm us with their problems, divide us and make us want to escape. Successful cities attract different ages, incomes, races and cultures in the meeting places of strangers and friends. Streets, squares, parks, courtyards, alleys, gardens become 'the outdoor public rooms, within the otherwise private realm of the city'.[23] Cities have many elements, but the public areas link our homes, our work, our social lives, the economy. They tell us a lot about how a city is working. When they are neglected, they quickly become dirty, noisy, traffic-ridden, disordered spaces that divide communities and drive people away.

Cities and their inner neighbourhoods are not static structures, to be cast off when worn out; they are an important cradle for creative talent. Our search for a future for cities led us to the signs of rebirth in cities everywhere. For cities have an immensely powerful pull on humanity, the potential to solve our most divisive problems of land pressures and social breakdown. English cities provide our test cases but the lessons apply to most urban communities.

Since we moved en masse off the green land into the brown brick streets over a hundred years ago, we are three times more populated as a country and the world's population has increased eightfold.[24] It is short sighted to imagine that, in one of the most populated countries of the globe, we can sustain anything other than more compact lifestyles. We are surely capable of building our future better than we built our past. Manchester is rebuilding its centre. But rebuilding its collapsing inner neighbourhoods, pock-marked by demolitions, modernist planning and sheer abandonment, is another story. Chapter 2 looks at the social changes that have driven people out of cities.

2 Social change and fragmentation

2 Paradise Row

In 1800, Lower Holloway in north London was the cattle route to the city's meat markets from the farms around. The tall, narrow Georgian terraces of Paradise Row, surrounded by fields, housed the skilled artisans of the early industrial revolution. The raised pavements kept the cattle to the narrow winding road.

By 1900, the area had become a crowded suburb of London, with Irish and Scottish immigrants, two families to a house, jostling within the local Cockney culture. By 1930, public health officials had declared it a slum to be demolished at an unspecified date. By 1950, there was a plan to widen the road and create a park. The area became part of a slum clearance plan covering a thousand homes and two thousand families.

By 1970, Paradise Row was an even more crowded and run-down inner city slum. There were forty-five children and thirteen families in a single terrace of six houses. It was blighted by the road-widening scheme and backed on to other clearance areas and multi-occupied terraced streets, housing new immigrants from the Caribbean, Mauritius, Turkey, India, and Ireland. Holloway was one of the poorest and most-crowded wards in inner London. It had the least open space of any ward and the highest concentration of 'new Commonwealth immigrants'.[25] The terrace had a factory and a warehouse at one end, two unofficial backyard factories within the row and a nineteenth-century courtyard mansion block at the other end. Every corner was occupied and in use. There were five shops, a pub and three primary schools.

In 2000, the threats of road widening and slum clearance have long disappeared. So have one of the local schools and all of the corner shops. The pub is boarded up and the children and their families have gone too. The houses are preserved, listed and upgraded. The site of

▲ *previous page*

Collapsing industry leaves behind bare contaminated land – potential space for new uses
Ulrike Preuss/Format Photographers

◀ Paradise Row, Holloway: a
street with great urban potential
John Hills

the Woodbine factory is now an adventure playground, a city farm and a small park. The area has been transformed. But its social infrastructure has fragmented. The community has been dispersed and the neighbourhood has thinned out to a point where many amenities are too costly to maintain for so few people. Paradise Row would still make ideal family housing: four bedrooms, back gardens, opening on to a park, close to public transport and central London. But it is too expensive for most ordinary families and too depleted for richer families. Wide social changes are played out in many similar small areas.

The relentless damage to our cities and countryside caused by industrial expansion in the nineteenth century was followed by the dramatic social and economic upheavals of the twentieth century that Paradise Row epitomises. The impact has been much greater in and around cities, for they were the heartlands of the brutal industrialised methods we pioneered. These have led to a cumulative collapse in conditions in the least-popular urban neighbourhoods, leaving whole cities with a feeling of unease. This unease makes cities unpopular with many families, creating a 'geography of misery' that they want to escape.[26] People believe that city neighbourhoods are getting worse, and aspire overwhelmingly to own a house in a secure and attractive neighbourhood.[27] Economic and social changes are driving this exodus.

Our urban legacy

Britain led the industrial revolution, which struck the world with a social and economic impact so powerful that it changed for ever the way we live and the way we see things. Its physical effect on the landscape was devastating. Having been first off the mark, we paid a terrible price in urban squalor but reaped vast rewards in wealth, power and scientific supremacy. We invented the steam engine, railways and the factory system.

Our race to the top at this turning point in modern history gave our industrial towns a unique urban form. The sudden explosion of dense, crowded slums created not just wealth but social hazards too. People in cities lived shorter, more dangerous lives than they had before: casual labour, constant movement in search of shelter and work, adulterated food and the lack of heat, light, clean water and drains caused unparalleled misery and disease. Death rates in urban slums rose between 1800 and 1850.[28] Gradually we found ways to control urban conditions, to tackle health, safety and shelter, through public intervention and civic co-operation. Local government emerged, a godsend in the eyes of many reforming Victorians.[29] But a transport revolution – the extension of tram and rail services to new suburbs – unleashed an urban exodus. Industry began to expand more slowly and less profitably as our cities began their long decline.

The industrial legacy we have inherited offers huge potential alongside chronic liabilities. First, a vast and largely obsolete industrial infrastructure left over from two centuries of constant growth litters the urban landscapes and cries out for attractive new uses. Second, our model of city government, derived from the need for control and prohibition of abuse, delivers vital services to every citizen, but today inspires little confidence in the cities.[30] Most urban voters do not turn out at local elections. Third, a folk memory of industrial squalor and urban overcrowding persists in the minds of public and planners alike and fuels an almost obsessive desire for low-density suburban homes.[31] We look at these three legacies in turn.

Industry has bequeathed us 45,000 hectares of damaged, contaminated, derelict and unreclaimed land and nearly a million unused buildings, many of them very large.[32] One hectare is two and a half acres, roughly the size of a football pitch. More than a quarter of our houses date from before the First World War, representing an attractive asset in most towns and cities but an unsellable liability in collapsed former manufacturing areas. More than three thousand miles of canals link our major cities in a priceless but now barely used network, offering vast scope for housing, recreation and environmental protection.

Local authorities gradually created order and greater equality after the extreme divisions of the nineteenth century. Britain's universal health, education and planning services were landmarks in world development. As a result, public support for a universal safety net is still very strong. But early in the twentieth century local authorities became the executors of a government-driven dispersal of the population. There were four main mechanisms: tight controls on private renting; the subsidising of suburban owner-occupation beyond existing city boundaries; slum clearance and the consequent displacement of inner city communities; and the concentration of public housing estates for low-income families within existing city boundaries. This concentration of poor people in the inner cities, coupled with the dispersal of better-off citizens, is part of the reason why urban schools and health care, having once set the standards, now fall far below the national average.[33]

Britain's civic planning offers a model to the rest of the world because of our invention of green belts, garden cities and new towns, because of the attractive centres of our historic cities, and because of that appealing single-family housing form, the terrace. However, such was the squalor of our industrial cities that visionary plans for new communities often generated uncontrolled sprawl.[34] The strong incentives to build outwards led to the 'thinning-out' of cities, destroying not only their electoral and financial power-base but also their social and political rationale. We are only just waking up to the damage. Can we turn this urban legacy to the good? To understand the scale of the challenge, we look at ten main changes in turn.

Depopulation

In 1800, only 10 per cent of the population lived in cities. At the end of the nineteenth century, 90 per cent did. Today, nearly half the population lives in suburbs.[35] From 1900, cities became less dense and more extensive, while the countryside was developed to house the outflow. Urban boundaries spread outwards and many smaller towns grew, often joining up with each other. While inner city populations plummeted, the overall population of built-up areas increased by 40 per cent. These built-up areas now cover 45 per cent more land than at the start of the twentieth century – an additional two million acres – but the urban population has grown by less than a third.[36] Inner London fell from 4.5 million in 1901 to 2.2 million in 1991, although unlike most other cities it began to grow again from the mid 1990s. The populations of Salford, Liverpool, Manchester, inner Newcastle and Glasgow tumbled by two-thirds over the same period. But from the 1950s, whole conurbations shrank too, particularly Greater London, which lost 20 per cent of its population between 1951 and 1991.[37] Much of this population loss was planned.[38] But the serious marginalisation of urban populations that resulted was not planned.[39] Chart 2.1 shows how the conurbations shrank from the 1950s, reflecting the migration into the countryside, smaller towns and cities.

Until about thirty years ago, most politicians, planners and developers thought it was a good thing to get people out of cities. Much of our investment in housing and infrastructure was directed towards pushing not just people, but also jobs and investment, outwards. But in the late 1960s a major shift in attitude began:

against clearance and new building and in favour of inner city renovation and the protection of traditional communities.[40] But the depopulation of inner cities – except that of London – has continued since then, as unstoppable as a giant oil tanker. Well-intentioned decisions often have unexpectedly far-reaching consequences. Inner city housing, built to replace slums, is now being abandoned and demolished in the least popular areas of towns and cities, often before the loans raised to build it have been paid off. Whole streets of sound, potentially attractive housing are emptying of people.[41] Chart 2.2 shows how the steep decline in city populations in the last thirty years has been paralleled by job losses. Leeds is an interesting exception, partly because its boundaries were drawn more generously than those of other cities, allowing more suburban growth within the city.

As far apart as Hackney and Newcastle, local authorities are battling against the outward flow of the people who have choice and jobs, who leave behind depleted services, boarded-up shops, half-empty classrooms, derelict homes and spaces – an ever more concentrated form of poverty. The story of Easterhouse, an outer Glasgow estate built to house fifty thousand people, is eloquently told by Bob Holman, a community and youth worker living there.[42] Five out of six secondary schools have gone, the population has halved, demolition is a daily occurrence and people struggle to survive and maintain control. These conditions may seem extreme, but Easterhouse is not an isolated example.[43]

If depopulation continues at the current rate, many city neighbourhoods will collapse completely. The scale of the infrastructure – roads, buildings, abandoned spaces – comes to dwarf the shrunken population, creating a sense of emptiness and dereliction. Cities become a prey to crime, social breakdown and collapsing property values, as the vicious circle of exodus and emptying tightens.

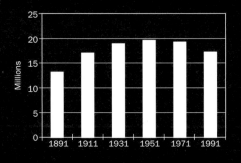

◄ **Chart 2.1 Population of conurbations (all metropolitan counties)**
Source: Office for National Statistics (2000)

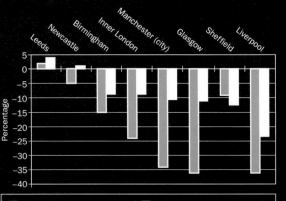

◄ **Chart 2.2: Population in the urban areas of England 1961–1994 and employment change 1981–1991**
Source: UTF (1999); DoE (1996)
Note: Population change covers the period 1961–1994. Employment change covers 1981–1991

Accelerating abandonment of the worst inner areas now affects many towns and cities.[44]

Job change

We are in the midst of a massive change in employment patterns that is global in its reach and local in its impact. The new world economy is driven by international financial and production systems beyond the control of national governments, let alone city authorities. As we create new jobs and new services and use new technology, manufacturing continues to shrink. Our industrial work force and our old industrial cities are adjusting only slowly and painfully. The impact is relentless, but there are positive developments in employment too, offering opportunities for new workers with adequate training. Chart 2.3 shows how the steep decline in manufacturing affects conurbations more than the rest of the country. It also shows the rise in service jobs, slower in cities but none the less beginning to gather pace.

The proportion of non-manual workers in the work force rose from a quarter before World War One to two-thirds by 1996. Manual workers represented three-quarters of all workers in 1911, but only one-third in 1996 (Chart 2.4). Yet three-quarters of all adults in inner Manchester and Newcastle still class themselves as manual workers.[45] The skills of the people left behind in cities simply do not match the jobs available to them.

Older manufacturing areas have been far worse hit than the rest of the country. Between 1980 and 1996, two-thirds of all manufacturing jobs disappeared in Manchester and nearly half of those in Newcastle. As a result, many people have dropped out of the labour force altogether, simply giving up the quest for work.[46] These people no longer show up in the statistics as unemployed. That is why, with

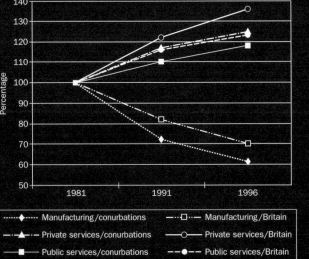

◄ **Chart 2.3: Employment decline in manufacturing and rise in services**
Source: Turok, I & Edge, N (1999)
Note: The baseline against which changes are measured for all types of employment is 100 in 1981

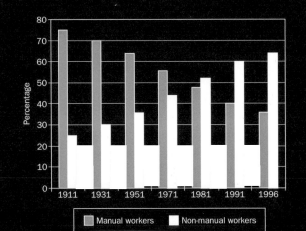

◄ **Chart 2.4: Workers as a percentage of occupied population 1911–1996**
Source: Halsey, A H (1988); Office for National Statistics (2000)

unemployment apparently now down to 5.9 per cent, we still have one in five families with no one in work, many of them headed by a lone parent. It is largely in our cities and former industrial areas that this drama of inactivity is being played out. The effect on morale, on the community, on young people, is devastating.

As we have moved from a manual, industrial economy to a service-based one, from a predominately male work force to one that is half female, there has been a deepening cleavage between the old, once relatively secure but now impoverished inner urban communities of our industrial past and the more dispersed suburban hinterland – wealthier, more mobile, more employed. One major cause has been the low skill level of the population. More than one in five people in Britain cannot read simple instructions or add up a short shopping list. In areas of deep poverty in the inner city, the basic skills problem is far worse.[47] We could become as polarised and racially divided as the USA, unless we can attract jobs and skilled people back into the heart of our cities and at the same time build the skills of the people who live there already. Chart 2.5 shows the loss of male, city-based jobs and the expansion of outer and female jobs.

Income gap

The global information age is unlocking huge new potential: cleaner, more prosperous, more interconnected cities. But the pace of change pulls apart incomes and conditions. New social and economic pressures are gathering strength as we struggle to adapt.

Since World War Two, wages have usually kept ahead of the cost of living, making those in work gradually wealthier. Since 1979, however, those out of work have gradually fallen behind. Their relative poverty has grown because social security benefits in the 1980s and 1990s did not keep up with increasing wealth, only with the cost of

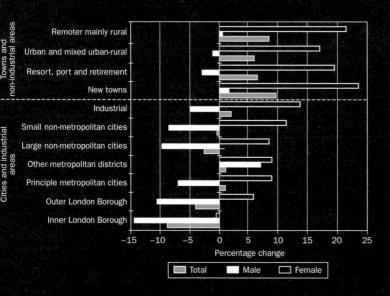

◀ **Chart 2.5a: Employment change 1984–1991 by area (full time equivalents)**
Source: DoE (1996)

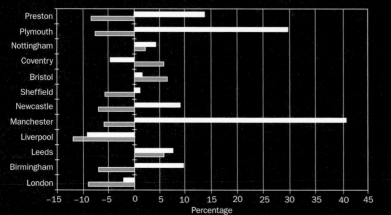

◀ **Chart 2.5b: Employment change for the inner and outer areas of twelve cities, 1984–1991 as a percentage**
Source: DoE (1996)

necessities.[48] The competition for a shrinking pool of low-paid jobs pushes real wages down at the bottom (Charts 2.5a, b). The least-skilled males are the worst affected, which means that old manufacturing cities are hit hardest.[49] Thus the legacy of our industrial past is unemployment and poverty.

Chart 2.6 shows how incomes diverged in the 1980s and 1990s. Overall we became 40 per cent richer in just fifteen years, but the bottom 10 per cent may actually have become poorer. People in this category are almost entirely without work, and they are almost entirely concentrated in cities.[50]

Ethnic change and race relations

While becoming more socially fragmented, urban communities have become more racially mixed. Two million new and racially distinct migrants came to Britain in the generation after World War Two.[51] Today, the inner areas of London, Birmingham, Manchester, Bradford, Leicester and many smaller towns house large numbers of people from ethnic minorities, often at four or more times their concentration in the population overall.[52] Chart 2.7 shows the concentration of different ethnic groups in major conurbations compared with their proportion in the population as a whole. The Chinese, who are much more dispersed, make an interesting contrast.

Overt racial discrimination played a part in the concentration of black and Asian people in the inner cities. Migrants were forced to crowd into the poorest, most unpopular areas, paying high rents for atrocious accommodation or buying unwanted property, often in targeted slum clearance areas.[53] The newcomers were deeply resented by local people for their greater willingness to take low-skilled jobs and to put up with poor conditions.

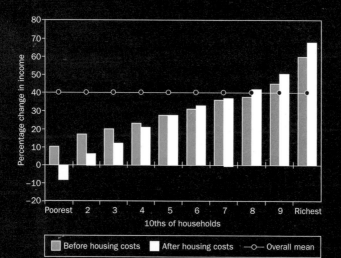

◄ **Chart 2.6: Change in real net income 1979–1994/95**
Source: Hills, J (1998)

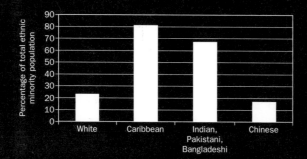

◄ **Chart 2.7: Percentage of population of different ethnic origin living within four main conurbations – Greater London, West Midlands, Greater Manchester, and West Yorkshire**
Source: Modood, T et al. (1997)
Note: 3% of total population is Asian, 2% black (including Caribbean), less than 1% other groups including Chinese

Today, most areas with high concentrations of ethnic minorities suffer acute deprivation.[54] Immigration and race have become linked with inner-city poverty and disadvantage, even though some members of minority ethnic groups have managed to achieve wealth and status, outperforming white people in educational attainment and integrating into the wider community. Increasing concentration is happening alongside increasing dispersal, and different ethnic groups follow different patterns, as Ceri Peach and Tariq Modood have shown.[55]

Only the enterprise and energy of incoming migrants has kept some inner-city areas going.[56] Certainly, many more schools and shops would have closed. Migrants are self-selecting: only those with the skills and the 'get-up-and-go' tend to migrate. Places like New York, where perhaps a million immigrants have arrived since 1990, show the contribution that they can make to the revival of a city's fortunes. Other US cities have had similar experiences.[57] But immigrants pay a huge price for their boldness, in the shape of ubiquitous discrimination. This is an injustice and a waste of talent that the Race Relations Act of 1976 only partially remedied.[58]

Change in the family

Changes in population and employment since the nineteenth century have been accompanied by a transformation of the household.

Household size has more than halved in a century, from nearly five people per family in 1900 to just over two today.[59] Single-person households made up one-seventh of the total in 1961 and almost one-third today.[60] This shrinkage of the family has many causes: more elderly people are surviving, but they live separately from their children; later marriage and childbearing; fewer children per family; more broken marriages and more lone parents; more economic independence for women. Though many women have part-time, low-paid jobs, employment has none the less increased their independence and their status in the family. This has partly compensated for the loss of male breadwinners in the inner cities, but it has shaken male confidence and forever changed the internal dynamics of the family. Charts 2.8a–g summarise the changes in the family.

The effects are starker in cities because childless households and lone-parent families are concentrated there. Cities attract young people and new immigrants, but tend to lose established working families. They also retain an elderly, 'left-behind' population.

Our increasing wealth means that we can, and usually do, build houses or flats for virtually every household, no matter how small. Overcrowding is half what it was twenty-five years ago, even among the poor. Even so, one in five of the poorest households – mainly families with children and ethnic minority families – still live in homes with more than one person to a room, almost double the level for rest of the population.[61] This overcrowding is concentrated in cities.

The past century has seen radical changes in the way we live, yet we have not adapted our view of housing to match. Much of the debate about housing need is based on fixed assumptions about the kind of homes we should provide. If people are living thirty years longer than they did in 1900, and many more of them live alone, we need to design our homes and communities to meet their requirements. Chart 2.9 shows that married couples will soon, for the first time, make up fewer than half of all households, although they will still form the biggest single group.

The effect of new household patterns

Even though our population is expanding slowly and within thirty years may even begin to decline, the number of households is bound to

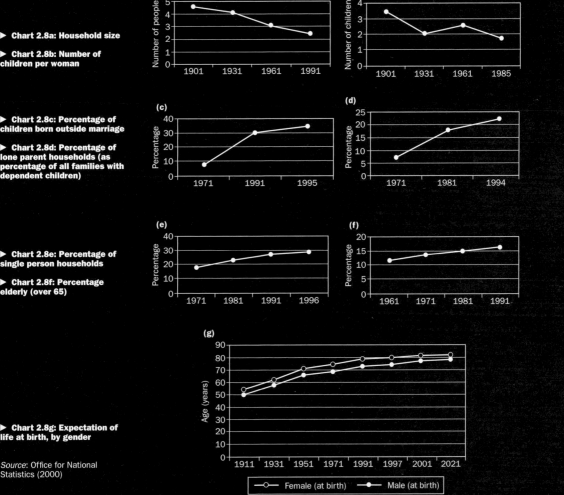

▶ Chart 2.8a: Household size

▶ Chart 2.8b: Number of children per woman

▶ Chart 2.8c: Percentage of children born outside marriage

▶ Chart 2.8d: Percentage of lone parent households (as percentage of all families with dependent children)

▶ Chart 2.8e: Percentage of single person households

▶ Chart 2.8f: Percentage elderly (over 65)

▶ Chart 2.8g: Expectation of life at birth, by gender

Source: Office for National Statistics (2000)

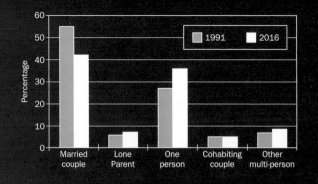

◄ **Chart 2.9: Projected breakdown of households by household types, England (1991 and 2016)**
Source: Office for National Statistics (2000)

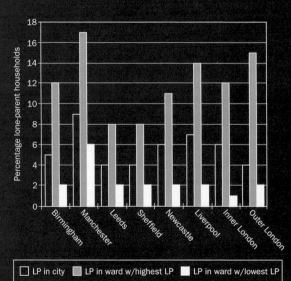

◄ **Chart 2.10: Lone-parent households as percentage of all households**
Source: DoE (1996)

increase if more people are living alone or in pairs than in larger family groups. This will have a dramatic effect, not just on the number of homes needed, but also on the demand for services, the type of space we occupy and the ways we interact. If we simply build new homes for the new small households in the same way as we used to build for much bigger households, people will become more and more isolated and the 'thinned-out' community will have too few people to justify facilities and support. New building will be costly, land-hungry and socially isolating unless we create new forms of housing to match the social revolution that has occurred.

Smaller households and fewer children mean less informal support from relatives and more demand for organised services. These services are only viable at higher housing densities. People who live alone feel more secure with near neighbours and familiar concierges. The streets feel safer with regular policing; public transport feels safer if it is full. In urban communities, a 'critical mass' of people is essential to maintaining order on the streets and sustaining services.[62] We discuss this further in Chapter 3.

Family and social breakdown

The recent increase in family breakdown and lone-parent households is insufficiently acknowledged or understood. As a result, society's response is inadequate. In the poorest neighbourhoods of our cities, lone-parent families make up half, or even more, of all families with children.[63] One third of children in the inner city are in lone parent families, compared with one in ten in the rest of the population. Chart 2.10 shows the difference in the concentration of lone parents in the poorer and richer wards of the same cities.

The sheer scale of family breakdown presents us with wholly new problems: lone parents struggle with poverty and the burden of parenting; children have more disrupted family lives; more and more elderly people live alone during their last and most vulnerable years; partners whose relationship breaks down require emergency housing and access to their children; young people try to become independent, often from families where a new step-parent has made them feel unwanted. These problems make it far more difficult for families and parenting to succeed.[64]

The loss of stability in families, the isolation of single-person households and the decline of family support – still by far the most valuable and reliable recourse in time of need – leave more and more people vulnerable and exposed.

Schools and insecurity

Schools are often a lifeline for families in trauma. But they too have to struggle with multiple problems: the disorganised behaviour and poor concentration of children in difficulty, the high levels of aggression, the peer pressure to underachieve.[65] Not just teachers, but also doctors and other public sector workers in inner cities, are swamped by problems. This leaves urban services doubly vulnerable – to higher demand and lower staff morale.[66]

Overall, schools – including those in cities – are achieving more exam passes and better standards of literacy and numeracy. But schools in the poorest inner city areas are only reaching one-third the level of performance of those in the rest of the country.[67] As urban populations become more segregated and better-off parents increasingly choose areas with better schools if they can, so the poorer areas are left with fewer and fewer children who have strong family support or parents with an educated background.[68]

Poverty and underachievement go together: Chart 2.11 shows that the proportion of children receiving free meals at a school is in inverse proportion to the number of GCSE passes the school achieves. Such statistics do much to persuade parents to opt out of cities.

Schools depopulate just as neighbourhoods do. Newcastle had 3600 spare school places in 1999.[69] Chart 2.12 shows how a school's problems interact with neighbourhood decline to influence house prices and the outflow of families.[70]

Some schools defy this trend, however, and there are inspiring example of progress. David Blunkett, Secretary of State for Education and Employment, with his instinctive understanding of disadvantage and declining communities, must keep his nerve.[71]

Urban malaise

Cities collect strangers. Major population movements concentrate vulnerable people in the places where other people choose not to go. Crime exploits this phenomenon. As social cohesion and informal controls weaken, so our ability to contain disorder and violence declines.

▲ Crime and decay generate urban malaise

People rank crime as their biggest worry. Charts 2.13a–c show that, in the most decayed inner city neighbourhoods, a majority of people are worried about crime and one in eight feel in danger of attack by a stranger. These are not baseless anxieties: there is a much higher incidence of recorded crime in cities, particularly in their poorer neighbourhoods.[72]

The general lack of supervision and the high incidence of anti-social behaviour make built-up areas where people are forced to share a collective space with others particularly difficult to manage. As we suggested in Chapter 1, these social and organisational problems

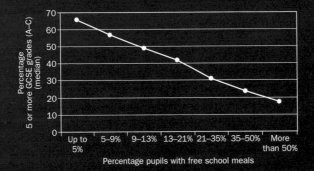

◀ Chart 2.11: Free school
meals and GCSE results, 1999
Source: DfEE (2000)

Percentage pupils with free school meals

◀ Chart 2.12: Parental choice,
neighbourhoods and schools

Cities lose families because of poor schools

House prices directly affected
by competition to move to
neighbourhoods with good schools

Parents want best education
for children

Area empties, partly affected by
schools – but bad schools empty
ahead of area

Slack in school places in cities
since 1960's

Poorest schools empty as capacity
expands relative to numbers

Parents opt for better performing,
more popular schools, putting
pressure on those schools

If necessary and possible, parents
are even willing to move house to be
in right catchment

Schools able to select/screen
if oversubscribed

Parents with cars increasingly
willing to drive

Reputations rise/fall even further –
more popular schools rise
while poorer schools lose pupils

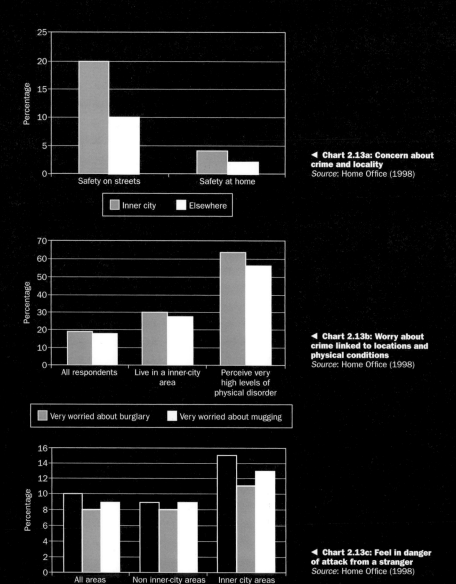

◄ Chart 2.13a: Concern about crime and locality
Source: Home Office (1998)

◄ Chart 2.13b: Worry about crime linked to locations and physical conditions
Source: Home Office (1998)

◄ Chart 2.13c: Feel in danger of attack from a stranger
Source: Home Office (1998)

impact powerfully on the design of public spaces and buildings. How we run our cities and prioritise their public spaces affects the way we use our streets and consequently how secure we feel.[73]

The squalor of inner city neighbourhoods reinforces what Peter Hall calls our 'urban malaise'.[74] It makes people reluctant to be out on the streets, thus encouraging even more crime. Charts 2.14a and b show how people rank neighbourhood problems. People in affluent suburban and rural areas experience far fewer social problems than those in urban areas, whether rich or poor. Cities tend to concentrate their problems, which helps to explain both the continuing exodus and the urgency of the problems. Reviving inner city areas, such as Hoxton and Shoreditch in London and Hulme and Moss Side in Manchester, battle constantly to overcome the effects of 'urban malaise'. The juxtaposition of 'new' wealth and 'old' poverty exacerbates the tension.

As communities become more marginalised, the empty buildings and empty spaces encourage vandalism and crime. Excluded teenagers form gangs and more hardened criminals prey on the vulnerability of the poorest people.[75] Some families have such chaotic lifestyles that they and particularly their children run amok – the so-called 'neighbours from hell'.[76] Where social controls are weak, policing inadequate and levels of fear high, matters can get completely out of control.[77]

Social exclusion

Social exclusion is primarily an urban problem. The one hundred local authorities in the country with the most-difficult conditions are all urban, and the twenty most deprived are all in major industrial conurbations and inner London.[78] Changes in the family and employment patterns have turned many inner-city areas, and some

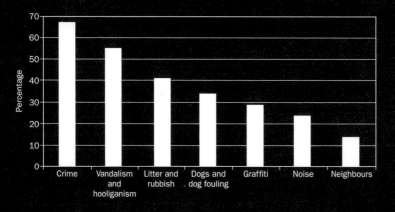

◀ **Chart 2.14a: Rank order of problems identified by householders in their area**
Source: UTF (1999) based on British Crime Survey

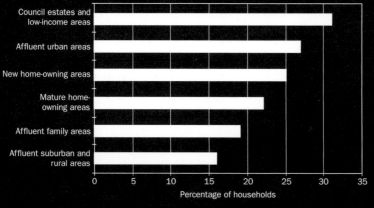

Percentage of households

◀ **Chart 2.14b: Percentage householders perceiving problems of crime, vandalism etc.**
Source: UTF (1999) based on British Crime Survey

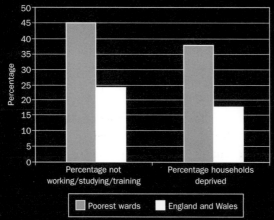

◀ **Chart 2.15: High concentration of workless and deprived households in the poorest wards compared with England and Wales as a whole**
Source: Glennerster, H et al. (1999)

large outlying council estates, into pressurised receptacles for social problems.

Social exclusion is about our inability to keep everyone within reach of what we expect as a society. It is about our tendency to push the more vulnerable, less able and more difficult individuals into the least-popular places, furthest away from our common aspirations. It makes certain people feel excluded from the mainstream. Social exclusion is concentrated in decaying areas, along with under-used buildings, boarded-up shops, broken glass, rubbish and vandalism.

The 'wealth gap' within cities is often dramatic. Their poorest neighbourhoods can be three times as deprived as the city-wide average.[79] These neighbourhoods may not stand alone, but be part of a much larger 'cluster' of poor neighbourhoods. Chart 2.15 shows the differences in unemployment and deprivation between the poorest neighbourhoods in cities and the national average. Chart 2.16 shows how 'clustered' poverty is in some cities.

The incidence of poverty in London – now a hugely wealthy global city – demonstrates the polarisation of population, the impact of changes in employment patterns on less-skilled people and the pressures on minority communities. The poorer eastern side of inner London grapples with extraordinarily high levels of unemployment, while the city as a whole grapples with the beginnings of a labour shortage.[80] Inner London experienced by far the highest rate of job losses in the country during the 1980s, resulting in the exodus of better-off people, racial polarisation and a concentration of people with few skills.

London is different from other regions and cities because of its wealth, the result of its vast financial, labour and housing markets. But it shares most of the major urban problems. Its wealth is distributed desperately unevenly: over half of the twenty most-deprived local authority areas in the country are in the capital.[81]

Nonetheless former industrial conurbations are even more acutely affected, because they lack London's economic strength and variety to counter the strong outward pressures.[82]

The exodus from the cities carries away not the poor, but the successful. To move out, you need money and contacts. Cities have long been the stage on which these social failures are played out. The poor image of our cities, the result of poverty and social exclusion, reflects one of the deepest cleavages in our society.

Society is now more individualistic, and as a result is more fragmented and harder to control. In the cities, signs of breakdown are visible everywhere. People are determined to exercise their right to go where they want and live how they please. Instant communications weaken social ties.[83] Does progress make these costs, disproportionately borne by the poorer and more precarious urban communities, inevitable? Do cities cause these problems? Or can cities help to remedy the damaging loss of social cohesion? We have a unique chance to adapt the way we design, build and recycle our cities to fit the new living patterns we have described. Social breakdown is not inevitable if we revise our living patterns to match our smaller, 'thinner' households. This does not necessarily mean having less living space, but making a more compact use of space. People's confidence may continue to leak away unless we can redesign the built environment to match the galloping social changes. If we don't intervene now, fragmentation will accelerate.

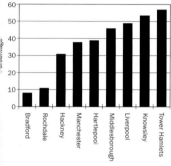

▲ **Chart 2.16: Percentage of Local Authority population living in the poorest wards in the country**
Source: Glennerster, H et al. (1999)

◄ Physical dereliction equals social exclusion
David Hoffman

3 The escape to the suburbs and the demise of compact cities

Byker

The physical fabric of cities

The ordering of cities

Britain's unique terraces

Garden cities

Suburbs

Disinvestment and slum clearance

Large public estates

Unsustainable cities

3 Byker

In the 1950s, the Byker area of Newcastle was still a settled, close-knit working-class community. Its steeply sloping old terraces overlooked the docks and the Tyne, where at least one member of most families worked. The houses were let by private landlords at controlled rents that barely funded basic repairs, and they lacked bathrooms or indoor toilets. Byker eventually became part of the city's large slum-clearance programme. Four thousand residents were to be uprooted and rehoused in a large new council estate on the site. There was resistance, because people liked where they lived and had a sense of pride and solidarity.[84]

An inspirational young Swedish architect, Ralph Erskine, promised to design the new Byker so that everyone who belonged in the community could fit in. It would be built in phases, that so no one would have to move away, and as an expression of faith in the new architecture, the architects themselves would live on the new estate for a year to see if the design really worked and to help with any teething troubles

The new Byker was a dramatic break with tradition. Noise from the planned motorway through the area – which was never built – was to be blocked out by a high, north-facing brick wall, giving a new name to the whole estate: the Byker Wall.

▲ *previous page*

The Byker Wall: model estate replaced old terraced streets (architect Ralph Erskine)
City Repro, City of Newcastle-upon-Tyne

The new flats cascaded down on the inner, south side of the wall in steep terraces, not at all like the former sloping streets, yet somehow recreating their intimate atmosphere. Once inside the huge wall, you feel as if you are stepping into a real community. All the flats face the sun, and the many small gardens, pathways and courtyards have an enclosed, informal yet orderly air. Everything is within walking distance.

The inner side of the giant wall is neatly packed with individual homes, tucked in behind the wooden staircases and gardens, the balconies and play spaces. Everything has a worn-in, settled feel that seems to work. But the attempt to avoid uprooting the original community was not entirely successful. Only about 40 per cent of the previous inhabitants stayed in Byker. One old lady summed up the problem: 'Why knock down all these streets and houses when we needed bathrooms? Why make us move? Couldn't they put in pipes?'[85]

The estate is large: nearly three thousand homes. It has very high unemployment. There are many lone parents. It is now twenty years since the estate was finished, and it cries out for a face-lift. It needs careful maintenance and 'community lettings' to prioritise people with links in the area, particularly the children of existing residents.

In 1999 the council proposed to knock some of the estate down: a pretty but dilapidated little court of flats that had not been let or managed for months. A group of residents got together and fought the demolition proposal. The old Byker had gone. The new Byker had survived better than had been predicted, for all its current difficulties. Why break it up again? In its own way, the Byker Wall had become a community, with its own roots and problems. To the people who liked it, knocking it down was not a solution – it was simply chasing the old problem round again. The residents have won for now: partly because the architect who designed the Byker Wall, Ralph Erskine, is famous and English Heritage has listed the estate because of its unique design; partly because the residents organised themselves this time and stood up for the right of poor communities not to be continually displaced; and partly because the way in which city governments relate to their citizens is changing. We are becoming more sensitive, less confident and perhaps more open to different ways of doing things.[86]

The physical fabric of cities

The upheavals of the past two hundred years are reflected in the physical fabric of our cities. Far from being orderly, attractive and well designed, our urban landscape is full of unplanned ruptures and broken street patterns. Many older neighbourhoods are decayed; post-war estates are often crudely implanted in neighbourhoods or added around the edge, where they form part of the general urban sprawl. Grand civic buildings are neglected, or have been replaced by intimidating concrete structures. Green spaces and public parks have lost their keepers and feel uncared-for and bare.[87] Cities have lost the connected, dense style that characterised them in the past. People long for nostalgic images of 'community', which explains why *Coronation Street* and *East Enders* have been our most popular television programmes for decades.

Most great architects of the twentieth century were 'anti-urban', because cities were so awful. Frank Lloyd Wright, Le Corbusier and Gropius dreamt of sun, air and light. They wanted to 'plant cities in gardens', as did visionary planners like Ebenezer Howard, inventor of the garden city.[88] Yet a compact sense of place and order is still the hallmark of popular inner neighbourhoods, smaller cities, market towns and historic villages. Multi-purpose, mixed and closely knit neighbourhoods ordered around streets and squares are the archetypal human settlement, as demonstrated by the very earliest cities.[89] But the chaotic growth of our industrial cities made them harder to control.

Throughout the twentieth century, governments responded to people's desire for order by creating civic institutions to run cities and by simultaneously encouraging people to move out of those cities. The owner-occupation of single-family dwellings confers a strong sense of control, and the flight to the suburbs has been fostered,

▲ Estate on the edge: poorly-designed high-rise, yet low-density blocks gobble up land
Paul Herrmann/Profile

even driven, by governments, as the famous poster shows (see below, p. 67).

Over time, this re-ordering of settlements has tried to separate work from home by increasing the distance between them. We have lost that blend of commerce, manufacture, leisure and home life that still makes certain areas and cities so attractive. The newer suburbs created by these dispersal policies, to which people still move in millions, offer individual space, control and social order, but often have a deadening feel because they do not have the dense mixture of activities.[90]

This chapter briefly examines how we have changed the face of our cities. We look at three strategies in detail: the abandonment of terraced housing and planned garden cities in favour of unplanned suburbs; the adoption of large-scale clearance instead of more incremental renewal; the construction of mass housing estates as the dominant low-income housing form in every inner-city area. These three strands of policy have shaped the cities of today in ways that were not foreseen. They help to explain some of the extreme polarisation we are now attempting to reverse.

The ordering of cities

Within cities, there has been a constant struggle to impose a structure on spaces that are constantly changing their functions as the local economy evolves and social conditions change in their wake. In smaller, more-slowly evolving communities, the collective ordering of the physical environment provides a powerful framework for individual behaviour and community relations. The church, the pub, the village street and its shops, the green, the square, the cemetery and the bus stop make up a pattern of public spaces that help people to organise their lives in a connected way. They are the landmarks people recognise and orientate themselves by.

The more slowly the physical structures adapt, the more blended and harmonious they become.[91] Surviving medieval street patterns in London, York and Edinburgh are still functional and appealing today. These ancient patterns have often inspired civic leaders, city planners and architects with visions of planned utopias that they then imposed upon the urban landscape. Poorer, less-ordered earlier settlements were swept away and populations displaced to deliver imposing, well-ordered urban plans. The proportions, scale and grain of the buildings, their juxtaposition and their interaction with the environment create a powerful sense of place. Edinburgh's New Town, the Cambridge colleges, Renaissance Florence, St Petersburg, central Paris and London's Nash terraces have a harmony and a physical beauty we find hard to replicate in modern cities.

Powerful patrons – the church, the nobility, the governing élites – commissioned these 'grand plans' and modern democratic govern-ments no longer wield sufficient power over entire urban communities to be able to imitate their example. We therefore need to broker what we do. This does not mean that we cannot plan, just that we need to do it more carefully. Too often, however, local and national governments still try to wipe out slums simply by clearing away run-down neighbourhoods. In Britain it is often the inner-city estates of the 1960s and 1970s, rebuilt to replace cleared slums, that are rejected as 'modern slums'.[92] We discuss this further below.

Today in Britain we are left with a variegated pattern of settlement: surviving Georgian neighbourhoods; medieval towns, villages and street plans; extensive older suburbs and bland, orderly, dispersed modern developments; half-abandoned Victorian 'by-law' terraces in old industrial cities; large slum-clearance estates imposed on older urban patterns or simply dumped at the edge of town; strong surviving public spaces and street patterns that struggle against traffic and commercial pressures.

◄ Victorian high-density model dwellings: still popular and fully occupied
Richard Townsend

► Changing urban landscapes

▼ 1900 bye-law housing: high-density 'Coronation Streets', often recycled
Katharine Mumford/Anne Power

In turbulent, fast-changing cities, where landmarks come and go, people find it difficult to orientate themselves. When order breaks down, people try to escape. Governments struggle to make cities work, while the inhabitants vote with their feet, causing the inner city to lose its cohesion. It then becomes difficult to recreate urban communities or to restore the physical conditions that will attract people back. Public spaces erode, city cores shrivel, outskirts become cluttered with unsightly developments and left-over spaces. The rest of this chapter explains how Georgian terraces, garden cities, New Towns, suburbs and inner estates fit together in the patterns we see today.

Britain's unique terraced style

Despite their present appearance, Britain's urban neighbourhoods did not emerge from a haphazard mixture of ideas. The dense and dignified layout of Georgian towns – Dublin's squares, Bath's crescents or London's terraces – demonstrates a sense of balance and grace. The four and five storey houses – narrow, deep and light – are remarkably compact, adaptable and imitable, built economically around usable public spaces. The Georgian terrace was carried over into the Victorian city and was constructed in more elaborate styles for the newly-emerging middle class, while millions of 'Coronation Streets' were built for the newly-arrived industrial masses.

Georgian and Victorian terraced and semi-detached housing has given a distinctive character to our cities and towns. In spite of large-scale demolition and two world wars, about five million pre-1914 houses have survived,[93] and in popular areas they are the most sought-after properties. Even today, they house between one and two hundred households – about three hundred people – per hectare in streets that are popular, compact and adaptable to new uses. Terraces are convertible, re-usable and good for families and single people alike, offering a sense of both privacy and social contact: a peculiarly British creation.

In England, as distinct from continental Europe and Scotland,[94] very few flats or tenements were built for the expanding population. The terraced form was adapted so that poor people could be housed in incomparably better conditions in long rows of two-up, two-down terraces, in narrow streets with back alleys to allow the soil carts to collect waste at night. These formed the early inner suburbs of skilled artisans – the aristocracy of our industrial work force. A thousand people could fit into every hectare of land.[95] This was a huge improvement on the single-roomed dwellings or 'rookeries' that had been added on to the older terraces, often lacking piped water or sanitation.[96] The new terraces allowed dense occupation as well as individual control, unlike the blocks of flats built by model dwelling companies and by philanthropists such as George Peabody, which required on-site supervision.

Cities quickly encircled these new inner suburbs. The neatly-built rows of terraced house did not rid the inner cities of their reputation for poverty, disease, ignorance and disorder. Slums were not primarily defined by their design or construction. Far more significant were a lack of basic amenities, disrepair, disinvestment, overcrowding and simple poverty.[97] Many of the terraces were well built and later proved to be structurally sound.[98]

We subsequently abandoned closely-woven terraced streets in favour of less friendly, more obtrusive council estates – which often managed to fit in fewer homes while giving individual families less space or privacy – and extensive low-density suburbs lacking the civic planning and social mixture of the inner city.

Older terraced housing only began to recover its popularity when slum clearance reached its peak in the 1960s. Widespread demolition had created such havoc that communities, politicians, architects and investors alike began to fight for more traditional inner-city design, for the rescue of surviving blighted neighbourhoods and for the re-instatement of traditional streets. Georgian and Victorian neighbourhoods have regained their popularity, particularly in London, Edinburgh and smaller cities such as York, Norwich and Bristol, where housing pressures are strong and the historic compact urban style survived. The beautifully-restored Georgian areas of Islington had once been part of a giant slum-clearance programme.

Garden cities

When city dwellers are under pressure, the peace and quiet of the countryside seem alluring. In 1898, the visionary planner Ebenezer Howard invented the garden city as a way of bringing order to cities and giving workers space. His utopian idea was to inspire planners around the world throughout the twentieth century.[99]

A town in the country, combining the virtues of both town and country while avoiding the 'backwardness' of rural isolation or the chaos of urban congestion, would free the toiling masses from squalor and allow industrialists to prosper. The initial investment needed to build garden cities would come from private enterprise, which would see their obvious benefits. All profits from the land would be re-invested in the community. Ebenezer Howard and his architect Raymond Unwin planned their garden city at twelve homes to the acre (thirty to the hectare), less than one-eighth the density of traditional city streets. They wanted to allow space for large gardens – which would encourage leisure, vegetable growing and agriculture – and also for wide avenues, public facilities and caring institutions of every kind. Charts 3.1 and 3.2 present Ebenezer Howard's own design, reflecting both his utopian ideals and practical approach.

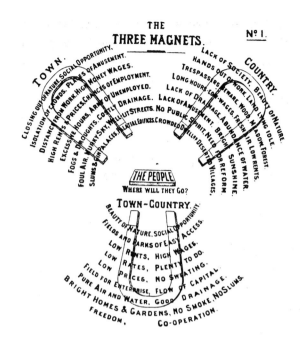

► **Chart 3.1: The Three Magnets**
Source: Howard, E (1985; new illustrated ed.) *Garden Cities of Tomorrow*

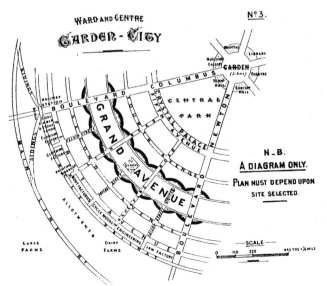

► **Chart 3.2: Garden City**
Source: Howard, E (1985; new illustrated ed.) *Garden Cities of Tomorrow*

Only two garden cities were built in England, Letchworth and Welwyn Garden City, and they proved costly and difficult to establish on a large scale. But the idea has retained a powerful grip on the public imagination, inspiring imitations in many countries. Howard's original concept of planned, self-contained towns integrating jobs, homes and social facilities still offers a comprehensible and inspiring model.[100]

Mark Swenarton's study of 'Homes Fit for Heroes', the government's ambitious house building programme after World War One, chronicles the gradual corruption of this vision.[101] We can see the consequences in and around our cities today: separate, single-function, low-income estates with too much land and too little physical or economic variety, lacking the diversity of people and activities to create a viable community. Nothing could have been further from the original idea.

After World War Two, the New Towns, modelled on the garden cities, exerted a similar magnetism. In all, twenty-eight were developed. Abercrombie's famous plan for post-war London (Chart 3.3) shows how captivating space can be on a flat sheet of paper. The aim was to decongest crowded cities and simultaneously create integrated, mixed, high-density communities where work, home and social life would create a functioning new community, not a dormitory town for nearby cities.

The reality of the New Towns was messier than the plans, and they proved harmful to cities, in spite of the improved conditions they offered, because they sucked out better-off, better-qualified workers along with expensively-relocated industry.[102]

New Towns became increasingly difficult to impose on open countryside, so a different concept, the 'expanded towns', was adopted – much like the government's current proposals for places like Ashford and Stansted. Many earlier New Towns are becoming the

▶ Homes fit for heroes: turning our back on cities and fleeing to the suburbs, 1918

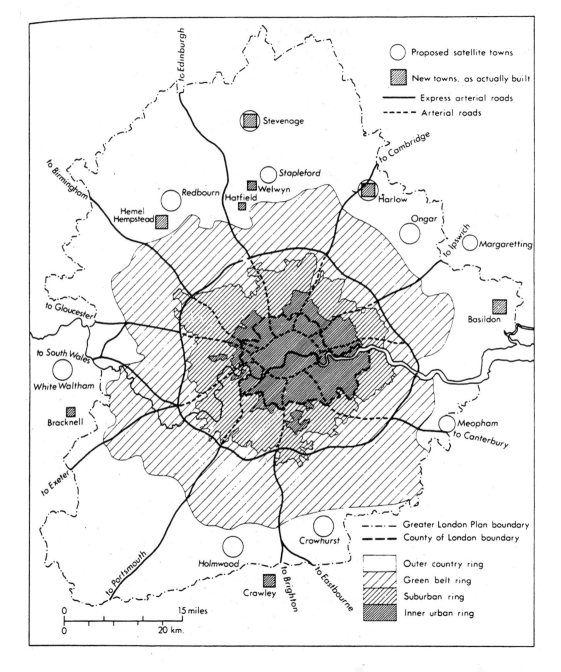

Legend:

○ Proposed satellite towns
▨ New towns, as actually built
— Express arterial roads
--- Arterial roads

Stevenage

to Edinburgh

to Cambridge

Stapleford

Welwyn

Redbourn

Hatfield

Harlow

to Birmingham

Hemel Hempstead

Ongar

to Ipswich

Margaretting

to Gloucester

Basildon

to South Wales

White Waltham

Bracknell

Meopham
to Canterbury

to Exeter

Crowhurst

Holmwood

Crawley

to Portsmouth

to Brighton

to Eastbourne

-·-·- Greater London Plan boundary
- - - County of London boundary

☐ Outer country ring
▨ Green belt ring
▨ Suburban ring
▨ Inner urban ring

0   15 miles
0   20 km.

'expanded towns' of tomorrow – a mark of their success. New Towns and garden cities are more compact than private suburbs, with a greater mixture of uses and incomes. But the complexities of creating these towns on a large scale has meant that successive governments have resorted to subsidised but unplanned private suburban building and inner-city slum clearance, described in the next two sections.

Chart 3.4 shows how Britain's urban patterns were influenced by the desire to impose civic order while at the same time driving people out of cities. This strategy is epitomised in the suburbs that now house half the population around all our older urban areas and in the mass clearances and council building that affected every inner city in Britain. We analyse these two very different ideas in turn.

Suburbs

Suburbs are residential areas built outside the core of the inner city, at distinctly lower density but linked to it through continuous development. They have a simple, repetitive form with single-family, usually owner-occupied, semi-detached or detached houses with gardens. Early suburbs grew up around public transport links, but

◀ **Chart 3.3: The Green Belt and New Towns around London**
Source: The Abercrombie Plan for Greater London, 1945

most newer suburbs are heavily dependent on the car. Suburbs are so pervasive that they shape our idea of home as something separate, private and predictable. Open land is divided into regular plots, houses are set back from the road, costs are minimised by uniformity and direct or indirect subsidy.[103]

Suburbs are resilient and enduringly popular. Their rapid expansion was a straightforward response to the acute housing shortages of World War One. As five million soldiers returned on the promise of 'homes fit for heroes', we subsidised every kind of house building on land beyond the inner terraced suburbs.[104] 'Semi-detached' became

Pre 1750 ORGANIC URBAN GROWTH – 'Medieval' cities

– often built on surviving Roman patterns
– dense, compact, narrow streets
– market squares
– merchant institutions

e.g. Canterbury, York, Chester, City of London, Old Town Edinburgh

1750–1820 PLANNED URBAN GROWTH – 'Renaissance cities'

– often added to and around earlier cities
– Georgian terraces, squares, crescents
– wide avenues and small streets
– churches and parks

e.g. Bath; Pimlico, London; New Town, Edinburgh; Georgian Dublin

1800–1850 CHAOTIC URBAN GROWTH – Industrial cities

– grafted onto towns, villages, earlier cities
– employer 'model' housing
– subdivided earlier terraced housing
– new Victorian terraces
– crowded back to backs

e.g. Manchester, Birmingham, Bradford, East London, Liverpool, New Lanark

1845–1912 CIVIC ORDER AND DISPERSAL – Reforming cities

– public health laws, clearances
– model dwellings
– bye-law housing: the new inner suburbs
– water, sanitation, street lights

e.g. Newham, London; Mosside, Manchester; Byker, Newcastle

1890–1919 UTOPIAN PLANNING – 'Garden cities'

Garden Cities →
– town in country
– low density
– open space and amenities
– costly, hard to execute
e.g. Letchworth

New Employer Settlements →
– close to work
– amenities
– health
e.g. Port Sunlight, Bournville/ New Earswick

Garden Suburbs
– added to existing towns
– model for council housing
e.g. Hampstead Garden Suburb

1919–1980 GOVERNMENT HOUSING – mass building

Subsidised Owner Occupation
– repetitive, bland, suburbs

Council building
– outer 'garden estates'
– inner clearances and dense block rebuilding

New Towns
– modelled on garden cities
– selective migration
– planned integrated growth

a status symbol. By 1930 it was almost as cheap to buy a house as to rent. Speculative development for owner occupation became standard practice.

The inter-war building boom was heavily influenced by the garden-city model of houses in green spaces. But the civic ideals that drove the first 'garden suburbs' were quickly lost in the speculative rush to build as cheaply and simply as possible with minimal planning or design. Nine out of ten suburbs came about this way. We have built nearly ten million suburban houses since World War One and many working-class people have benefited.[105] The suburban dwelling has become the single most common form of British housing.

Thanks to this rapid expansion, we are extremely well-housed as a nation. We have virtually universal basic amenities, there are two habitable rooms per person, and nine out of ten families live in single-family houses with gardens, compared with fewer than half in other European countries.[106] Chart 3.5 shows a continuing surplus of houses over households from the 1960s to the present, thanks to continuous building in ever-more suburbs.

◀ Chart 3.4: The evolution of Britain's urban patterns

The multiplication of smaller households has only just begun to modify our building patterns, even though Cullingworth alerted us to this new trend in 1969.[107] We live with the consequences. The plus points of suburban housing are that it is popular, relatively cheap and serviceable, and gives maximum individual control. The minus points are its extensive use of land, the expensive duplication of infrastructure, and the weaker links with town centres, civic life and core services. Land close to the city and the main public transport routes has run out, so suburbs have become more dispersed and more sprawling, with double the road space of more compact patterns yet lacking the critical mixture of uses. This has made travel times and road and car costs rise steeply, as we discuss in Chapter 4.

If we costed in the travel, infrastructure and service requirements of continuing to build this way, the price of each new suburban home would go up very significantly.

In the USA, where sprawl is a far greater problem, the additional federal subsidy needed for basic infrastructure, roads, sewers and utilities is estimated at $25,000 for each new suburban home.[108] The social costs to the city are extremely high too: intense segregation, concentrated poverty and a general loss of confidence.[109] Britain's dispersed housing, greedy of land and heavily polluting, is fuelled by hidden subsidies, both for the immediate capital costs, such as additional schools, major roads and service infrastructure, and for the long-term running costs. We discuss this further in Chapter 6.

The cash cost of ever-extending suburban sprawl is not counted in Britain, but its deadening impact on our landscape and its divisive effect on our social lives are hard to escape. Commuter traffic erodes our city streets and public spaces while making suburbs less attractive (see Chapter 4). By investing so heavily in new building in the outer areas, we divert vital resources from sustaining and recycling older, more compact and often more attractive urban neighbourhoods, including our inner suburbs. These older suburbs, many of them seventy years old, are closer to public transport and are a major resource for cities. Yet we are in danger of undermining them through ever more outward movement. As they age, they can decline too. These areas need revaluing and can be made to work, as we outline in Chapter 7.[110]

We have to come to look on buildings as stand-alone objects that we place on available land, rather than seeing the development of new settlements and the regeneration of existing neighbourhoods as a way of reinforcing social relations and public life.[111] For the growth of

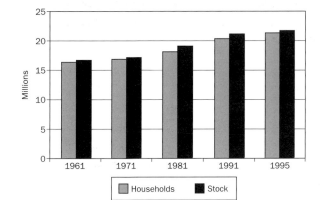

▶ **Chart 3.5: Number of households and size of stock (millions)**
Source: Glennerster, H and Hills, J (1998); Power, A (1987)

▼ Inter-war estates: building low density communities – 35 homes to the hectare
Paul Herrmann/Profile

suburbia runs directly parallel to the long-term decline of inner cities. And suburbs by definition do not work as stand-alone areas. They depend on cities, and thriving cities make thriving suburbs.

Disinvestment and slum clearance

When suburban growth began in earnest after World War One, 90 per cent of the population rented from private landlords. The role played by these private landlords has been crucial to the evolution of modern cities and suburbs. In Britain, almost uniquely in Europe, we drove most of them out of business,[112] thus pushing the inner cities towards mass estate building. Draconian rent controls had been introduced in 1915, to quell unrest in key cities where the wartime boom in shipbuilding had been pushing up rents.[113] Controlled rents, in place for seventy years, blighted virtually the entire inner-urban stock by discouraging essential repair and modernisation, leading eventually to 'twilight zones' in every city by the 1950s.[114] Throughout the twentieth century, rented properties disappeared at an alarming rate. Too few new landlords emerged to take the place of those that gave up. Not until 1988 were private rents finally freed from undue regulation. After that, private renting began to expand for the first time in many decades.

The proportion of homes privately rented fell from more than 90 per cent in 1900 to under 10 per cent by 1990, a dramatic decline in a period of vast expansion in housing. The number of privately rented homes dropped from over 7 million to 2 million, while the total number of homes tripled from 8 million to 23 million. Over 2 million inner-city private landlords sold up their decayed terraced stock into home ownership, fuelling this decline. Another 2 million lost their properties in slum-clearance programmes.

Chart 3.6 shows how little private renting we have compared with other European countries (and the USA), and how few flats we have built as a result.

Today, the shortage of private renting creates problems for jobseekers, newcomers and households undergoing change, all of whom need quick and easy access to housing. Most people, rich and poor, need to rent at some stage in their lives. Better-off people can more easily find a rented flat, but they pay a high premium for merely reasonable conditions. Until rent controls were relaxed in 1988, it was often simpler and cheaper to buy. This made our housing system doubly inflexible.[115]

A shortage of private renting is a major cause of homelessness in cities. People with immediate housing problems cannot 'live in a queue' while they wait for subsidised or rent-controlled housing – they must shelter somewhere. Many of the problems of homelessness would be eased if there were off-the-street, ready-access rooms to rent. New York City has pioneered this approach by organising single-room lets to a mixture of income groups, including previously homeless people. Hotels and hostels in downtown Manhattan have joined this programme.[116]

As we fragment into more and smaller units – perhaps during transitions or crises – we need a variety of routes into permanent homes, many *ad hoc* lets. Young people often need to share, to keep costs down and to accommodate their flexible lifestyles, while they try to find a foothold in the city. This requires adaptable homes to match, as the new housing-capacity study for London emphasises.[117] Cheap rooms and flatlets, hotels and hostels, shared accommodation and lodgings, as well as luxury flats and serviced hotel suites, are critical to urban vitality. They can be part of a mixture of commercial and social uses.

Most private renting is provided by small landlords with one or two properties. It maximises the use of the housing stock and its investment potential by encouraging small-scale entrepreneurs and owners whose homes are simply too big. In Germany, owners willing to provide a rented home within their property can offset some of the cost against tax. In Britain, by contrast, there are still tax disincentives.[118]

By controlling private rented housing of all kinds, through the combination of hostility to private landlords and reliance on councils as main providers, we ran down our historic stock of rented homes. The chronic disrepair of inner city terraces and the gradual withdrawal of private landlords from renting drove many people out of the cities, but also caused intense decay and shortages, leading to slum conditions and eventual demolition on a vast scale.[119]

Large public estates

There was no Big Idea for solving these problems of chronic dilapidation, disinvestment, poverty and overcrowding until, in 1930, a desperate government decided to obliterate the slums – literally. Demolition became the new way forward.[120]

At first, only the very worst, most-crowded areas were targeted, and money was conditional upon councils rehousing the families. Outer suburbs usually objected to the arrival of large public housing estates of ex-slum dwellers. So council housing became tied to inner-city demolition and rebuilding on the spot. The government gave an extra subsidy to encourage the building of flats on clearance sites. In the 1930s, 1950s and 1960s, costs were cut to the minimum to enable maximum building and minimum rents for the poorest families.[121]

In fifty years we have displaced four million families and built ten thousand large estates, many of which stand out harshly on our urban

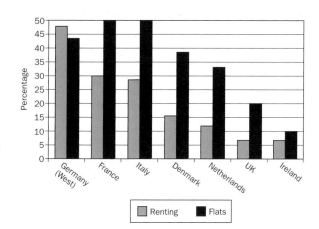

► Chart 3.6: Private renting and flats as percentage of stock
Source: Power (1993; 1996)

▼ Typical new private estate: extreme low density, wasted spaces – 25 dwellings to the hectare
Photo: Llewelyn-Davies

Renting ☐ Flats ■

landscape with a utilitarian stamp. Urban conditions are still strongly shaped by the crude weapon of the bulldozer. A million terraced properties were blighted by official clearance plans between 1930 and 1939. A further million were added to that in the 1950s. More were added in the 1960s until the programme ran out of steam in the early 1970s.

It took ten to twenty years from the declaration of an area for clearance to rebuilding it.[122] Many more areas were declared than could be handled, in an attempt to create enough space to rehouse the people from already-declared slums.[123] The conditions for residents while they awaited rehousing became worse than they had been in the original slums. Childhoods were passed waiting for rehousing and watching bulldozers. Little care was taken to preserve community links – people were literally forced to go.[124]

Newcomers, single and childless households, and 'problem' families were excluded from rehousing because of the shortages that clearance created.[125] In other words, clearances caused homelessness. Areas of ethnic-minority settlement in the inner cities were avoided, and ethnic-minority residents within clearance areas were largely excluded from rehousing until 1976, when the Race Relations Act outlawed discrimination by public and private bodies. This led to much greater ethnic concentrations.[126] Neighbourhoods adjacent to clearance areas became overcrowded as the threat of demolition spread and excluded people were pushed out of the rehousing programme.

Many local authorities, closer to their voters than central government was, resisted demolition, but clearance only ground to a halt after the economic crash of 1974. Meanwhile, the sheer scale of clearance and rebuilding meant that management, repair, environmental maintenance, and caretaking had extremely low priority, and the need to settle disrupted communities was ignored. So estates began to decay almost from Day One.

Richard Crossman, minister of housing in the 1960s, boasted in his diary of forcing Islington to tear down the elegant Packington Square.[127] Towns like Wigan and in the Rhondda were pressurised into declaring slums in settled, low-income communities where people wanted to stay.[128] Cities like Liverpool, Birmingham, Manchester and Newcastle wiped out up to 40 per cent of their inner-city stock. Some of this no doubt needed demolition. The inner areas were so overcrowded that 'deconcentration' was inevitable. But estimates of slum conditions varied widely between local authorities, suggesting that both local and national politics played a significant part. About 60 per cent of the 'slums' the GLC declared in the 1960s were structurally sound.[129] The Westbourne Road area of Holloway was declared in 1968 because, according to the Medical Officer of Health, it was 'full of pimps and prostitutes'.[130] Both Byker in Newcastle and Moss Side in Manchester had sound terraces but serious poverty.[131]

Slum clearance unleashed a new form of public investment: mass council building. Neither this country nor anywhere else in the Western world had ever attempted such an ambitious, publicly-funded, publicly-managed housing programme before.[132] Only centrally-planned economies have ever countenanced such large scale interventions. Only Britain tried to do it within an almost entirely urban framework, displacing whole communities.

Many of the new estates were carefully designed and have stood the test of time. London County Council architects had a world-wide reputation for moderate cost, moderate density and high-quality design. Most of their estates would work well today with more careful management, continual upgrading and a broader mix of inhabitants.[133] But some estates were assembled without any architects at all. A bill of quantities and a 'bed-space requirement' was all that developers were given; Haringey council developed the Broadwater Farm estate with Taylor Woodrow Anglian in this way.[134]

The physical and social consequences are plain to see. On too many estates, the forcibly-imposed physical structure is designed to sort people and their individual behaviour into a uniform pattern. It paid no heed to informal human relations or to people's capacity to organise and to solve problems for themselves. It disregarded traditional patterns and transplanted entire poor communities into alien environments. This rigid, minimalist urban form coincided with an era when those with choice could move out – seeking something they could own, in a suburban neighbourhood that was more private and less vulnerable to the heavy hand of public intervention, less dominated by private squalor.

The clearances did untold damage to services and jobs, as well as to homes and communities: one demolition area in north London, now the Elthorne Estate, contained ninety shops before clearance, but only six were rebuilt in the new development. Liverpool lost 40 per cent of its population and at least as much of its small-scale employment.[135] Glasgow moved most of its low-skilled population away from centres of employment and wiped out many businesses and workshops.[136]

By 1974, demand for the enormous supply of new council housing was declining in most large cities.[137] Too many estates were concentrated in restricted inner areas. Council estates became single-function, low-income islands within cities. For this reason, they often failed to create a viable community. They are heavily dependent on state support: physical investment, rent subsidy, income subsidy, public ownership and management. They therefore lack the independence, diversity or wealth of more mixed communities. In London, people from ethnic minorities have become disproportionately concentrated in the worst estates.[138] Outside

London, council housing remains predominately white, in spite of the large ethnic-minority populations in cities such as Leicester and Bradford.[139] White prejudice has caused the concentration of ethnic minorities in some estates and their exclusion from others.

According to Patrick Dunleavy, it is slum clearance and mass estate building, with all their consequences, that have earned councils their reputation for waste, insensitive planning, poor design, impersonal delivery and lack of contact with the people directly affected. The process of mass public housing reduced the legitimacy of local authorities and stigmatised many inner-city communities.

City councils became the largest landlords in the country, owning over two-thirds of all rented housing and nearly half of all inner-city housing. Cities such as Glasgow and Birmingham, which had the largest clearances, and inner London, which had the greatest municipal activism, are still deeply enmeshed in the problems of council housing.[140] Chart 3.7 shows the concentration of council housing in cities.

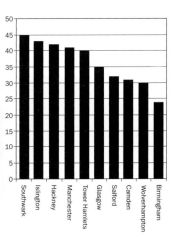

▲ **Chart 3.7: Percentage of city stock owned by local authorities (1999)**
Source: DETR (2000)

Today, council housing is in turmoil. It is unlikely to last in its present form (see Chapter 7). The number of council homes has shrunk by over two million since 1980, from 33 per cent to 16 per cent of the total housing stock, mainly due to the 'right to buy', which enabled the better-off tenants of better housing to become owners. Council housing has become a 'little-choice option' for the most needy. Demolition of large modern estates is becoming common.[141] The supply of affordable homes is shrinking and poorer urban communities are being wiped out, sometimes only twenty years after they were rebuilt. The Hulme estate in Manchester, built to replace the cleared Moss Side terraces in the 1960s, was demolished in the 1980s after acute failures of management, social relations and physical conditions.[142] There are hundreds of estates in a similar condition.

One of the biggest challenges for city governments is to reconcile the need for affordable housing with the avoidance of single-class, segregated estates. Opening up estates to a broader range of social groups and managing them more carefully would make many of them more viable.[143] At the moment, low demand and empty properties affect at least 11 per cent of council housing, even in inner London.[144]

In the short term, it is impossible to demolish and replace more than a small number of the very worst estates. Even the least-ambitious programme would take decades. Yet tenants in structurally sound estates in Islington, Hackney, Southwark, Tower Hamlets and Lambeth, and in other cities all over the country, are being offered expensive regeneration packages that wipe out their estate and reduce the supply of affordable homes. The question is put to tenants in this way: 'Do you want your estates to be demolished? If you do, you can get a new three bedroom house with a garden.'[145] The demolition that follows this 'vote' halves the available properties and concentrates scarce regeneration resources on unsustainable, unaffordable, low-density new homes that many of the displaced tenants will never live in.

◄ Islington's tree planting along rescued old streets: extremely popular houses at 100 dwellings to the hectare
John Hills

Adding new and adapting old buildings keeps neighbourhoods alive. Some demolition is inevitable, but most inner-city estates could be renovated for around half the price of building a new home, providing twice the homes on half the land. The full costs are between £80,000 and £150,000 for a new home, compared with between £15,000 and £50,000 for a refurbished home.[146] The politicians' love of 'flagship projects' takes precedence over the daily needs of low-income communities and the demand for constant care of urban environments. Council estates are not only a vital source of affordable housing; in many cases they are convertible into attractive, marketable housing appealing to a much wider group of people than are currently allowed access. All over London, unpopular lower blocks are being rescued and reused by socially mixed groups.[147] Creating a viable mixture of uses, incomes and tenures within estates is essential to their revival.

Mixed tenures greatly improve the prospects for more compact cities, as by definition they involve more diverse uses. Nearly half the population says it would prefer to live in mixed tenure areas. An overwhelming majority prefers owner occupation because of the choice and control it offers. This is why council housing must change, as Charts 3.8a and b show.

Unsustainable cities

The changes in the structure of cities have caused the overall density of buildings and people to plummet. We now build one new home on the land we used for eight homes in 1900. We house one person for every twenty people we housed in the same space in 1900. Everyone supported the reduction in overcrowding at the beginning of the twentieth century. We now face the opposite problem in many areas: unsustainable low density, with too few people to keep services going. Chart 3.9 shows this.

Unless we increase the number of households in a neighbourhood to make up for the fall in household size, shops will continue to close, bus services will shrink, banks will close their branches and classrooms will empty. Which is exactly what is happening in most inner cities today.[148] Some families will opt out of cities anyway. But many would stay if their neighbourhoods were more viable. Chart 3.10 shows the impact on society, the economy and the environment of outer sprawl and inner decline.

The continental European practice of building apartments has created a need for concierges and wardens. Our low-density housing makes this difficult. But small households at low density result in less

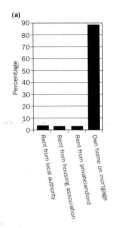

(a)

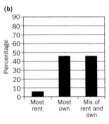

(b)

▲ **Chart 3.8a: What do you hope for your children in 20 years . . .**
Source: IPPR (2000)

▲ **Chart 3.8b: I would rather live in an area where . . .**
Source: IPPR (2000)

Date	No. dwellings per hectare	No. people per hectare
1900 (bye-law housing)	250	1200
1950 (new towns)	35	120
1970 (inner city estate)	100	330
1990 (inner city renovated streets – Islington)	70–100	185–250
1999 (national average planning requirement for new housing)	25	57
Ratio of dwellings 1900–99	10:1	
Ratio of people 1900–99	20:1	

▶ **Chart 3.9: Estimated densities at different times**
Source: Urban Task Force (1999)

Impact on country	Impact on towns
Increased road traffic	More traffic inflow/commuting/ congestion
Increased air pollution, speeding, roadaccidents	Skewed population loss – poverty
More energy consumption and emissions	Exodus of employers
Noise and loss of tranquillity	Empty buildings and land
Impact on water and land use	Negative effect on schools
Loss of countryside – damage to wildlife	Loss of shops and amenities
Village and town encroachment	Decline in property values
Weak public transport in displaced settlements	Buses become less viable
Tendency to over-supply through speculative development	Falling demand/over supply problems
'Rationalisation' of services	High cost of services
Increased demand for some services e.g. health	Polarised, fragmented neighbourhoods – depleted elderly care/disorder
↘	↙

High social costs
High environmental costs
High economic costs

▶ **Chart 3.10: Environmental, social and economic impact of suburban sprawl and inner city decline**

informal 'policing' than with denser and more compact urban forms. There are simply not enough people on the streets to deter anti-social behaviour. Britain has three times more vandalism than Germany, twice as much as Holland and Scandinavia, and nearly a third more than France or Spain. Graffiti and vandalism are perhaps part of the more general lack of respect for the public spaces that are vital to civic survival. Chart 3.11 shows how badly Britain suffers compared with other European countries.

The loss of popular inner-city terraced streets, the loss of much of the private rented sector, the blight of slum clearance, the creation of increasingly-impoverished council estates, the concentration of minorities in the least-popular inner areas and the constantly expanding supply of low-density suburban private homes all compound the problems of cities. Successive housing decisions have locked us into ever more entrenched patterns of behaviour, which so far no government has been able to modify. The line of least resistance is simply to go on building outside cities while trapping the lowest-income tenants in a vicious circle of declining confidence, declining status and declining conditions.

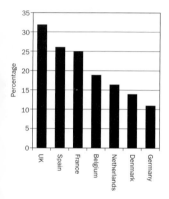

▲ **Chart 3.11: Complaints about vandalism to houses and gardens, as percentage of housing stock (1991)**
Source: UTF (1999)

◀ The line of least resistance: a new housing estate in the middle of the countryside, Stockton, Warwickshire
Martin Bond/Environmental Images

We are reaching the limits of dispersal, and this is forcing us back to the idea of compact, dense, mixed, integrated cities. Traditional urban patterns survive in most towns and cities, and we need more compact, more flexible homes. Many more can be fitted into the existing streets and buildings.

If people could live in the modern equivalent of a spacious but densely-structured Georgian terrace, with tree-lined streets and squares, beautiful buildings and public spaces, close to good schools and public amenities, with access to public transport and with a strong sense of community and security, the benefits of city living would become clear. This must be our ultimate goal – to bring people back to the heart of our towns and cities.

4 Cities and traffic

4   Copenhagen

It is easy to despair of making cities attractive and workable because of the decay, congestion and environmental damage that traffic inflicts upon them. Copenhagen, the capital of Denmark, tells a different story. Today it is the only European capital to have prevented growth in car traffic over the last thirty years.

The story begins in 1962 when the city decided to pedestrianise its main shopping street, Stroget Street, with the aim of controlling traffic throughout the city and making the city centre more attractive to its citizens. The core idea was that if traffic were restricted in the main commercial centre, if public transport improved simultaneously and if physically separate cycle paths ran alongside the pavements, people would only drive into the centre when strictly necessary. Year on year, the city cut parking spaces by 2 or 3 per cent, incrementally changing people's habits.

At first people said, 'We are Danes, not Italians – we don't have a street café culture.' But the new policy became both popular and commercially attractive. Gradually, cars were pushed back and people encouraged to use the space created. Two further streets were pedestrianised by 1973. Since then, the city squares have been closed one by one to traffic, leaving the remaining streets for buses and other vehicles. In 1968, the squares had been mainly car parks; by 1998, they had become outdoor leisure areas – for café life, street entertainment, civic events, picnics or just sitting and strolling. There is now seven times the amount of pedestrian space in the city – 60 per cent of it in squares, 40 per cent in the shopping streets. Four times the number of people stop, sit and enjoy the life of the city as thirty years ago – and there are 25 per cent more pedestrian journeys in the centre. Cycling has increased 65 per cent since 1962; a quarter of all journeys in the city are now by bike.[149] Taxis have to fit cycle carriers so that they can pick up cyclists in bad weather.

▲ *previous page*

Copenhagen: spaces for people rather than cars
Lars Gemzoe

City engineers had the primary target of cutting congestion. Vehicles can now move more freely around the city, and parking is less of a problem, precisely because most journeys across the city have been cut out. Previously the centre was used as the shortest through route, but this no longer works because of the traffic controls. Improving the quality of public spaces followed directly from 'taming the traffic'. The freed-up spaces are now 'public rooms', with trees, more attractive façades, street benches, cafés, balconies and small shops.

Copenhagen's centre is compact: only one kilometre across in each direction, an easy twenty-minute walk. Of the city's one and a quarter million inhabitants, only five thousand live in the centre. The city's commercial district continues to thrive, suggesting that the need for parking spaces for casual traffic is far less than normally assumed. Part of Copenhagen's charm is the mixture of different activities side by side in the same space. Traffic calming encourages more dense use because of the freedom from traffic noise, pollution and danger.

One of Copenhagen's most effective strategies has been the quiet gradual approach: 'Each year the city becoming a little better than the last, encouraging more people to come and use city spaces.' The city centre has become 'a well used living room . . . a meeting place for citizens, a civic forum, among the highest valued attractions a city can offer'. Oxford is the only city in Britain to have prevented traffic growth over the last fifteen years, though York and Edinburgh are both battling towards the same goal.

The Paddington rail crash

The Paddington rail crash in July 1999 killed thirty-five people and created national panic. Yet on the roads, sixty-six people are killed *every week*. Every day, nine hundred are injured.[150] In search of safety and mobility, more and more people drive, yet cars have become 'mobile fortresses', putting us all in danger. Because of the fear of road accidents, only one in fifty children now bikes to school, compared with two-thirds of all children in Denmark and Holland, where clearly separated cycle tracks make it safe. Fewer than half of all schoolchildren walk to school now, compared with the vast majority thirty years ago (Chart 4.1).[151] The consequence for streets, for families, for the countryside and for public transport is ever more traffic.

Cities cannot exist without movement. They develop on the back of large inflows and outflows of people, goods and the vehicles that carry them. The cycle of mobility, congestion and invention has been with us since the Industrial Revolution. Yet our transport methods have not changed fundamentally for a hundred years, since cars, bicycles, railways and undergrounds first brought mass mobility to cities. There is now a strong consensus that new transport solutions are needed. Even car manufacturers recognise this.[152] But there is little consensus on how to charge or distribute the costs of mobility. For up to now we have not paid the full costs to society of moving from place to place.[153] The community at large has accepted these wider costs: the disruption, dirt and dangers. However, we may now be reaching crisis point. Traffic congestion forces us to think again about who will pay. People are keen to reduce the impact of traffic but reluctant to limit their personal freedom.[154]

Public transport aims to expand the gains of travel while limiting its wider costs. But although public transport took off eighty years before cars, it is now insignificant by comparison. Cars account for four fifths of the miles we travel in Britain.[155] The dominance of the car, the relative decline in public transport and the loss of public space for pedestrians and cyclists damage cities, harm the environment and undermine social relations. In this chapter, we look at traffic and congestion, public transport, walking and cycling as they affect cities.

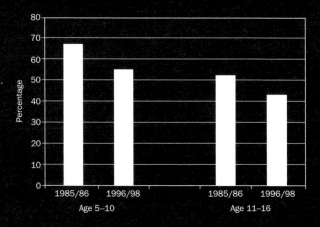

▲ Chart 4.1: Walking to and from school by children aged 5–16, 1985 to 1998
Source: DETR (1999i)

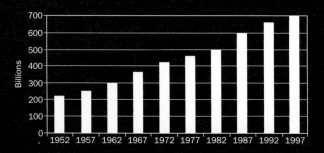

◄ Chart 4.2a: Total passenger km travelled (billions)
Source: DETR (1998f)

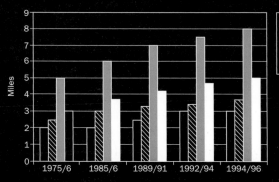

◄ Chart 4.2b: Average journey length in Great Britain
Source: UTF (1999)

The traffic problem began in earnest when railways and roads encouraged the development of suburbs and created the illusion that movement, spread over ever wider areas, would for ever support a dilute form of urban development – the benefits without the costs. Nothing could have been more wrong. The number of journeys we make has almost doubled and the distance we travel has more than tripled since the 1950s (Charts 4.2a and b). The length of journeys is rising steadily, although most are still under two miles.[156] The volume of traffic we generate now seems to be out of control. We travel further to school, to shop, to work.

The proportion of journeys we make by car has risen steeply, from just over a quarter of all journeys in 1950 to two-thirds today. Buses provided twice as many passenger miles as cars in the 1950s but only one-twelfth as many in 1997 (Chart 4.3).

Easy access

Britain's cities draw traffic from an ever wider hinterland, resulting in ever more people moving about within the city. As a result, the centres of our cities are dominated by excessive concentrations of traffic and attempts to expand road capacity. Many cities are bisected by fast through roads. Bradford is one of the worst examples, and as a result its city-centre functions are all but impossible to connect up. Core urban activity – street life, social and commercial interchange – is blocked by traffic. Poor inner-city neighbourhoods are marooned.

The growth in outer-city jobs has greatly increased travel around and across cities. The M25 orbital road around London was jammed within months of its completion, mainly for this reason. The motorway around Birmingham is one of the biggest bottlenecks in the country. Building more roads is not the answer. They simply generate more traffic to fill the extra space.[157] The less dense cities become, the

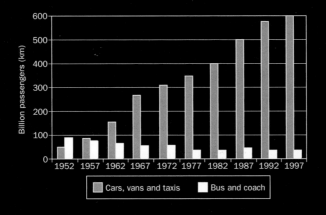

◄ **Chart 4.3: Share of passenger km travelled between cars/vans/taxis and buses**
Source: DETR (1998a; 1999f)

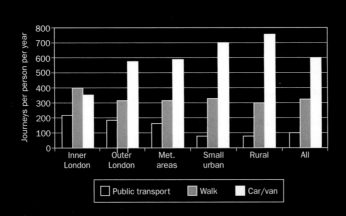

◄ **Chart 4.4: Journeys by type of transport and type of area (1994/96)**
Source: DETR (1998m)

worse the traffic problems are, as people move over wider areas to do their business. American cities show this.[158] We are stuck between traffic jams in ever more depleted cities and speed-bound sprawl into the countryside. In cities, people use cars three times as often as they take a bus and nearly twice as often as they walk – in small towns and rural areas the figure is ten times as often. The resultant traffic encourages yet further flight.

A more vibrant city with higher density and more intense economic activity is forced to rely less on cars, as it would otherwise become gridlocked. Today, cars in London travel at roughly the same speed as horse-drawn carriages in 1880 – around eight miles per hour in the central areas. Bicycles are faster, and sometimes walking too! In inner London, people make more journeys on foot than by car, but they still use buses less than cars; Chart 4.4 shows this. Cities and towns outside London have nearly double the car use.

Cars and danger

Cars damage health, the environment and the streets. They are also dangerous – far more so than any other form of transport. In Britain, cars killed 3,421 people in 1998 and seriously injured 40,834. Six thousand children a year are killed or seriously injured on the roads. Traffic accidents in cities kill two pedestrians, cyclists and motorbike riders for every car occupant killed. Speed is a major factor: 85 per cent of pedestrians hit by cars travelling at 40 mph are killed. At 20 mph, this drops to 5 per cent. Yet very few built-up areas have 20 mph speed limits, and drivers constantly exceed the 30 mph limit.[159]

Most people are car owners. They depend on cars and seem to love them. Over the next fifteen years, road congestion is expected to increase by a further two-thirds as car ownership and car journeys continue to expand. Limited availability of land and the political impossibility of building many more roads make congestion inevitable. Cars, like sprawl, have a powerful momentum of their own. The world is grabbing what it can of the car miracle while it lasts. Those who can buy cars do so in spite of the problems. Thus in Britain there is a rapid shift from one-car to two-car households, as well as from no-car to one-car.[160]

In the USA, 93 per cent of all journeys start from people's front doors by car. Europeans, including Britons, are less car-prone than Americans because of the more concentrated urban living and the smaller distances between cities. But in continental Europe, car use is lower than in Britain because public transport is better.[161] Even so, there is now one car to every two people in Western Europe. World-wide, the number of cars has doubled since 1980 to over 700 million (Charts 4.5a and b).

The rapid growth in cars across the world is contributing significantly to global warming through carbon dioxide emissions. The threat of climate change is now so real that we have reached international agreement on limiting emissions.[162] The government vacillates between trying to limit cars without provoking too much outcry, encouraging public transport without doing anything radical enough to hold back the increase in cars, and supporting walking and biking without spending real money on protecting either. There is a fear of appearing to prevent the onward march of free choice and of being outflanked by countries with fewer land pressures, better roads and better public transport.

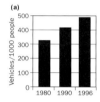

(a)

▲ **Chart 4.5a: Growth in vehicles in Western Europe**
Source: UNEP (2000)

(b)

▲ **Chart 4.5b: Growth in vehicles in the world**
Source: UNEP (2000)

More roads?

Each new green-field development devotes nearly half its land to cars: roads, garages, drives, junctions and turning spaces. Road expansion requires land, often in beauty spots, environmentally sensitive areas or already built-up areas. With each new road scheme, the protests become more strident and more unified. Our very density of population, particularly in southern England, makes roads far more contentious than the mere space they occupy. It is almost impossible to win agreement to build more of them, even much-needed bypasses that reduce urban through traffic and protect historic centres. Just to park the cars we own, nose to tail, would requires 280 square kilometres of space, enough to accommodate 1.4 million new single-family homes. A conflict has grown up between housing people, employing people and moving them – a tug of war between movement and activity.

We have already lost most of the tranquil areas of England, as Chart 4.6 shows. Development of all kinds – housing, employment, roads and air travel – has caused this. But roads are critical to all the others.

One of the first acts of the incoming Labour government in 1997 was to halt all current and planned road building. Unfortunately, this bold action was not matched by the offer of any real alternatives, and the fear of alienating car-owning voters has tamed any real commitment. Since July 2000, there has been a lot of new money for road repair, improvement and expansion. Yet the latest British Social Attitudes Survey shows an acute awareness of traffic problems and of the need to improve public transport (Charts 4.7a and b).

Traffic-bound neighbourhoods

People want to have their cake and eat it: they want to live outside dirty, congested, traffic-bound cities and earn enough to do so by driving in to work, then driving in again for leisure and evening entertainment, turning historic meeting points into traffic islands. As

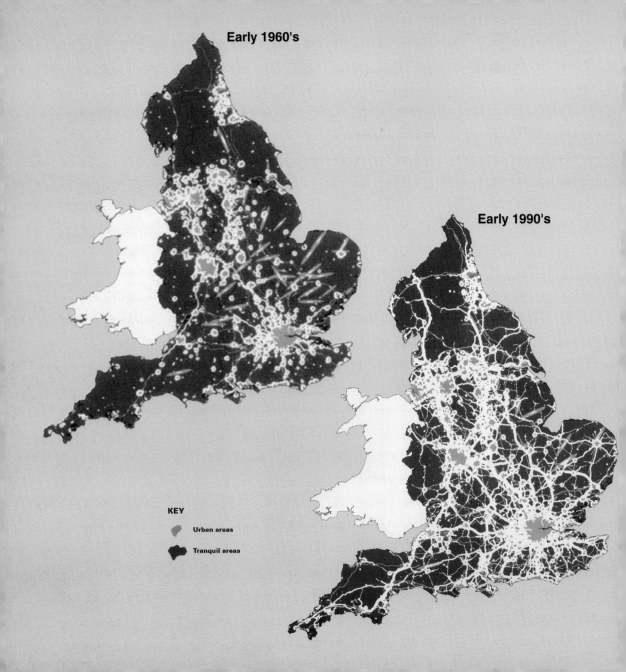

Early 1960's

Early 1990's

KEY

Urban areas

Tranquil areas

◀ **Chart 4.6: The steady erosion of tranquil countryside in England**
Source: CPRE (1994)

▶ **Chart 4.7a: Problems of traffic**
Source: Jowell, R et al. (1999)

▶ **Chart 4.7b: Importance of improving public transport and cutting car numbers in Britain**
Source: Jowell, R et al. (1999)

▼ Divided communities: wide roads, heavy lorries, fumes
Paul Herrmann/Profile

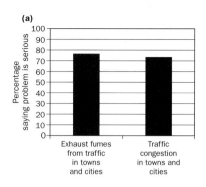

(a)

Percentage saying problem is serious

- Exhaust fumes from traffic in towns and cities
- Traffic congestion in towns and cities

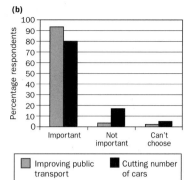

(b)

Percentage respondents

- Important
- Not important
- Can't choose

☐ Improving public transport   ■ Cutting number of cars

urban densities fall, cars can become more dominant than people. The results are devastating. When only cars use the space, there is vandalism, litter and dirt. Cars themselves add dust, fumes, polluting particles, even cigarette butts and sweet wrappings. If you don't live where you drive, it is harder to care. Commuters use residential city streets as free car parks. So poorer communities have to live with the air pollution, noise and disruption imposed on them by outsiders.

Traffic in city neighbourhoods is hostile to family life. Children cannot play safely, cannot cross a road. A famous study of San Francisco streets carried out by Don Appleyard as long ago as 1976 showed that the density of friendships and people's sense of neighbourliness decline with increased traffic; see Charts 4.8a and b. In Britain, we have been slow to introduce traffic schemes that prioritise pedestrians. However, the experience of traffic restrictions, play streets and giving priority to pedestrians and public transport in German, Scandinavian and Dutch cities confirms that people feel more secure and more socially integrated in low-traffic streets.[163] Copenhagen shows that limiting unnecessary traffic is the key to change.

Traffic has a serious impact on health too. Cities have far worse air pollution than the countryside. It is mainly caused by traffic. Air pollution aggravates breathing problems. The lack of exercise among children caused by the fear of traffic leads to obesity, softer bones, weaker spinal development and general restlessness.[164] But traffic also affects the health of workers. Many cities in the USA and Europe now have to stop motorists when air pollution rises above a certain level. So cities, and particularly their centres, bear much of the environmental cost of dispersed car driving. This creates yet another polarising pressure, because the air pollution both results from and causes urban flight. Traffic and the shortage of land are causing a gradual shift back to higher-density living, and creating demand for alternatives to the car.

Public transport is a great equaliser, as it creates links for lower income people. However, the belief took hold that, as they became cheaper, cars could replace public transport. As a result, we have disinvested in public transport. In developing countries such an idea is unthinkable, but in developed economies car ownership reaches far down to the lower income levels. Thus we often overlook the fact that one-fifth of the population of Britain does not own a car or have access to one. In many inner-city neighbourhoods this proportion rises to well over a half. Some groups are particularly disadvantaged: the elderly, lone parents, young single households, people living in council housing, people in inner-city neighbourhoods and outer estates.[165] Poorer people in poorer neighbourhoods are triply penalised because public transport is both inadequate and expensive relative to their incomes, and a car is often unaffordable. This has a drastic effect on employment, mobility and social exclusion, as people without cars are trapped. Cars are also a powerful status symbol. For young men in particular, they represent everything that society values: independence, success, dominance. The alternatives are seen as inferior, slow and unpopular, demonstrating relative powerlessness. The desire to own a car lies behind much car theft and joyriding.[166]

Until we organise a fast, clean, reliable public-transport alternative for every urban community, people will constantly be driven to become car owners, for want of an alternative and to become part of the culture of success. Otherwise they will feel excluded. But public transport, like neighbourhoods, has to attract all sections of the community if it is to work. When the New York subway became safe again in the 1990s, rich bankers were persuaded to travellers with the mass of low-income workers.

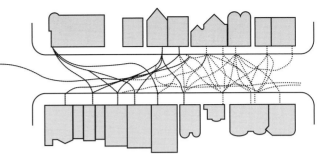

Light Traffic
2000 vehicles per day
200 vehicles per peak hour

3.0 friends per person
6.3 acquaintances

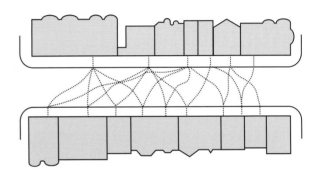

Moderate Traffic
8000 vehicles per day
550 vehicles per peak hour

1.3 friends per person
4.1 acquaintances

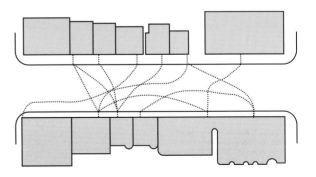

Heavy Traffic
16000 vehicles per day
1900 vehicles per peak hour

0.9 friends per person
3.1 acquaintances

► **Chart 4.8a: Social contact decreases with increased traffic.**
Source: Appleyard (1981)
Note: dots = frequency of occurrence of outdoor activities; lines = contact between friends and acquaintances

Light Traffic
2000 vehicles per day
200 vehicles per peak hour

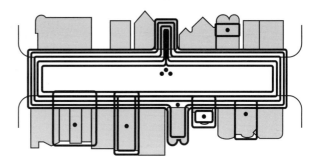

Moderate Traffic
8000 vehicles per day
550 vehicles per peak hour

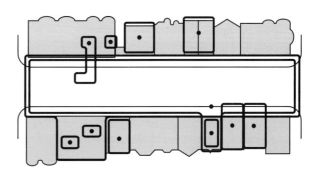

Heavy Traffic
16000 vehicles per day
1900 vehicles per peak hour

► **Chart 4.8b: Perceptions of home territory are also affected by traffic**
Source: Appleyard (1981)

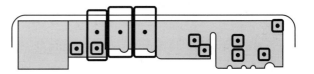

The costs of congestion and its impact on jobs

In the USA, employers are counting the costs of traffic congestion. The lost working time, accidents, ill health and delays cost an estimated $385 per person per year.[167] The subsidy provided by the federal government to each 'sprawl' home – those built outside an existing settlement – in the form of roads, infrastructure, utilities and services is estimated at $25,000.[168] The cost of new schools in these new and far-flung communities – $90,000 per additional classroom, funded largely through local taxes – is increasingly contentious.[169] In both Britain and the USA, traffic congestion has become an electoral issue. In 1999, a US local election was for the first time fought and won on an anti-sprawl platform; and the new head of the Confederation of British Industry recently appealed to the government to tackle public transport in cities, particularly London, to reduce the cost of congestion.[170]

The social consequences are at least as serious. US cities have lost population and jobs, and now contain 85 per cent of the poorest neighbourhoods. 70 per cent of the urban poor are from minorities.[171] This intense segregation of US cities was directly assisted by the building of roads with federal funds.[172] The extreme poverty and decay of US urban ghettos, the spread of these problems over ever wider areas and the impact of inner-city collapse on economic and social conditions have caused a reversal in attitudes since the mid 1990s. US employers and investors are now looking towards the inner cities as new centres of opportunity. Their inability to find enough workers in the sprawling suburbs and the need to transport them across ever-greater distances has partly driven this change. Unemployment is now falling steeply in the inner cities, and investment in urban public transport is growing.[173]

However, the habit of economic investment in the outer areas is strongly entrenched, and jobs are still being created faster outside es, as we showed in Chapter 2. The cost of traffic and within cities deters major investors and employers. parking problems in towns provided the rationale for out-ping centres. The creation of green-field business parks en by the poor public transport of cities. The balance bility and prosperity is critical. The environmental and of traffic are now starting to affect economic progress, loyers, governments and citizens to question the viability ny further outwards (see Chapter 5). The balance of cost awl and city densification could shift significantly.

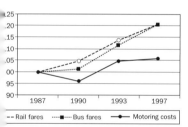

▲ Chart 4.9: Earnings relative to motoring costs (in real terms)
Source: DETR (1998a; 1999f)

▲ Chart 4.10: Relative travel costs (in real terms)
Source: DETR (1998a; 1999f)

The cost is a major influence on the amount we drive. Once we have paid the purchase price of a car, it is often cheaper to drive, particularly if more than one person is travelling, than to use the alternatives. Motoring is cheaper than it was ten years ago relative to incomes, in spite of the high taxes on fuel and the road tax, parking charges and insurance (Chart 4.9). As a result, the government has decided to increase fuel tax annually.

The cost of motoring relative to public transport has also fallen over the last ten years, contributing to the dramatic drop in bus use we showed in Chart 4.3. Public-transport costs have risen in line with the rise in average incomes (Chart 4.10), heavily penalising poor people whose incomes have not risen as quickly.

There are many other costs. The corrosion of city buildings by traffic pollution costs an estimated 3 per cent of GDP.[174] Hospitals, doctors, police, insurance companies, employers and employees between them bear the costs of road accidents, running into hundreds of millions of pounds a year. These costs are direct and indirect, environmental and social as well as economic, out of the traveller's own pocket and out of exchequer subsidy. Are there cheaper alternatives?

Public transport

Mobility in and around cities is as vital as it always was. In the service and knowledge-based economies of today, cities are the command centres[175] of a world-wide network of communication and exchange. Far from 'wired-up' communication making cities redundant, it appears to enhance their value.[176] Although cities would die without interchange, and traffic is part and parcel of that interchange, traffic can also help cities to die. So what can our public transport infrastructure do to help?

Around two-thirds of all journeys are under five miles, and half are under two miles – distances over which a bike or a bus is often faster. Capturing a small proportion of these journeys would make buses viable on most local routes.

In inner London, but not in other cities, there is strong support for congestion charging to deter cars.[177] Parking in the centre of the capital is either unavailable or very expensive – a major deterrent that already exists. A city the size of London simply cannot cope without a comprehensive, interconnected transport system.

Support for radical public transport solutions is growing. But on a crowded island we have to trade some individual freedom of movement for collective provision. Real alternatives must be available. There are three problems: enticing the public out of their cars into buses and trains; giving public transport sufficient priority to make it economical, reliable and comfortable; making walking and cycling safe and enjoyable.

Buses

The simplest, cheapest and most flexible form of public transport is the bus, which accounts for nearly 70 per cent of public transport

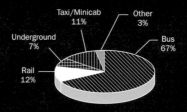

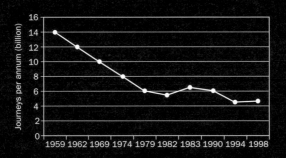

◀ Chart 4.11: Bus share of
total public transport journeys
Source: DETR (1998a; 1999f)

◀ Chart 4.12a: Local bus
passenger journeys
Source: Office for National
Statistics (2000)

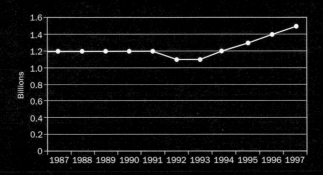

◀ Chart 4.12b: Local bus
passenger journeys in London
Source: DETR (1999f)

journeys. Super-buses can provide convenience, comfort, speed, connections and reliability. They can go along most roads. They can be given priority over cars without expensive tunnelling, tracks or engineering.[178] There are some avant-garde experiments: Curitiba, Copenhagen, Strasbourg and Oxford are cities that have cut car travel by greatly expanding public transport. Chart 4.11 shows how buses dominate the public transport system.

Yet in spite of this, bus journeys fell by two-thirds between 1959 and 1998. The decline has slowed as traffic worsens, but it still continues in all areas except London, where there are now 400 million more bus journeys a year than in 1993. Charts 4.12a and b show the rapid overall decline in bus use and the steep, recent rise in London, helped by the franchise system and the introduction of bus lanes and new information systems.

Investment in faster bus lanes can pay off quickly. The dedicated express bus route from Edinburgh to Leith saved twenty minutes, bringing a 60 per cent increase in passengers in the first year.[179] Only by displacing cars and strictly enforcing bus-only lanes can we enable buses to gain ground. Surprisingly, the Heathrow fast bus lane is reported to have cut both bus *and* car journey times by 'smoothing' the traffic bottlenecks.

▲ *previous page*

Strasbourg: well-designed public transport
TRANSDEV

Light railways and trams

Every major British city has an extensive network of suburban railways constructed in Victorian times. These link many smaller towns within our larger conurbations, and before we started to close 'unviable' railway lines or stations in the 1960s, almost every settlement was within reach of a station. In addition, cities and industrial towns were criss-crossed with electric trams and trolley buses, running along dedicated routes that guaranteed fast, safe travel across built-up areas. These systems provided models for the rest of the world, and our technology was widely exported. Brussels, Amsterdam and many other European cities still rely heavily on trams. We, however, had dug up all our tramlines by 1962 – except for a mile or two along the seafront in Blackpool and Brighton.[180]

Suburban and local railways offer cheap and easy access to jobs, shops and leisure facilities in the cities. British Rail tried to close these lines, but the combination of public protest and the lines' economic importance saved many of them, and they now offer vast potential for rapid transit systems along dedicated routes. The north London orbital rail lines were kept open, and some closed lines may now be re-opened.

Unfortunately, many of our suburban and branch lines are seriously run down, slow and inefficient. They have unmodernised rolling stock, much of it forty years old, and antiquated stations and services, some of them over a century old. The signalling and safety systems are inadequate for new demand.[181] They use main-line tracks, slowing inter-city trains and at the same time being delayed themselves.[182] More than one in ten delays on the national rail system are caused by problems on local lines. The suburban lines out of all our conurbations offer slow, unreliable, uncomfortable journeys – and they need frequent bus links to work properly.

Birmingham lies at the heart of the cross-country rail network, and 12 per cent of all train delays and disruptions are caused by its inadequate connections. The fact that the city is the hub of a huge conurbation and suffers from notorious motorway blockages creates exceptionally high demand for rail journeys. Yet the competing claims of inter-city, cross-country and suburban trains along a single short rail route into the city snarl up both the national and local systems. The price of under-investment and lack of modernisation is cancellations, delayed trains and congestion on the railways as well as the roads.

Many cities are trying to create integrated 'metros' out of their old railway networks, combining existing suburban railways and new light rail systems, all running on the same or interchangeable tracks and linked to buses. Manchester has relaid tramlines across the centre of the city, and Newcastle, Oxford, York, and Leeds are pioneering integrated transport systems. Most other major cities are following suit. This is having contradictory effects. The more easily people can travel in from Northumbria, Cheshire or the Scottish coast to Newcastle, Manchester or Glasgow, the less incentive they have to live in the declining inner city. Better suburban metro and rail lines can reduce road traffic from the suburbs into the cities and attract new investment and jobs, but if cities continue to decay, they can also facilitate the flight of the better-off and the employed to the outer suburbs and the nearby towns. Therefore new urban transport must be linked to employment and physical and social regeneration.

Trains between cities

The same kind of traffic problems that exist within cities occur between cities; over-use of cars, accidents, delays, pollution and damage to villages, small towns and the countryside. One way to secure additional investment in repopulating the inner cities is to build fast rail connections. Lyons and the other French cities now connected by *trains à grande vitesse* (TGV) all show economic growth.[183]

The main advantages of trains are that they provide direct links between city centres, with more predictable journey times, less stress and pollution and lower energy and environmental costs. Trains use less than a third of the energy per passenger mile that a car consumes, and for carrying heavy goods, far less energy than

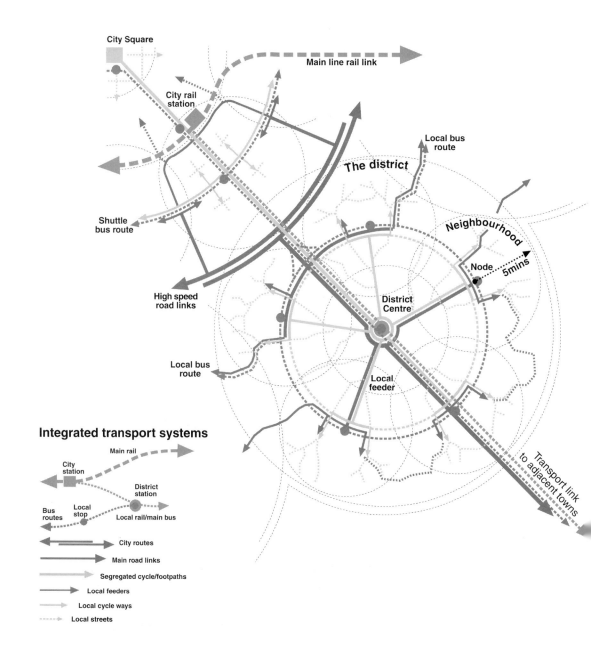

City Square

Main line rail link

City rail station

The district

Local bus route

Neighbourhood

Shuttle bus route

Node   5mins

High speed road links

District Centre

Local bus route

Local feeder

Integrated transport systems

Main rail

City station

District station

Local rail/main bus

Bus routes

Local stop

Transport link to adjacent towns

City routes

Main road links

Segregated cycle/footpaths

Local feeders

Local cycle ways

Local streets

lorries.[184] Now that slow transport connections are hampering economic growth in all regions in Britain outside the booming south-east, the speed and reliability of trains have become crucial.

When businesses make decisions about investment, they take into account the cost of traffic jams and delayed trains. Potentially attractive cities in the Midlands and the North-west have space and ambition, but antiquated railway infrastructures. Birmingham, Manchester, Liverpool and Glasgow are all served by the West Coast Main Line, the worst-performing operator in the newly-privatised rail network (mainly because essential modernisation was blocked prior to privatisation). Thus the three largest conurbations outside London are inefficiently connected, holding back the shift of new development northwards.

The bias of the new economy away from the old industrial centres and the growing importance of links with Europe make many firms consider that relocation northwards is too risky. The rail connections around Britain are far less developed than in Europe. But investment can change this, as Richard Branson is keen to prove; Virgin's massive investment in new, tilting trains will by 2002 start to cut journey times by 25 per cent and greatly increase the number and quality of journeys.[185] The electrified eastern line from London to Edinburgh, which predated privatisation, has brought major economic benefits: the cities along the east coast, with the notable exception of Newcastle, have all fared better than the cities along the western lines, and the upgraded line has certainly played a part. The European rail map (Chart 4.13) shows our rail links.

◄ An integrated transport system
Andrew Wright Associates for the Urban Task Force

Unfortunately, rail privatisation was driven by the desire to reduce government subsidy, creating a narrowly profit-oriented service that is fragmented and unreliable. The privatisation package of 1993 made it easier for the Franchising Director to fine the twenty-four operating companies for failure to run on time than to stimulate investment

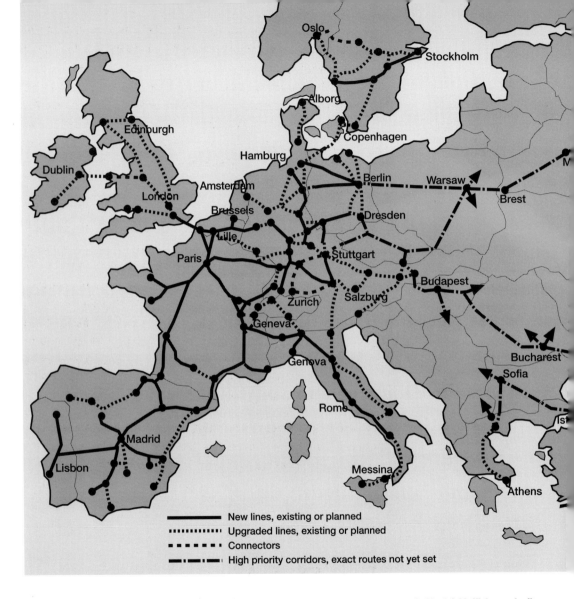

▲ **Chart 4.13: High-speed rail linking Europe's main conurbations**
Source: Scientific American (1997)

in track, signalling and rolling stock. There has been a massive increase in late trains: nearly half a million in 1999, up by a quarter on the previous year – although after the Paddington crash these fell back by 10 per cent as a result of more careful management. One in five Virgin trains arrive late, making it impossible to plan key journeys. This is partly caused by the attempt to run more trains. But it is also caused by under-investment. As a result, our rail system has fallen behind the European high-speed rail network, of which we are supposed to form an important part.

In spite of this, over the past three years the number of rail passengers has risen by a quarter and there are 1500 more trains per day than before privatisation.[186] This unexpected explosion in passengers has left the government floundering for a response. The congestion on the roads is predicted to cause a further 50 per cent rise in rail travel over the next ten years.[187] Running more trains requires more modern signalling, more trained staff, additional rolling stock and more integration between companies. All this will take years of investment: according to the head of Railtrack, there is a shortfall of around £46 billion in funding. The government is now offering over half of this.[188]

Until we link all aspects of transport – rail, bus, road, and in the future, trams – into a seamless inter-connected web, cities will remain difficult of access. The public transport systems we so recently ran into the ground still offer a framework that can help cities economically. Chart 4.14 summarises the advantages of railways to cities.

Walking and cycling

Connectedness between cities is vital, but it is equally essential within cities, where a multiplicity of small and local journeys are made. Until very recently, most people in cities made most journeys on foot. People without cars walk at least two-thirds more than those with cars. There has been a striking decline in walking since 1985, as Chart 4.15 shows; the link with rising car ownership is strong.

Walking is popular when it is quicker and more convenient, when it is attractive and safe, when it involves short journeys, and when it is for leisure. In London, congestion forces people to walk more than in any other city in Britain. But greater proximity between work, shops, banks, restaurants, and public transport makes walking even more attractive. People rarely want to spend more than fifteen minutes – three-quarters of a mile – walking to a shop, a transport link or a social event. But more than a quarter of all journeys are under a mile. If walking were safe and pleasant, instead of dangerous and unpleasant, people who need to make short trips to local shops and schools would use the city pavements. If buses and bicycles had priority over cars, then the 50 per cent of all journeys that are under two miles could combine walking with bus or bike.

Walking, like cycling, does not mix with traffic, so many smaller streets, roads and lanes have become unsafe and unpeopled. Britain has fewer car accidents than any other European country, but our record for pedestrian accidents *caused by cars* is terrible.[189] Where cars are controlled, speed limits reduced and paths and pavements provided, people use them. It took Copenhagen twenty years to shift the balance in favour of pedestrians and cyclists, so we should not delay.[190]

Reliance on fast-moving one-way systems, on penning pedestrians into traffic islands like sheep and on saving seconds for motorists while endangering pedestrians' lives cannot be the right way. Under the pressure of new greenhouse-gas targets, many European cities are extending the areas where pedestrian and cyclists have priority. Strasbourg has linked its highly popular modern trams to a range of

Railways connect city centre to city centre	Trams, protected bus routes and light rail link into railways	Railways counter congestion costs – delays, unreliability, health	Railways open up new opportunities for declining cities	Railways carry skilled workers into new city jobs from suburban conurbations	Railway tracks once laid become increasingly valuable as land pressures mount

CITIES

Railways carry bulk goods cheaper than any other method apart from boats	Railways are expensive to build and maintain but relatively cheap to run at higher volume	Railways with modern stock and signalling have expanding capacity, improving return on investment	Large existing railway infrastructure encourages advanced systems, e.g. Heathrow express, Channel Tunnel etc.	Inter-city fast rail substitutes for air and car at lower time and energy costs

▲ Chart 4.14: The advantages to cities, the economy and the environment of railways

▶ Cycling is dangerous in British towns
Richard Townsend

new transport methods, including boats and pedestrian and cycle ways.[191] Cycling in the city has shot up.

Areas of the city that are walkable, bikeable and serviced by public transport, and where cars are controlled, are social magnets. Creating such areas helps people with disabilities, who should always be given priority; it also helps people on lower incomes, children and the elderly. Limiting car movement to the essentials would *de facto* prioritise pedestrians. At the moment the balance is wrong. Since we are being forced to convert to lower-energy systems, we can make a virtue out of necessity and make our cities more accessible and greener at the same time.

Cycling has experienced an even more dramatic decline than walking. In the 1950s, a quarter of the population went to work on a bike. Now fewer than 2 per cent do. Yet the cost of a typical bicycle has tumbled from twenty times the average weekly wage to less than half. Usage is still extremely low, even though non-car owners cycle 70 per cent more than car owners.[192] The decline is not just about the increasing preference for cars, since many low-income people still do not own or have access to a car. It is about poorer people being crowded off their bicycles by better-off people using cars over ever longer distances. Both the number of journeys by bike and the distance covered have dropped dramatically, as Chart 4.16 shows.

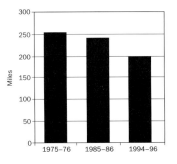

▲ **Chart 4.15: Total distance walked per person per year**
Source: DETR (1998m)

People clearly like bikes and want to use them. Alongside the fall in journeys by bike, there has been a massive rise in bike purchase. About 40 per cent of households now own one, even though they rarely take them out. Chart 4.17 shows the increase in bike sales.

Both cycling and walking are dangerous. Pedestrians have to cross roads, which is when many accidents happen. Cyclists are three times more likely to have an accident, be killed or seriously injured than their numbers suggest. Walking, cycling and motoring simply do not mix safely in the same space, yet for the vast majority of cycle journeys the public road is the only option. Attempts at separating bikes and cars are too fragmented to stand a chance. Sheer survival instinct tells many people not to cycle, however much they like bikes.

The biggest barriers to cycling are the lack of dedicated cycle routes, the speed and fumes of cars and a lazy, pro-car culture. Bikes could easily account for a much bigger share of journeys if cyclists were better protected and city leaders promoted cycling more actively. Within cities, bikes offer the freedom and flexibility of a car at a fraction of the cost and environmental impact. Younger and fitter people enjoy it. Cities such as Amsterdam, Copenhagen, Gothenburg, Freiburg and Strasbourg – which have seen bike journeys double in ten years – show how easily cycling can be extended, protected and sold to a very wide public. In the whole of Germany, cycling has risen from 5 per cent to 10 per cent of journeys in ten years. Other European countries have a far higher rate of cycle use than Britain, as Chart 4.18 shows.

Oxford, Cambridge and York are probably the only cities in Britain that give the same kind of support to cyclists; a quarter of their residents go to work on a bike.[193] Oxford is unique in Britain for having reversed the growth in cars in favour of buses, cycling and walking by interconnecting all three. In June 2000, Sustrans's first five thousand miles of dedicated cycle tracks across Britain showed the way to the future.[194]

Walking and biking seem simple. People like both activities, as the increases in off-road leisure walking and cycling show.[195] They choose them as alternatives to cars when congestion makes them more attractive, when distances are short and when they are pleasurable. Cities that have introduced pedestrian areas and cycle routes and have controlled traffic have benefited economically – more

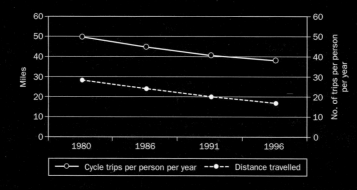

◀ Chart 4.16: Decline in cycling
Source: DETR (1999e)

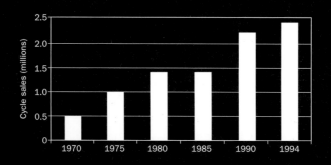

◀ Chart 4.17: Volume of bicycle sales per year
Source: DoT (1996)

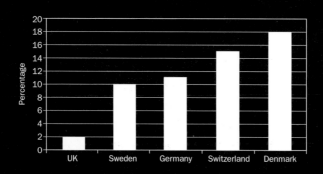

◀ Chart 4.18: Bicycle use in Europe
Source: DoT (1996)

services, more tourists, more investment in infrastructure, the arts and culture. Jobs grow from such changes.

International limits to growth

Built-up areas all around the world have traffic problems. In poor cities, development is seriously hampered: informal settlements are displaced to make way for new roads; the demands of parking and traffic on scarce urban space push poorer people to the periphery, far from work, leading eventually to even greater congestion and inequality. Explosive traffic growth world-wide threatens our delicately balanced ecosystems.

European cities have four times the population density of those in the USA. As a result, there is less than a quarter of the urban traffic – although this does not stop our cities from being choked with cars. The extreme impact of sprawl on car use and petrol consumption in the USA contrasts sharply with the much-lower energy use in European and Asian cities. The differences are partly attributable to the low cost of petrol in the USA and the long distances between cities and suburbs. Political support for cheap petrol and cars is overwhelming. Hence the huge investment in roads.[196]

In Britain, attitudes are changing. Fewer people find driving a car 'too convenient to give up'. Only a third agreed with this statement in 1999, down from over 40 per cent in 1994. Nearly a third are unsure, up from a quarter (Chart 4.19).

Italy has introduced car-free Sundays in most city centres. Some US cities are pulling down urban freeways. Strasbourg is relaying its tramlines, as many British cities are now planning to do. Home Zones in Holland now turn residential streets into extended 'pedestrian crossings'. Some Oxford buses can be flagged down by pedestrians

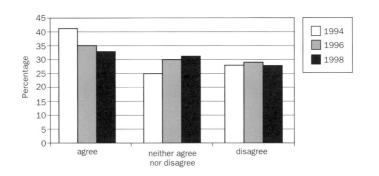

between stops. Interlinked transport decisions can connect cities and enhance their economic prospects.

We all hate streets jammed with cars. We like cities with fast, efficient and interconnected transport, pedestrian and cycle routes. Yet in political terms the leap from where we are to where most of us want to be is vast. The depleted network of public transport makes it all but impossible to provide the complex links, the convenience and the individual control that a car can. We are hemmed in by our own choices. Or are we? We have adapted very quickly to smaller households and to reliance on cars. So we could adapt our living and travelling patterns to modern urban conditions in the same way. Good public transport would make this possible. But we need complementary planning policies that make settlements viable for public transport – compact rather than cluttered, connected rather than dissected. We can improve the transport links, the environmental conditions and the vitality of existing settlements simply by using them more carefully and enhancing their 'compactness'.

Traffic may prove to be one of the biggest problems of the twenty-first century. Of all urban problems, it is possibly the most contentious because it imposes unmeasured costs on other people's quality of life. Our goal is clear: less traffic, less congestion, better communication, greater ease of movement, more people-friendly public spaces. But progress towards it will involve real pain. For we have become a highly mobile, suburban, low-density society. Our cities and our environment are more and more damaged as a consequence – but not irrevocably. In the second part of this book we look more closely at why we are changing our cities and how we can make them work.

5 Cities and the environment – why we must change

5 Curitiba in Brazil is unique. It is a Third-World city with exploding population growth, inequality and environmental pressures, yet over thirty years it has become an ecological experiment, boasting the most advanced urban bus service in the world and social and environmental targets that put the rich world to shame, as well as parks, trees and an historic pedestrianised centre.

Curitiba is an improbable example of a city that works. It has grown from 150,000 residents before World War Two to 2.2 million today. In 1971, the repressiveness of central government inspired a radical local government. Curitiba elected a progressive local mayor, Jaime Lerner. Plans to demolish much of the historic centre and create a 'car-dominated' city were scrapped. Curitiba pedestrianised the centre, winning the backing of schools, businesses and residents. An anti-demolition policy protected homes and employment, and the city's limited resources were concentrated on simple and quick solutions. For example, the inability of rubbish collection carts to get down the narrow alleys of low income settlements was resolved by persuading residents to carry their rubbish to collecting points in exchange for free vegetables.

Pedestrianising the centre was only the first step in revolutionising transport. The central street had to be transformed overnight to prevent sabotage by hostile car owners. Curitiba became the world's first 'bused' city, with dedicated express busways, three-coach buses, multiple loading and unloading and cross-city connector routes. The fare structure favoured the poor, with flat fares from disadvantaged outer neighbourhoods. The first busway, covering 20 kilometres, was opened in 1972. It took two years to build. Virtually no demolition was involved. Since then, year on year, the integrated transport network has expanded to create more of these city-wide busways and 500 kilometres of linking routes. Thanks to transfer terminals along the busways, people only need a single ticket to move from one bus to another. The express routes are linked by hundreds of local buses.

Curitiba developed strong social welfare programmes to integrate its exploding population: crèches and child care, schools, training, investment incentives, environmental protection and recycling. Some of its most innovative ideas were extremely simple.

Children come to the pedestrianised main street every Saturday to paint on paper stuck to the pavements – this guarantees no cars and the involvement of all sections of community.

To raise environmental standards, the city planted thousands of trees down all the streets in exchange for the residents looking after them; green space increased from half a square metre per citizen in 1970 to fifty square metres in 1996.

Rubbish collection, disposal and recycling became a core task for all citizens, reinforcing the ecological message the city wants to promote. Curitiba cleaned up its rivers, providing sewage treatment and turning the flood lands into large parks.

City engineers designed special buses for maximum comfort and speed.

Like other fast-growing cities in the developing world, Curitiba is ringed by squatter settlements. It decided not to demolish homes or displace people, but to upgrade conditions as the cheaper, more universal option.

Curitiba has hundreds of homeless children. It developed day centres, shelters and open-access hostels to help protect and reintegrate them. The city also operates recycled buses as mobile adult education and literacy centres, using hundreds of volunteers.

Brazil has one of the most unequal societies in the world. Curitiba, now its fifth city, has broken the mould by prioritising an attractive, green, economically dynamic city where the poor play their part alongside the rich. Clever design played a key role. Jaime Lerner, three times re-elected as mayor, was an architect and engineer. His development teams scoured the world for the best design ideas and invented their own when no one else had the answer.

What is driving such changes? Cities can only work by introducing a more sustainable urban environment. The Brundtland Commission's definition of environmental sustainability is far-sighted: 'Meeting the needs of the present generation without compromising the ability of future generations to meet their needs'. Tackling poverty and inequality, within local communities and between nations and regions, must be part of this agenda.[197]

Cities are particularly harmful to the environment, producing 75 per cent of the world's waste and using 75 per cent of the world's energy. Although they occupy only 2 per cent of the land surface, they draw their resources from a vast hinterland and spread their waste over it too. Environmental pressures compound the problems of cities. But cities also compound environmental pressures as the illustrations show. Thanks to cities, their sprawl and their waste there is a deeply unequal use of resources, as Chart 5.1 shows.

Europe and North America have only one-tenth of the world's population, yet they consume over half the world's energy, as Charts 5.2a and b show.

According to Klaus Töffer, the highly regarded head of the UN environmental programme, we need a ten-fold reduction in resource use by developed countries to allow adequate resources for the developing world[198]. This imperative, which the Rio and Kyoto environmental summits addressed in the 1990s, is widely supported by environmental agencies world-wide. But it would require much more radical changes in resource use, distribution and life styles than those we are currently proposing. In Britain and many other European countries, land is a critical issue that forces us to re-examine our attitude to the environment. To meet both present and future needs, we may have to recycle it much more carefully than previously.[199]

Britain has one of the highest population densities in the world. There are serious pressures on land in its most populated regions.[200] Britain is also the second most-deforested country of the European Union, owing to the long-term exploitation of the natural environment for economic purposes – only Ireland has cleared more trees.[201] Yet parts of the North Circular road, a traffic-clogged ribbon around London, are now so polluted that the trees planted there by an environmentally-conscious local council will not grow. Curitiba shows that cities can be made far more energy-efficient and environmentally-friendly, but in Britain we are only just beginning.

For example, British local authorities only recycle 8 per cent of their waste, in spite of a 25 per cent target set five years ago. Now the government is to legislate to enforce the 25 per cent target, amid a storm of protest over polluting incinerators, illegal rubbish dumping and pollution from the four thousand official landfill sites. There are no proper sanctions against the 'cowboys' of the rubbish industry because we simply cannot process what we produce, and we are running out of landfill sites.[202] Land pressures have forced the Isle of Wight to recycle over 40 per cent of its waste. By separating organic matter and composting it, the island has become a fast-growing and profitable producer of organic vegetables, as well as Britain's best performing local authority on recycling.[203] Cities are doing much worse.

Until now, the principle of sustainability has not been applied to land and buildings, because it was assumed that land was there to be

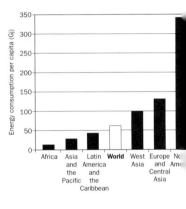

▲ **Chart 5.1: Unequal use of energy due to urban development, 1995**
Source: UNEP (2000)

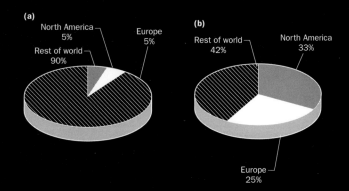

(a)

North America
5%

Europe
5%

Rest of world
90%

(b)

Rest of world
42%

North America
33%

Europe
25%

▶ **Chart 5.2a: Share of the world's population**
Source: UNEP (2000)

▶ **Chart 5.2b: Share of the world's CO_2 emissions – major greenhouse gases**
Source: UNEP (2000)

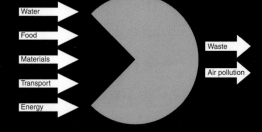

Water

Food

Materials

Transport

Energy

Waste

Air pollution

▶ **The city as consumer**
Most cities in Britain consume resources inefficiently (linear metabolism)
Richard Rogers Partnership with Andrew Wright Associates

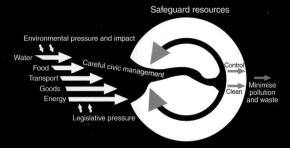

Safeguard resources

Environmental pressure and impact

Water

Food

Transport

Goods

Energy

Careful civic management

Control

Clean

Minimise pollution and waste

Legislative pressure

▶ **Conserve urban resources**
Cities can be made sustainable by recycling resources (circular metabolism)
Richard Rogers Partnership with Andrew Wright Associates

used as long as there was some of it available. Economic costs do not reflect environmental costs.[204] As a result, particularly in cities, we cast off buildings, used land, industrial waste and millions of other damaged, used products directly into the urban environment and its wide hinterland. Most of this is unnecessary. Careful recycling of land, buildings and waste could make a difference not just to the landscape and viability of both town and country, but also to our approach to cities in general. With care, buildings can last twice or three times their predicted life. The Peabody Trust still recycles its dense blocks, a hundred and fifty years old yet still fully occupied and popular. The two-hundred-year-old Georgian terraces of Barnsbury in London and Jesmond in Newcastle show that recycling the land and the cities that stand on it can work.

The government's target of having 60 per cent of new homes constructed on brown-field land or within existing buildings is motivated by the need to recycle land in a heavily built-up country, but it cannot be reached without recycling cities. And recycling land is only one part of the broader need to recycle energy, materials and buildings. Cutting emissions of greenhouse gas, reducing the use of toxic materials in buildings, cutting energy waste in heating and processing, and creating viable public transport are some of the other elements that are needed to form a pro-urban, environmentally sustainable strategy.

▶ Recycling land and buildings: canal-side warehouse, Rose Wharf, Leeds (architects: Carey Jones; developer: Caddicks)
Paul White Photography of Wakefield

Urban brown land is often more valuable than green-field land, and using it carefully offers wide social benefits. The Earth's systems depend on recycling and renewal. Traditionally, people were always obliged to recycle because of the limitations of transport, extraction and production techniques. Our rush for growth, the enormous increase in mass-produced goods and in mass consumption, have put us out of the habit of recycling. We are piling up waste and we are using up resources far faster than they can be renewed.[205]

Herring fishing

The environmental risks we are running by over-consumption and the waste of land have many similarities with over-fishing. Developers do to land what fishermen did to herrings in the Irish Sea in the 1970s. As the stock of fish and the catches declined drastically, a ban on herring fishing became inevitable. Fishermen reacted by fishing even more intensively, knowing that within a short while everything would have to stop. Traditional fishermen in Clear Island, County Cork, fished the sea dry because they could not stop foreign trawlers from scooping up the remaining herring shoals. As a result, herring virtually disappeared. A ban was imposed and a generation of Cork fishermen was ruined. Stocks eventually began to revive, but over-fishing, driven by predatory and uncontrolled competition, is again becoming a major threat. Herring has still not regained its position as the 'poor man's salmon'. Over-fishing is a situation that requires wider action. Otherwise one fisherman can be undercut by many others.[206]

Like the Clear Island fishermen, developers know that the tide is turning against green-field development. They understand that land is finite. They know that environmental pressures are becoming intolerable. Because they cannot stop others from green-field speculation, the developers can limit their 'catch' or they can go for bust as the fishermen did. In this situation, the government's recommended target of 60 per cent of homes on recycled land and in recycled buildings is an attempt to tilt the balance in favour of cities. Key players in the process are the local authorities that control planning decisions. In Newcastle, major developers have already asked to play a bigger role in regenerating the inner city and are reducing their green-field building. They see the way the wind is blowing.[207]

Sustainable development is everyone's goal and no one's job. Our cities are accumulating ever more severe problems, and it is

▲ *previous page*

City waste – economic costs do not reflect environmental costs, New York
Eugene Richards/Magnum

impossible to know how near we are to the point where they might suddenly slide out of control. We may have little choice but to make the brown-field target tougher and to enforce it more strictly. Largely because of green-field building, the abandonment of our inner cities is accelerating. Residents in depopulating neighbourhoods talked of a 'cancer' of abandonment, of 'infections jumping across the street' as the value of their property collapsed before their eyes.[208]

Over-development: the environmental risks

Britain, Europe and North America are not alone in facing this combination of urban and environmental problems. Change is sweeping the globe and affecting towns and cities everywhere. Chart 5.3 shows the current growth in world population and in urban populations. Most urban growth is now in the developing countries of the South, as the West and the North de-urbanise. The scale of this change is so vast and its environmental consequences so grave that 'sustainability' has everywhere become the watchword.

The dangers of over-development are as serious as the dangers of under-development. Consuming too much and wasting too much are linked to four main changes: global economic change, inequality, migration and environmental threats.

The effects of global economic change are unprecedented. We are immensely more productive, wealthier, more mobile and more interconnected than we were even twenty years ago. Technology has taken over many former low-skilled jobs, and industrial production has increasingly shifted to newer economies. But alongside wealth and freedom, the global economy creates unparalleled inequalities and dislocations.[209] These have some of their harshest impacts in the poorest urban neighbourhoods of Western cities.[210] We are only just beginning to understand how carefully we need to tread.

◀ Children washing cars, London
*EPL/Jo Lawbuary/Environmental
Images*

The inequalities of growth are exacerbated by the increase in international migration, particularly by poor people. More than five-sixths of the world's people live in developing countries with rapidly expanding populations, exploding cities and extreme poverty. Their search for work extends across the globe. About a million new migrants come to the European Union each year and a further million go to the USA. Most are from developing economies,[211] and a third to a half of them enter illegally. Developed cities absorb these migrants, legal and illegal, who struggle to compete, often in deplorable conditions, with redundant Western workers for a shrinking pool of low-paid jobs. At the same time, the congestion and high costs in these cities increasingly push manufacturing, computing and high-tech jobs out of Western developed economies and into the developing world. This two-way traffic in people and investment concentrates the problems in the cities, which do not always hold up under the weight of it. Riots in Spain, France, Germany and Denmark in the late 1990s were triggered by strong ethnic tensions caused by immigration.[212]

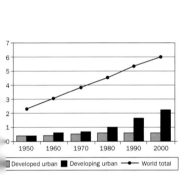

▲ **Chart 5.3: World population, urban population in developing and developed countries**
Source: World Bank (2000)

The outward migration from cities is driven in part by this inward flow of poorer people, as we showed in Chapters 2 and 3. This social and racial polarisation, and the inequality it causes, affect us all. We all depend on cities, even if we do not live in them. Keeping them healthy and functioning is vital to continuing economic growth and sustainability. European governments, including Britain, invest heavily in the physical, economic and social regeneration of cities for these reasons. Although the USA has prospered while its cities have wilted under the impact of a bitter racial divide, the social and environmental cost is as yet uncounted. The vast supply of virgin land has enabled Americans to abandon their cities. Now, however, they are attempting to 'regrow' them.[213]

Cities and towns have the potential to be the most efficient, the most ecologically sensitive and the most equalising environments. They have been so in the past.[214] We can adapt them to the population and consumption pressures of the twenty-first century. By living together in close proximity, we can accommodate far more of the world's population, use less energy, concentrate goods and services, design ecologically sensitive buildings and move around more efficiently.[215] However, the uncontrolled consumption of resources and production of waste in cities are now two of the biggest environmental threats throughout the world. Global warming, to which they massively contribute, is now accepted by almost all scientists as a reality. We know we have to change the way we do things[216].

These four trends – global economic pressures, inequality, migration and environmental threats – make the British government's target of at least 60 per cent of new housing on brown fields an absolute minimum. Even if we cut green-field building to 40 per cent and use land at higher densities, we are still eating away at a finite supply. By setting this target, the government is accepting that some new housing will continue to be built on green fields, but that we have to reorientate ourselves towards cities, towards a more sustainable future. It provides a baseline to work on now, not a distant rainbow.

Cleansing and recycling land, making it fit for use, is not all that is needed to make good the damage we are causing. Cities need natural reprocessing too, to restore the ecological balance in the air, the water and the animal and plant life. Without a wider hinterland that restores the balance of the urban environment, air and land pollution and 'water stress' – shortages, flooding and contamination – all become far more serious.[217] Many effects of over-consumption take a long time to correct. The Danube, flowing through eleven different countries, is now so built-up along its banks, so polluted by industrial waste, that it no longer works as an ecological purifier. Worse than that, giant dams are causing water disputes, silting and disastrous fish losses in the Black Sea. The consequences are so serious that the World Bank, the European Union and the UN are jointly helping to work out how to restore the environmental balance.[218] Recovery can only happen if green space is left. And the only way that space can be guaranteed is to protect it.

We need both to protect the land and recycle it. The Rio and Kyoto summits in 1993 and 1998 inspired many governments, including our own. In response to Kyoto, the Japanese are changing their building regulations to make houses last not twenty-five years as now, but seventy-five like ours. Japan is the world's largest purchaser of rainforest timber to support short-life building methods.[219] The developed world needs a much more custodial, real-cost approach to energy and land use and to sustainable development. There is a powerful tug of interdependence. We know that cities, communities and nations work better if they are integrated across social, physical, economic and environmental barriers. Increasingly, this is also true across continents,[220] as demonstrated by the increase in natural disasters attributable to climate change caused by the over-consumption of energy, largely in the West.[221]

Establishing the need to recycle land may inspire more ambitious people into cities, to broaden and re-integrate the population, to create more wealth, to heal the racial divide that obstructs opportunity, to challenge the conventional wisdom that cities can be over-used and then thrown away. The social rationale overlaps with the environmental concerns. Bruce Katz of the Brookings Institution in Washington, an adviser on cities to the US government, gives three justifications for stopping sprawl and shifting the balance in favour of cities. First, poor people are concentrated in cities and will only progress by means of the greater opportunity created by a greater mixture of people. Second, the economy is affected by an ageing population and there are growing labour shortages in suburbs. Third, free association, which generates civic life, requires density of contacts in institutions and public spaces in and around city centres. The third justifications is fundamental to the first two.[222]

Our human footprint

Many environmentalists argue that far too much damage has been done already and that every move we make should be restorative, avoiding all further growth. Extremists are willing to fight for zero economic growth and even attempt to disrupt the global system of capitalism to achieve this.[223] But few people want to stand still. Nor do they want to turn the clock back. For although there are environmental limits to growth, there are also economic and social limits to how far we can redirect the juggernaut of modern society, with its consumerism and its fears of international competition. The millions of jobs that we need to survive depend crucially on a modern economy, a satisfied work force and a more or less free market. The conflict creates a political stalemate in which each development decision becomes piecemeal, attempting to improve our environmental and economic performance at the same time, but in ways that bring us closer to the inevitable collision between finite limits and restless expansion. In the long run, however, jobs in developed, post-industrial economies depend as much on high levels of skill, on environmental care, on proximity, on good public services and attractive environments as they do on free movement and expansion. Care is a crucial component.

The impact of development and building is ubiquitous. The noise, smells and waste of modern activity, including intensive agriculture, permeate virtually every low-lying piece of land in Britain. Many of our villages, towns and cities are still charming, but only because they have been heavily protected. This is an argument for restraining unnecessary development and for protecting cities and towns, while reshaping them to meet new needs and new environmental imperatives.

The main debate is no longer about whether we need to scale back the damage cities do to the countryside, but about how far we should go. There have been alarms before and the world did not fall apart.[224] But scientists now believe that global warming is so entrenched that it will be half a century before the damage can start to be reversed. Eminent scientists such as Sir Robert May, the government's Chief Scientific Adviser, warn that the changes are accelerating and their impacts are becoming more serious.[225]

Some of the most disturbing signs of damage – the loss of songbirds in Britain, the rapid rise in temperature in the frozen bedrock of the Alps, the failure of Greenland's offshore ice shelf to form, the over-salination and consequent loss of fertility of irrigated land[226] – have causes that are unintelligible to the lay person, and their consequences will reach far beyond this generation. This makes them unmanageable unless we change in many small ways.

We are drawing on the credit of millions of years of natural capital without any idea of when that credit runs out or what it might mean when our ecological system goes into the red.[227] We are not charging the cost of use, precisely because we do not know how big the credit or the debt is; therefore we behave as though our environmental system, particularly our land, is an expandable resource. It can be recycled and used more economically, but it is not expandable. It can sustain higher densities if design and organisation support the goal of compactness rather than dispersal. Chapter 6 explores this further.

Many see the land as a resource to be exploited now, not protected for some unknown future. Because we are not monitoring the damage carefully enough or using what we know to change our ways, we do not plan our land use in a sustainable way. Because human demands are so fragmented, voracious and potentially conflicting, we do not manage our cities and their use sustainably. We prefer to allow diverse groups to spread, having first come together in cities.[228] But preventing environmental damage costs less than cleaning it up afterwards, as Chart 5.4 illustrates.

Why are attitudes changing?

As a completely clear horizon, free of buildings, roads, railways, pylons, power stations and the other clutter of development, becomes increasingly rare, attitudes in Britain and other European countries are beginning to change. In England, only the National Parks and a few other protected beauty spots have escaped – and even there, development and traffic pressures can be intense.[229] In urban areas it is hard to escape from vacant sites with hoardings around them, unwanted buildings with broken windows and battered frontages, closed-down shops, factories and warehouses, large car parks sprawling across waste ground, and tarmac and traffic dwarfing people (Chart 5.5). So our built-up areas look neglected while our countryside looks over-developed.

Meanwhile, there is new building on the outskirts of almost every settlement, large or small. New homes go up, frequently in clumps of 150 or 200, cluttering and damaging the land. They are often detached houses with a few feet of space between them and their neighbours; they have wide drives, double garages and large turning areas. New private estates provide the type of homes that families find attractive. Children play in cul-de-sacs; people quickly get to know each other; and if you have a car, such suburban homes are a safe investment. But they would be less land-hungry, more energy-

▶ Chart 5.4: The economics of cleaner production
Source: Rabobank, (1998)
Note: The costs of cleaner production diminish over time, while the costs of controlling pollution and cleaning up after the event become increasingly high as new regulations are introduced. Modern industry is switching to cleaner production as a result.

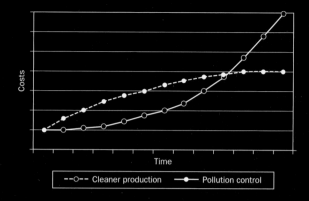

▶ Chart 5.5: The rapid change in percentage of empty property in six small areas, Newcastle and Manchester, 1995–98
Source: Power, A and Mumford, K (1999)

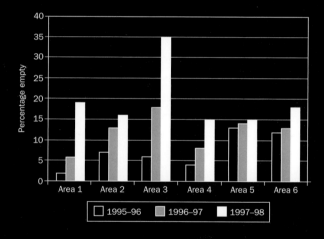

efficient, less car-dependent and potentially more attractive at double the current density (see Chapter 6). The Danes now actively discourage detached houses.[230] We could do the same.

Around three million families have moved into new homes in the suburbs over the last twenty years. This means that, on average, three new private housing estates of between one hundred and two hundred homes have been added to every small neighbourhood of three thousand homes with seven to nine thousand inhabitants across the whole country. That is one new development every seven years in every community. The impression of ubiquitous building is not a false one. But the building has not been evenly distributed. A majority of it has used green-field land.

Our generosity with our land – for the benefit of speculators, developers and those that end up living on it – kills the tranquillity of the countryside through insensitive encroachments. Where overcrowding was the problem in 1900, under-use of space is the problem today. Yet many of the new houses are in regions where they are not needed; some are empty, unsellable or unlettable. The collapse in property values in some inner-city neighbourhoods of the North and Midlands shows the absurdity of this competition between town and country, sucking people away from good-quality homes in depleted urban areas.[231] We watched this classic vicious circle played out over two years in Manchester and Newcastle, in small neighbourhoods and streets of thirty-five to five hundred homes.

To grab green fields we have committed the self-defeating error of neglecting spare buildings and brown spaces. In most parts of the country we are still far from achieving the 60 per cent brown-field target. In London we achieve 85 per cent simply because there is little green-field land available. This shows how much capacity there is in modern cities.[232] The new planning guidance could transform the situation, as it requires local authorities to withhold green-field permissions as long as brown-field sites are available (see Chapter 6).

Over-supply and the Manchester syndrome

A popular density for houses with gardens is between forty and sixty to the hectare, as reflected in the prices asked for older, more central properties at this density. We went from a guideline of forty to sixty per hectare after World War Two to twenty-five per hectare in the 1980s. As our planning system lowered building density and released more land, suburban authorities competed to attract development.[233] The experience of the North West – the region with the most available brown land, the lowest demand and the greatest number of empty properties – shows the consequences of releasing too much green land. The planning system releases land ahead of household projections; developers build new homes ahead of household formation; and the number of existing empty properties dwarfs either projected demand or projected new supply. Key local authorities in the region show a housing *surplus* of around 20 properties to every projected – not actual – new household.[234] It is therefore not surprising that in every city and industrial town in the North West – Britain's largest conurbation – there is boarded-up but perfectly sound housing, large-scale demolition, the abandonment of poorer inner neighbourhoods and a devastated urban landscape. Chart 5.6 shows starkly the over-supply of homes, mostly built on green fields – one of the most important pieces of evidence uncovered by the Social Exclusion Unit's action team on unpopular housing.

Large parts of Manchester, Salford, Preston, Liverpool and Birkenhead and scores of towns in between are affected in this way. The over-supply of green land, low-density building and urban dereliction work together, increasing people's desire to move out and

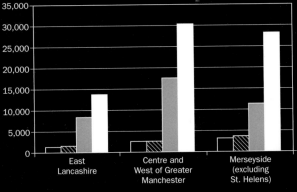

◀ **Chart 5.6: Figures for housing provision in the North West showing the large over-supply of new homes, land and empty dwellings**
Source: DETR (1999n)

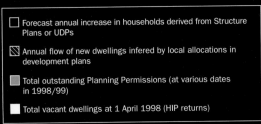

☐ Forecast annual increase in households derived from Structure Plans or UDPs

▨ Annual flow of new dwellings infered by local allocations in development plans

▨ Total outstanding Planning Permissions (at various dates in 1998/99)

☐ Total vacant dwellings at 1 April 1998 (HIP returns)

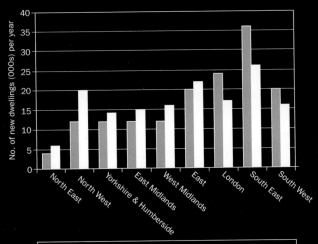

◀ **Chart 5.7: Comparing annual rates of projected household growth with past trends in house building completions**
Source: UTF (1999)

▨ Annual additional households projected to form (1996–2021)

☐ Average annual number of new dwellings completed 1991–1997

their ability to afford it. House prices in the North West conurbations are the lowest in the country.[235] The drift out of the cities to new suburbs is far stronger than the drift to the south, as Alan Holman's work at the Cambridge Property Unit has demonstrated.[236]

Empty, unused spaces in cities beget trouble: vandalism, fires, illicit activity.[237] Intense social polarisation, anti-social behaviour and unmanageable urban conditions afflict many inner-city neighbourhoods as they struggle with inadequate regeneration projects in the face of hidden competition from heavily subsidised new green-field housing. Communities in Burnley, Bolton, Pendle and Colne, four Lancashire ex-cotton towns near Manchester, are fighting proposed large green-field developments that will not only destroy their countryside but also undermine their towns.

There are other regions besides the North West where more land is being released and more homes are being built than we need: for example, Tyneside and Teeside, Yorkshire and Humberside, the West and East Midlands. In these regions, the government must increase the target for brown field sites. Chart 5.7 shows the recent rate of house building compared with the projected rate of household growth. Only London, the South East and South West build at below the rate of household formation.

We only recycle when we have to, not by choice. This is as true of houses in Newcastle and North Tyneside as it is of rubbish and landfill sites. It is always easier, so long as the supply of land is there, to start from scratch and build from scratch. House buyers prefer the predictability of new outer homes to the uncertainties of old inner homes. Recycling involves careful planning and execution; it requires community participation and support; it needs wealthier people, as well as lower-income people; it involves complex partnerships and land preparation (see Chapter 6 on tackling inner-city sites). Only when the cost of recycling falls below the cost of new building will habits shift decisively.

Supply creates demand

The government has blamed the 'predict and provide' approach to land use for creating this state of affairs. Government forecasts calculate how many new households are likely to form over twenty-five years, based on present trends. In line with these 'projections,' the government requires local planning authorities to identify sufficient land in advance for building development to meet future, as yet unrealised, demand. Yet the demand for housing fluctuates with economic conditions. At least a quarter of the predicted households may not form at all, depending on social and economic conditions.[238] For example, couples that split up now find new partners faster than had been forecast, thereby reducing demand. Loss of student grants leads to more students living at home. Conversely, some households form simply because housing is available, particularly in low-demand areas.

In high-demand areas, competition for homes pushes up prices beyond the reach of low-paid households. These problems of housing shortage encourage more sharing, with its accompanying pressures, particularly on low-paid workers and poor households. The unevenness of this pattern across the country makes accurate forecasting difficult and may throw calculations out by hundreds of thousands.[239]

Because more land is allowed in the system than will be required to meet future needs, developers create 'land banks' so that they can plan over several years and meet future demand.[240] This favours green-field development over brown field, as green land is available more predictably, is easier to develop and has already been 'banked' in many cases. If the government encourages building for fear of housing shortages, which it repeatedly does, then planners will cast around for land to put into their development plans, and builders will build on it rather than attempt the much messier job of recycling. The spare land in the planning system encourages lower densities simply because land is available.[241] In addition, planning permission transforms the value of agricultural land, making farmers increasingly keen to sell. Speculators make a windfall profit just on the enhanced land value.

Brown land has built-in disincentives and risks as well as additional costs. The Newcastle growth strategy plans executive homes on former green-belt land north of the city, because it is more attractive to developers and they fear that higher-income people will not move back into the emptying city as it stands. But it is arguable that only by recycling the inner city from the centre outwards will actual growth occur. It is development around the edges that has undermined the city. The costs of brown development can be far outweighed by the gains if we draw up a 'sustainable' balance sheet; see Chart 5.8.

Shrinking households create new life styles

The shrinkage in household size makes brown-field building more achievable, more attractive and more essential. It makes city centres more appealing for more of our lives. It makes interminable strings of almost indistinguishable 'family houses' less attractive. But it also changes the meaning of density. Now that the population is only increasing very slowly, we have halved the density at which we build since the 1970s in terms of the number of houses per hectare and simultaneously quartered the number of people per hectare. We predict that almost four million additional homes will need to be built over the next twenty-five years, but nearly three-quarters of these additional households, if they form at all, will consist of single people.

Costs/Barriers	Gains/Attractions
• Complex uses and ownerships	• Connected, linked sites
• Need to fit in with what is there	• Part of historic urban frame
• Existing obsolete, damaged infrastructure	• Potential re-use of much of existing structure
	– land
	– roads
	– surroundings
	– building materials
• Awkward size and shape of sites	• More interesting, challenging sites
• Difficult access and transport	• More accessible to other activity
• Tighter, more complex planning requirements – time-consuming appeals	• Contribution to rebuilding the city
• Restrictions on design and use due to proximity	• Design challenge and potential – need for vision
• Contamination problems – low or high level	• Techniques to overcome most contamination
• Higher costs and lack of incentives	• Potential for avant garde energy and transport plans
• Uncertain sale value due to environment	• Highly marketable product – some savings
• Unfavourable subsidies and taxes	• Regeneration funds available

▲ Chart 5.8: Costs and gains of brown-field development

Nearly half the projected new single households will not be able to afford a home themselves, suggesting that new ways of building and of converting existing homes may have to be found.[242] The experience of London shows that, in practice, many single people share, for both social and economic reasons.

This shifting pattern creates a disparity between density of buildings and density of people. A private estate of a hundred homes built to house three hundred people in three-bedroom houses may now be occupied by only 220 people. A decline in people density on estates, private and public alike, creates an empty, lifeless feel. On the other hand, if an estate is for families with children – the staple market for suburban developers – there will be a lot of young life, maybe a hundred and fifty to two hundred children, in the hundred houses; a total of four hundred people. Families with school-age children like this, but it can put off older people and younger childless households. There may be an increasing divergence between the needs of families with children and those of childless households.

However, families with children now form a minority of households. Most of the housing we need from here on is for the new, smaller households we are forming. Developers are already casting around for suitable sites in the centre of cities, for that is where most of the new single-person households may want to be, and where single young people naturally group and form new partnerships. Although most people on occasions seek solitude, everyone needs human contact and support. This is particularly true of people who live alone, as most of us will at some time in our lives. We cannot fragment beyond a certain point without destroying our links with each other. We need a critical mass of people to support services, and this may persuade older people as well as younger to live near basic facilities in more compact neighbourhoods. Some developers are building 'granny' and 'student' flats into new homes in recognition of

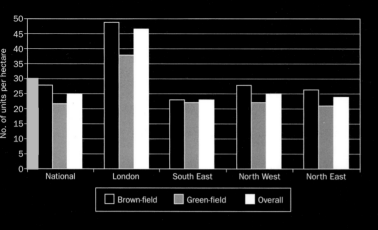

◄ **Chart 5.9a: Average densities of new housing development, based on trends up to 1998**
Source: UTF (1999)

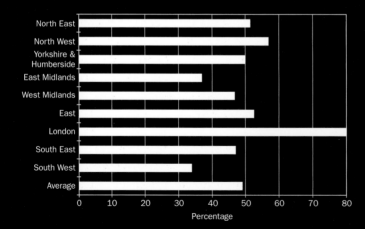

◄ **Chart 5.9b: Percentage new dwellings on recycled land in 1994**
Source: UTF (1999)
Note: The percentage brown-field building has risen since 1994 but is still below 60%. London far overshoots the 60% target. The London Planning Advisory Committee has produced evidence that London can continue with a very high percentage of brown-field building

these changing trends. Studies in Germany have found similar shifts.[243]

But we are being very slow to tackle sprawl. Between 1991 and 1996, we built only 40 per cent of new dwellings on urban brown-field land. Ten per cent of the green land converted to residential use came from 'urban green fields', precious spaces within towns and cities not previously built on. The densities outside built-up areas were so low that the 60 per cent green land produced less than 50 per cent of new homes.[244] About 40 per cent of the rural green land used was given over to tarmac and garaging.

These dispersed new developments, together with rural car culture, have had the perverse effect of closing down country services as well as city ones – particularly buses, health services and shops – because better-off people can drive to shopping centres, health centres and commuter railway stations. It is uneconomic to provide traditional local services, such as shops, schools and post offices, in dispersed settlements. Chart 5.9a shows the very low densities we build at outside London, with even lower densities on green fields. Chart 5.9b shows that, according to the most recent figures, every region except London fell short of the brown-field target.

Many argue that there is not enough brown land to satisfy demand, that many of our old industrial sites have already been reclaimed, that the cost of reclamation is too high or that sites are in the wrong places. But a small island can use most sites; good transport can link most areas. Land and buildings can be re-used many times over as their former uses disappear. There is immense potential in recycling, as the government's new interest in the Thames estuary shows.[245] Some of the largest derelict sites in the South East lie only a few miles from London along the Thames Gateway (Chart 5.10). Ambitious transport plans are proposed for the area.[246] The potential

Northamptonshire

Milton
Keynes

Cambridgeshire

Suffolk

Buckinghamshire

Luton

Stansted

M25

Essex

City Airport

Heathrow

Thames Gateway

A406

Greater London

Surrey

Gatwick

Kent

Crawley/
Gatwick

Ashford

Hampshire

West Sussex

East Sussex

Chan

Isle of Wight

● Area for Plan Led Expansion

(APLE)(diagrammatic)
Thames Gateway

Priority Areas for Economic
Regeneration (PAER)

is huge, but to realise it, a bold vision of compact, integrated new development grafted on to the old is needed.[247]

The cost of the problem

Public bodies and newly privatised utilities provide and pay for most of the vital infrastructure for new developments, connecting new homes to essential services: roads, sewers, street lighting, water and gas. Schools, health centres, police stations and other standard services also have to be provided. Although developers often meet the direct costs of site development and may contribute to community facilities, they do not pay the wider and longer-term costs. Schools and transport links are two obvious examples. The wider community is funding many of the costs of sprawl.

In most cases developers evade the requirement for affordable housing within their private schemes. They often trade sites or pay lump-sum contributions, or offer community facilities elsewhere so that the social housing is segregated and built on the least desirable sites. Planning authorities could quite simply insist, as they do in Holland, that an agreed proportion of affordable housing is fully integrated. New Towns have shown that this works.[248]

▲ Chart 5.10: Thames Gateway: the great urban potential
Source: DoE (1995)

A strong argument in favour of complex, multi-purpose re-use of brown field sites is that it connects new development to the wider environment, committing developers to taking a longer-term view – including revitalising existing infrastructure and services– if they are to market their buildings successfully. Urban Splash, the innovative developer in the north, is recycling imposing ex-industrial buildings in Manchester, Liverpool and Newcastle. This works because the developer, Tom Bloxham, is plugged into wider city-regeneration ideas, the recovery of canals and providing the services and security that new residents require.[249]

No one in government has worked out exactly how big the hidden subsidy is for green-field development. Treasury officials do not monitor the direct or indirect costs, nor apparently do local authorities or the DETR. But the American figure of $25,000 per 'sprawl home' suggests at least as high a figure here, given the much stronger public support for basic services. The parallel cost of keeping deprived city neighbourhoods going, with their falling populations and growing deprivation, is clear. Education in the most disadvantaged inner areas costs far more than the national average.[250] Even the administrative costs of social services and social security are higher.[251] But the main costs arise from the concentrated deprivation in cities and the need to replicate services in ever more spread-out new areas. The poorer the neighbourhood, the higher the differential.[252] So we are paying twice over for the public infrastructure we need.

If developers and home buyers no longer received a hidden subsidy for green-field development, redeveloping brown fields would become much more attractive. Its costs would compare more favourably with the more realistic cost of comparable green-field development. Of course, some green-field sites are more expensive to develop than others, and these problems are likely to increase as land becomes scarcer. None the less, the attraction of green fields will remain until we literally run out of space.

An absurd deterrent to recycling buildings is the fact that developers are allowed to build free of VAT – one of the few remaining business activities that is fully exempt – while the repair and renovation of existing homes carries a 17.5 per cent tax. If new building carried VAT like every other business has to, this would be a disincentive. The government is reluctant to do this because it would increase the cost of new homes, with a knock-on effect on all house prices. But if repair and upgrading were zero rated for VAT, there would be more incentive to maintain and improve existing homes. An option might be to charge all developers the same lower rate of VAT across the board on both new build and renovation. The rate would need to be calculated so that it maintained revenues to the Treasury and so would not affect house prices. A reduction of VAT to 5 per cent on improvements and repair could help to recycle many older homes in danger of abandonment. Thus there would be double benefit and minimal cost. There are strong additional arguments for charging an environmental impact fee or a 'green tax'.[253] But equalising VAT is a simple preliminary step. That way, at least the playing field would be more even and the incentive to recycle would thus be greater. The Isle of Man has just won this concession from the European Union.[254] Will mainland Britain follow?

Renovation would give us a higher density within attractive traditional streets, historic design and unusual landmark features. Surveys have found a strong preference for renovated property.[255] The actual costs of renovation are often cheaper than demolition and new building, as long as the main structural elements are sound – a powerful reason for equalising incentives, not penalising urban developers as happens now. To save a half empty, insecure, dilapidated but structurally sound tower block in London costs about £50,000 a flat. To build equivalent new housing costs at least £100,000 per unit and requires far more land. With improved security, energy efficiency, environmental care and maintenance, rescued blocks are proving attractive at higher rents.[256] Recycling appeals to young 'urban pioneers' and helps to protect existing communities. Disused buildings offer exciting opportunities for carving out lofts and warehouse flats that new residents fit out themselves. It restates our confidence in cities while preventing the displacement of those that want to stay. But we also need to build anew.

The barriers to brown fields

Brown-field building sites are intrinsically complex, carrying the imprint of their former uses, often lying within restricted building patterns, hemmed in by traffic and disrupted systems: closed-down stations, silted-up canals, dug-up tramlines, over-grown land, disused machinery. The brown land itself, its condition and its costs, are barriers to change. The high risks attached to these sites created the Docklands initiatives and led the Thatcher government to set up ten heavily subsidised Urban Development Corporations (see Chapter 6). Some sites are damaged by decades, or even centuries, of industrial pollution: lead, sulphur, gas by-products, oil and other chemical wastes, some of which are poisonous, inflammable or explosive. We should fund reclamation more systematically.[257]

Thamesmead, built in the 1960s on an old weapons testing ground, is close to contaminated land, which deterred investors for twenty years after the New Town was built. But the perceived risk far outstrips the actual risk. Thamesmead Town illustrates both the challenge and the immense potential of brown-field sites, with its riverfront, its train link to central London and its brown land. As the Thames Gateway project unfolds and both the Channel Tunnel rail link and the new river crossing are built, the area will become more and more valuable. In 1983 Thamesmead was the first council estate to create an independent town company, involving residents and mixing tenures and buildings on brown land. It points the way forward for many similar areas.[258]

Cleaning up brown land can involve dumping contaminated soil somewhere else, but techniques for treating soil are being rapidly developed. As yet, however, it is often uneconomic to use them. Our record is far worse than Europe's or the USA's.[259] We need to be able to guarantee brown sites against unreasonable health and investment risks without causing pollution elsewhere. This requires a major up-front commitment over the next two decades. The new strategy on waste, which reveals many of these problems, may push local authorities to act. Following the Urban Task Force report, the UK is at last introducing a single, simplified land condition licence to help developers through the minefield of regulations, laws and poorly enforced controls covering waste, water, land, contamination and resources.[260]

Brown land often has buried beneath it tons of debris, old infrastructure and other waste, which has to be removed, cleansed, dumped and relaid before new foundations and modern infrastructure can be installed. Some of the old infrastructure can be re-used or adapted, but much of it is obsolete, such as lead pipes or old electricity cables. There is no escaping the complexity of many sites, but it is rare to encounter insuperable barriers to development. Brown development can fit in with, and where necessary conserve, building lines, layouts and façades. Integrating imaginative new developments within cities helps to revalue the urban infrastructure. This requires intricate planning and a flexible reuse of the existing buildings to maximise their historic value.[261]

Business sprawl

It is easy to forget that the brown-field target must apply to jobs and businesses as well as to housing, otherwise it simply will not work. Jobs and houses are linked. Interestingly, some businesses are beginning to react against 'investment sprawl.'[262] It creates problems of communication; it can make it more difficult to recruit workers; and as cities regenerate, their attractions become more obvious. Victorian buildings that once housed large enterprises have become increasingly attractive, offering space, originality, grandeur and above all connections. They can often generate within the same building the clusters of services that new enterprises need.

▲ Greenwich Peninsula:
contaminated land cleaned up for
reuse
Courtesy English Partnerships

◀ Greenwich Peninsula: mixed
uses and transport links
surrounding the Dome
*Alison Sampson, Richard Rogers
Partnership*

▶ A sustainable development on
recycled urban land
*Greenwich Peninsula Master Plan
1996/Richard Rogers Partnership*

Issue	Percentage agreeing in different years			
	1987	1994	1997	1998
It is already built up enough round here			62	70
Would like a few more houses			28	21
Planning laws should be relaxed to allow people to live in the country	34	28		23
Countryside should be protected, even if it sometimes leads to fewer jobs	60	71		77
Industry should be prevented from causing damage even if it leads to higher prices	83	89		92

◄ Chart 5.11: British Social Attitudes on rural space and urban jams
Source: Jowell, R et al. (1999)

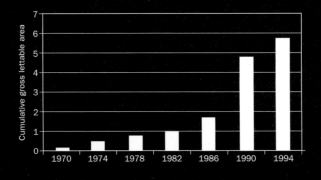

◄ Chart 5.12a: Growth in out-of-town retail provision 1970–1994
Source: UTF (1999)

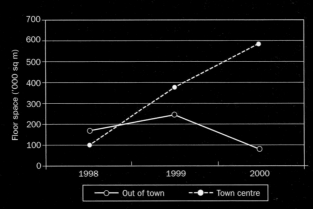

◄ Chart 5.12b: A policy coming good: predicted shopping-centre openings
Source: UTF (1999)

Green-field jobs have the same attractions and liabilities a[...]
field housing. New low-density factories and warehouses, [...]
parks and trading estates, supermarkets and superstores of [...]
have spread greedily across the land, creating new roundab[...]
car parks and more concrete, consuming space and having a [...]
visual effect on green spaces. Businesses find this approach cheaper
so long as they do not have to pay for the environmental impact.
However, as land becomes scarcer in the fastest growing areas,
businesses will have to change their approach. Concentrating
businesses around public transport links, strengthening town centre
investment and regenerating older business parks within cities –
these are already beginning to happen. This trend underlines the
importance of new skills for the traditional work force and an
attractive urban environment for business.

The British Social Attitudes survey found that a large majority of the
population opposed further green-field building where they live, apart
from a few additional houses (Chart 5.11). People say they would
sacrifice jobs to achieve this. Across the country as a whole, over two-
thirds of people think that we are already built-up enough. Three-
quarters believe that protecting the green belt around cities from new
building is essential. Overall, 78 per cent support using brown land
rather than green land.

The previous Conservative administration blocked new out-of-town
shopping centres unless there was no in-town alternative, a move
that many critics believed was too little too late. This cut back on a
practice that was destroying attractive town centres and gobbling up
green fields all over Britain. The adoption of a 'sequential' approach
to shopping centres forced planners to look at available inner sites
before allowing out-of-town developments. This same approach,
which prioritises brown-field sites and existing buildings, is now being
applied to housing. Charts 5.12a and b show the impact of the
sequential approach on shopping.

planners now insist on the re-use of brown sites before allowing new green field building, the brown-field potential rises to 70 per cent or higher in the regions with surplus brown land. If the sequential approach were applied to business investment, it would greatly accelerate urban revitalisation and reduce further the need for green building land. Since most new jobs are in services and 'clean' industries, the rationale for zoning employment away from housing has in most cases disappeared. Since new high-tech industries are more compact, they can fit more easily into brown sites.[263] The new policy would make northern cities with many inner sites very attractive, so long as other matters such as transport, public space, schools and the wider environment were also tackled.

Major companies struggle with the costs of the South East. As these pressures grow, they may find themselves less discouraged by the poor image and bad condition of brown inner-city sites on offer in the Midlands, the North and even parts of east London. At the moment businesses, like housing developers, receive a hidden green-field infrastructure subsidy. If this were replaced with an impact fee, as the Urban Task Force proposes, the balance would shift.

Some firms are beginning to change their thinking. Legal and General, the large insurance company, relocated a large part of its operation to Cardiff, where regeneration incentives together with available land, housing and workers made the inner city more attractive than the pressurised South East. The chief executive is himself Welsh.[264] The experience has been most positive: less congestion, better housing, lower costs, a large available work force. Chart 5.13 shows the skewed supply of brown land away from the booming South East.

Jobs create tugs of war: between areas, particularly the inner city and the suburbs; between regions, particularly northern regions where jobs are scarcest and the south; but also between brown and green

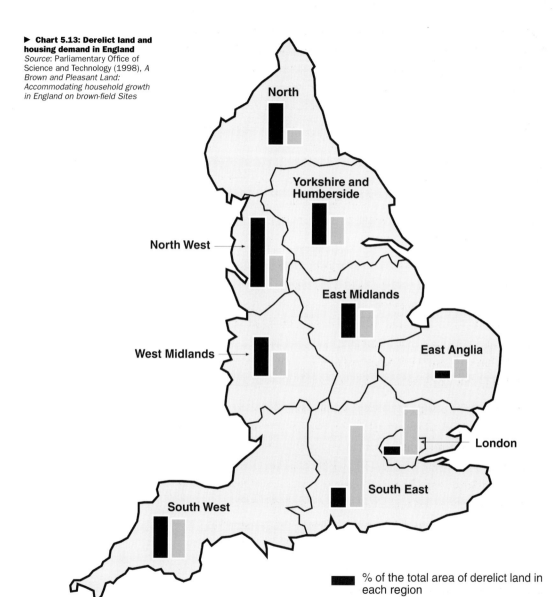

► **Chart 5.13: Derelict land and housing demand in England**
Source: Parliamentary Office of Science and Technology (1998), *A Brown and Pleasant Land: Accommodating household growth in England on brown-field Sites*

North

Yorkshire and Humberside

North West

East Midlands

West Midlands

East Anglia

London

South East

South West

█ % of the total area of derelict land in each region

▓ % of the total household growth in each region

locations; and between countries of the European Union. The regrowth of city centres is now generating thousands of new jobs, although as yet far from enough to replace the ones we lost.[265] The outflow of population has meant that the new workers often travel into work through the work-poor inner-city neighbourhoods. Employers argue that the people who were left behind are insufficiently or inappropriately skilled to meet their needs. Both the City and Stansted airports said that it was difficult to recruit new staff from the East End, in spite of very high unemployment.[266] Communities schooled in the tradition of manual work often lack the confidence to retrain or the contacts to make the break. Many of these barriers are inherited by the upcoming generation. But young Bangladeshis in Tower Hamlets are flocking to IT training in order to capture new jobs. Employers may become more open-minded as labour shortages increase.[267] Creating attractive business locations on brown land within cities while offering some of the essential assets and amenities of cities is a key to creating more urban employment. But schools have to improve and crime has to fall if this is to work.[268]

A younger, more skilled and more active work force that chooses to live in the city is already re-colonising places like London, Reading, Bristol, Cambridge, York and Leeds. British Business Parks is conducting innovative experiments in regenerating 'brown business parks' to meet this new demand. Walsall has successfully re-opened the first 'brown business park'.[269] But we currently offer the wrong incentives and the wrong conditions for a major regrowth of city jobs. Urban decay still acts as a powerful deterrent, making it seem risky to develop brown-field jobs. This leads planners to under-estimate what is possible on city sites, which in turn generates demand for more land releases outside cities for industry and commerce as well as homes. Jobs are the key to achieving the brown-field target.

Pressures on land

Cities and the countryside are interdependent. On a small island, it is impossible to allow the wastelands in and around our cities to stay unreclaimed for long. Having built so extensively and spread out so far from city centres, we need to reclaim if we are to pass any land on to future generations – we cannot create more of it. The brown-field target is a shaky one, but it should be strengthened rather than weakened.

There is bitter disagreement on this. Many argue that Britain still is a green and pleasant land. It is both selfish and patently wrong to argue that we do not have room to spread out. We could carry on building at current rates for another fifty years and still 70 per cent of our land would not be covered. Socially aware people argue this in the name of creating better homes and better conditions. Developers and free-market economists argue that we need to use space with minimal constraints if we are to grow and respond to the rational choices people make[270] (see Chapter 6). Planners argue that we could plan new settlements outside existing cities to provide the important social and environmental conditions we need, thus offering better models for twenty-first century urban living – 'sociable cities' as Peter Hall and Colin Ward have called them.[271]

The suggestion that Milton Keynes, Stansted, Crawley and Ashford should be the next generation of expanded towns must be weighed against the environmental and social impact such growth might have. This is not to suggest that no growth should take place. Rather it means that the environmental impact should be costed in, careful design should enhance the use of land, and a 'sequential approach' should be adopted. The emphasis should be on infill, adaptation, higher density, more mixed patterns, clever design and maximum reliance on public transport. There is an overwhelming case for recycling the available brown-field land first. More gradual and concentrated development make more sense because it allows the existing infrastructure to be used more effectively and forces us to make a careful effort on nearby brown sites. Clever development within these expanding towns may help to reduce the sheer volume of tarmac. Milton Keynes and Crawley could almost certainly absorb another fifty thousand households each without losing significant green space, just by using existing infrastructure and wasted land more carefully. If new building is carefully planned at sustainable densities and linked to amenities and public transport, then we can absorb significant growth and new development while minimising the use of new land, as we discuss in Chapter 6.

The South East is changing its habits the most rapidly. Building densities in London are rising sharply, sometimes reaching an extraordinary 400 flats per hectare in new developments in central areas. The proportion of flats being built doubled since 1980, many of them for higher income groups.[272]

There are three realities we must confront in order to reduce environmental pressures and make our cities more attractive. First, there is more green-field land in the planning system than we need, as shown by the major over-supply in the North West and the evidence of building in excess of household projections in all parts of the country outside the south. Secondly, the extremely low density at which we build everywhere, except in London and the very centre of cities, supports the claim of over-supply of land and underlines the fact that we are no longer building in a sustainable way. Thirdly, the large volume of empty property, which shows up dramatically in the North West and North East, affects every city and most towns. Even London has serious problems of empty property.[273] It suggests a hidden subsidy to green-field building, a hidden tax on re-using existing properties in cities, and an over-generous supply of land.

Land is the vital issue. Land is a finite resource and in some sense belongs to everyone. It must be conserved for future generations and used in a way that does least harm. There are major social as well as environmental costs to supporting the outward movement of those who can afford to do so. As more people become wealthier, this exodus is likely to continue unless we charge the true cost to the environment and cities of making it possible. We can concentrate our building, reduce our energy use, recycle waste, conserve our land, if we make cities work. Chapter 6 looks at how we can change the way we do these things.

▼ Land is a vital resource often badly used, Leicester
Courtesy English Partnerships

6 City centres recover – going against the grain

The grain of cities

Popular moderate density

Fitting the homes in

City recycling

City centres:

Historic city centres

Derelict dock areas

Planning

Impact

Inner neighbourhoods

Remaking city spaces

City virtues

The grain of cities

Christchurch is an ideal coastal retirement town. The ancient priory, the river Avon and its marshes, Hengistbury Head – a rocky promontory opposite the Isle of Wight offering sanctuary to migrating birds – wide mudflats, beaches and an attractive town centre of old terraced properties all make it an appealing place. But it bears the tell-tale signs of low-density sprawl, green-field building and car dominance. A large new out-of-town Sainsburys is reached by a wide, busy dual carriageway and giant roundabout just outside the town. Smaller, more local shops, including those in the town centre, struggle against it. New detached houses have been built on parts of the last surviving water meadows and along the marshes and mudflats that join the old town to the sea. Along the coast, building is virtually continuous to Bournemouth. Hengistbury Head, a wild preserve, is scarred with the paths eroded by the crowds who arrive by car and coach at its large tarmac car park. There is a notice explaining that this once unspoilt spot is still trying to protect wildlife. In the town centre, a new single-storey shopping precinct breaks away from the traditional shopping street, trying not very successfully to compete against out-of-town stores.

▲ *previous page*

Street life – enlivening city spaces
Christa Stadtler/Photofusion

The town council has just opened offices near the centre that have an ugly, over-sized car park in front and are of an insensitive, intrusive design that ruptures the street and blocks any imaginative mixed-use alternatives that might spare the remaining marshes and water meadows. Many homes could have been fitted in. People who moved into the new suburban developments on the edge of the mud flats in the last ten or twenty years do not like what is happening, but they do not know how to stop it. They feel powerless – and muted by self-interest. So they watch as the next piece of countryside they came to enjoy goes under the bulldozer. Trees, hedges, wild flowers, birds, animals are disappearing, to be replaced by brick, concrete and tarmac. It is their actual backyard that is going.

Who gains from this development? The south coast is under great pressure. Should demand simply be met? Clearly, it is an unsustainable demand that simply destroys what people come for – a self-defeating process. The alternative is to use brown land within the existing town more densely, following the traditional pattern of the town's streets, terraces, opening straight on to pavements, with gardens at the back. The green spaces and river banks in the town would need as strong protection as the outlying green areas. But even in such a desirable and high-value place, there are many empty properties and unused spaces over, between and behind shops. Residents are saddened and angered by what they see. A mini-green belt might help the planners.

Christchurch's problems are serious. But they are not on the same scale as Manchester's. The city's large northern and eastern neighbourhoods have more than twenty thousand homes and are afflicted with abandoned property and derelict land, low property values and neglected environment. Communities are crushed by the excessive provision of new housing in the surrounding small towns and countryside. There is little doubt that all the new homes that might be needed for the next two generations could be fitted within the existing urban frame. Manchester was first with almost everything that gave birth to the industrial revolution. North and east Manchester, beginning less than half a mile from the city centre, grew to world pre-eminence in the first half of the nineteenth century, only to collapse in the second half of the twentieth. Canals, parks and rivers cut through these old neighbourhoods. Nineteenth century industrial buildings cry out for conversion. Here are real urban villages dying before our eyes because Manchester is a divided city that cannot pull the levers to halt sprawl. The city's green belt cannot work because it does not encircle the city proper. Greater Manchester is made up of *ten* metropolitan authorities and many adjoining smaller towns. A maxi-green belt around the whole conurbation might help.

We *can* work with the grain of cities, we *can* restore their compactness. The post-industrial era is changing cities across the Western world. After declining since the 1960s, they are becoming more important to businesses, to people and to governments. Cities have become the nerve centres for both regional and international economies. Businesses and workers may communicate across frontiers, but they are always located in a particular place, invariably near or in a city or town. In that sense, cities may be as essential to economic well-being in the technological age as government or enterprise. How will they adapt to the new internationalised economy? Will they win back enough resources, skill and status to reform their conditions?

The politics of change require a strong consensus in favour of cities. Although only a minority of people now actually inhabit the core of cities, most us live within the orbit of cities, towns and their suburbs. So most people have a potential stake in their revival. Many activities can only happen in built-up communities where spaces are closely connected and where people can make easy contact. We cannot organise autonomous life-support systems, household by tiny household. We are collective, social beings and we could not survive such complete individualisation. As we have seen, people seek companionship as well as support through frequent changes of partner. For this to happen there must be a social nexus. So the fragmentation of families and households will make many of us more pro-urban. Indeed, it is probably already happening.

This inevitable shift in favour of cities provokes conflict. On one side there are those who support an even higher target for brown-field development. On the other are those who support continued building or who are ambivalent. Both sides would probably agree that if cities worked better and were more attractive, more people would want to live in them. Most developers support urban regeneration in principle,

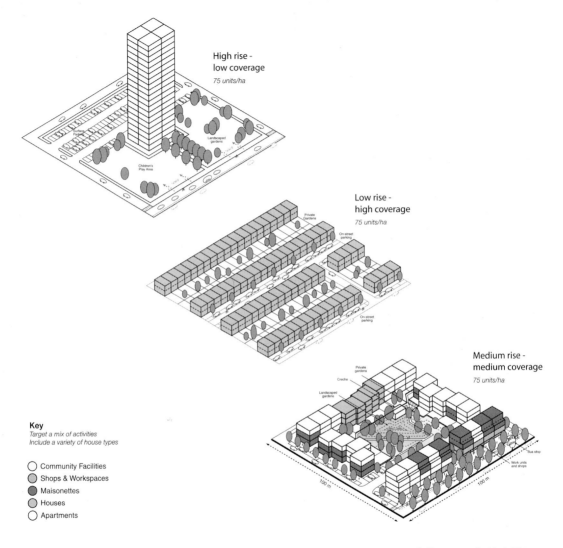

High rise -
low coverage
75 units/ha

Surface
Parking

Landscaped
gardens

Children's
Play Area

Low rise -
high coverage
75 units/ha

Private
Gardens

On-street
parking

On-street
parking

Medium rise -
medium coverage
75 units/ha

Private
gardens

Creche

Landscaped
gardens

Bus stop

Work units
and shops

100 m

100 m

Key
Target a mix of activities
Include a variety of house types

○ Community Facilities
◐ Shops & Workspaces
● Maisonettes
◓ Houses
○ Apartments

▲ Three ways of achieving the
same density
Andrew Wright Associates for the
Urban Task Force

Supporting continued green building

- The **builders** want more land to bank for future building. Green development is easier, cheaper, more profitable and until now politically popular. They want further green land releases as long as land is there. Green land will run out.

- The 'affordable housing' lobby wants enough homes for all and a proportion of affordable homes in all communities. New green-field estates should include affordable homes.

- The 'affordable movers' cannot access reasonable housing in popular inner-city neighbourhoods. They reject poorer, cheaper urban neighbourhoods where affordable housing is available but where social conditions are unfavourable. Green development offers a low-cost quality option.

- **Smaller cities and towns** and small **non-urban local authorities** often support some new green-field development so as not to stymie growth or drive investors away.

Supporting greater development on brown-field sites

- The **NIMBYs** (not in my back yard) argue that building destroys the countryside, not just for country-dwellers, but for urban migrants too. They oppose further green development.

- The **pro-city, pro-urban lobby** sees countryside and cities being destroyed by current patterns, and wants to use all the gaps and spaces in existing built-up areas.

- The **environmentalists** want to safeguard the natural environment as our prime responsibility. Green-field development is pro-car and damages a much wider environment. If we recycle land and buildings we will need far less green land. More environmentally friendly, less traffic-dominated cities attract people.

- The **social environmentalists** support pro-city policies as the only way to reverse social polarisation and make city environments attractive again to a broad cross-section of the population.

▲ **Chart 6.1: Where to build?**

and are almost certainly open to persuasion if conditions and costs are right. We need new-style developers with a more mixed approach to brown and green building than the standard volume house builder. There is a strong shift in this direction.[274] Chart 6.1 sets out the groups on each side of the brown-field debate.

Popular moderate density

Many people worry about being pushed back into cities or being forced into high-rise flats. But we are arguing for a revival of clustered, higher-density settlements of all sizes and shapes, including small towns and villages, that follow popular patterns. Density *per se* has never been the main problem, as the New Town in Edinburgh and Kensington in London show. Both have at least 250 dwellings to the hectare, many of them flats, fetching up to five times the national average house price. It was the combination of low incomes, lack of opportunity, the overcrowding of poor families and poor-quality environments that people like Ebenezer Howard rejected. Careful design and management produce attractive, high-density, mixed, compact styles within already built-up areas. But we must overcome poverty if people are to mix with ease. Tony Blair's aim to eliminate child poverty over twenty years is pivotal.[275]

Outside cities, a typical density in a village centre is about fifty homes to the hectare, double the average for new build. If we built to this density today, it would halve the amount of rural land needed, even if there was no increase in brown-field development. New developments would become less intrusive, more appealing and more 'typical'. The most attractive villages and market towns – in Devon, the Cotswolds, Cheshire, Yorkshire – have compact, closely woven centres with a mixture of houses, gardens, shops, small businesses and open space. It is the older homes at higher densities, clustered in the core of these established communities, that fetch record prices, because

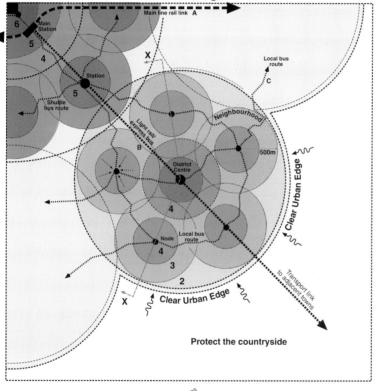

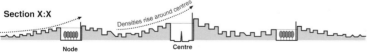

▲ In sustainable cities areas of highest density surround transport hubs
Andrew Wright Associates for the Urban Task Force

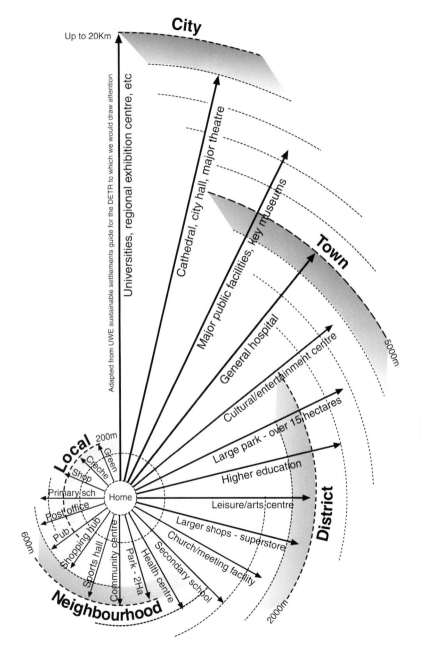

City

Up to 20Km

Adapted from UWE sustainable settlements guide for the DETR to which we would draw attention

Universities, regional exhibition centre, etc

Cathedral, city hall, major theatre

Major public facilities, key museums

Town

5000m

General hospital

Cultural/entertainment centre

Large park - over 15 hectares

200m

Higher education

Local

Green

Crèche

Shop

Primary sch

Home

Leisure/arts centre

District

Post office

Larger shops - superstore

Pub

Church/meeting facility

2000m

Shopping hub

Secondary school

Sports hall

Park - 2Ha

Health centre

600m

Community centre

Neighbourhood

◀ From neighbourhood to city: the basic ingredients of social life
Andrew Wright Associates for the Urban Task Force

of their age, their style, their 'blended' qualities, their position near the centre and their higher density. Many village homes are over shops. Attics are used. Houses are close to the pavement. Side passages to back gardens are narrow and usually abut the next property. There are even rooms built over them sometimes, making the most of usable space. There are rarely garages or drives in traditional streets – only the big manors had those. So cars get tucked in or parked on the street. This more compact, more clustered but less cluttered form makes cars less dominant and the style of building more imposing.

Land may be the most controversial issue, but making neighbourhoods work as communities is as important in the long run. Living at greater densities, in line with traditional patterns, could make new communities more viable and sustainable. At below fifty dwellings to the hectare, it is hard to keep shops, buses, doctors, even nurseries and schools, within walking distance of everyone. This is a critical measure of viability, as the Urban Task Force showed.

The ambition to live in the country with cars, garages and driveways, the resistance to having affordable housing next door and the threat of exported urban problems – all these played a part in the shift to lower density. Building less on more land, and thus pushing up the cost per home, is a blunt way of limiting the exodus to those who can afford 'executive homes'. Of course, large homes with plenty of space in exclusive areas are attractive to those who can afford them. But low-density building increases overall demand for land because it limits supply. Developers often want to put in more houses but politicians and planners often insist on less.[276] The politics of local planning in more-affluent outer areas has often been driven by the desire to keep out cheap developments, but the low-density solution, as our Christchurch example shows, is self-defeating.

Many people are in favour of more compact streets and settlements. Yet we are often told that new low density development is 'market-driven'. Planning restrictions seem a more likely cause, since there is evidence that builders try to create higher densities after planning permission is granted. Some of the best urban developments happen in spite of planners, when architects and developers go to appeal, surrounded by controversy, fighting for higher density and more mixed facilities, bolder street fronts and more compact environments. The rescue and conversion of warehouses, factories, old headquarters and hospitals were not originally planned; in fact they were often made possible by the suspension of planning powers in city centres where the last government declared Urban Development Corporations (see below p. 197–8).

Planners play a key role in land use and the layout of developments.[277] It is therefore vital to identify simple core goals that everyone supports so that we can escape the current circus of developers blaming planners who blame developers. Both blame politicians and argue that they are 'demand driven'. But we have shown that demand, land supply, green subsidies, brown barriers and the pressures of growth or decline all play a part. There is no clear market in such a constrained environment.

The leafy parts of older cities are dotted with small parks, squares and large abutting gardens, yet they have at least twice the density of modern private developments. Manchester, Liverpool, Newcastle and Birmingham all have attractive areas: Victoria Park, Sefton, Gosforth, Edgbaston. Communal gardens, mature trees, children's play areas, wide pavements, streets and squares encourage outdoor social activity. It is absurd to imagine that this is too high a density! Building at fifty homes to the hectare has created all the attractive spaces we like best. It should be the minimum at which we build in cities. Nothing would more quickly enhance the attractions of city neighbourhoods than a more limited supply of green land and an urban density target of fifty dwellings to the hectare. In March 2000, the government made it the top of their range, a big improvement on the earlier target of twenty-five. Chart 6.2 shows the official densities.

Traditional southern European towns and villages usually have double, triple or quadruple the density of a typical English town. Continental cities are also built at much higher density – from Brussels to Rome, Lisbon to Berlin. Their attraction lies in their easy access to the town centre via public transport, their links with neighbours, who are often adjoining, and the shops on the doorstep. The style is partly cultural. People like the density. Such cities have a sense of place. They are a built environment that is clearly marked out from the surrounding landscape. They offer greater security, more street life and quicker access to open spaces. For this reason they offer a useful model for future planning. Britain is not only shorter of land than Europe, it is socially more unequal and its inner cities are more decayed. So we can learn from Europe.[278]

Many new urban schemes in Britain are adopting a continental European pattern: concentrated buildings, mixed uses, sharp, clear openings on to the street, attractive façades, planned public spaces, clusters of activity, much higher density and a dominant human presence.[279] New housing and commercial developments in the centres of Birmingham, Nottingham, Leeds, Liverpool, Glasgow and Manchester follow this dense urban form and have proved popular. The South Bank, the canal area, the neighbourhoods immediately around the city of London are also burgeoning on this mixed pattern. Density no longer means overcrowding, because the numbers of people per home have fallen so dramatically.

Fitting the homes in

If an average density of fifty dwellings per hectare were applied to all built-up areas, including villages, and to all new developments, our requirement for green land would already be virtually satisfied by what is the pipeline for the next twenty years, even assuming that all the projected single households form and require separate units.[280] Developments of one or two houses would obviously still happen, and there would be variations within any average. None the less, shifting density upwards to between thirty and fifty homes to the hectare, as the government has just done, cuts the amount of additional green land we need down from the present 43 per cent to almost zero, as Chart 6.3a shows. The much higher proportion of childless and single households means that even those who favour low density accept that forty homes to the hectare can give space, privacy, gardens and single-family dwellings. Chart 6.3b shows how an increase in density to moderate levels affects the 60 per cent brown-field target and the 40 per cent green-field target. Overall figures in the chart do not reflect regional variations. However, a shift away from the South East may be helped by capacity in the rest of the country.

If we change the way we look at density, we can revolutionise cities. Friends of the Earth and UrbEd argue convincingly that at least 75 per cent of new development can be fitted into existing built-up areas.[281] The London Planning Advisory Committee has shown that all the homes London needs over the next twenty years can be fitted within the boundaries of the capital, almost entirely on brown land. This is remarkable, given that London has the shortest supply of land, is already the most crowded part of the country and has the highest demand. Land shortage and finite boundaries generate high demand for recycled housing and higher densities. However, this does push up costs and limit-supply, so strategies are needed to protect the large supply of low-cost 'social' housing and to uncover new capacity within

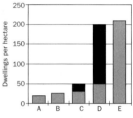

A: 60% of recent green-field developments (1990s)
B: Planning guideline to 1999
C: New government guideline 2000
D: City centre developments – 2000
E: The CASPAR model – Birmingham 2000

▲ **Chart 6.2: Officially planned densities**
Source: DETR (2000b); JRF (2000)

Conditions	Split of development	
	Brown-field %* capacity	Green-field % requirement
Based on patterns in place in May 1999 – 25 dwellings per hectare	55	45
By increasing density by 20% in line with the minimum in the new Planning Guidance, March 2000 – 30 dwellings per hectare	65	35
By increasing densities 50%† – 37.5 dwellings per hectare	82	18
By increasing density by 100% in line with upper planning recommendations in March 2000 wherever possible – 50 dwellings per hectare	100	0

▶ **Chart 6.3a: Changing supply of brown-field housing**
*Brown-field includes recycled buildings, infill sites of less than 1 acre and already used land.
†As recommended in New Town plans. We assume that the playing fields, school and open space requirements reflect lower child densities.
Source: UTF (1999); DETR (2000b)
Note: The green-field land already in the pipeline would provide housing for all the projected increase in households to 2021, if used at New Town densities.

	Units
Homes required by DETR 1999 forecast:	3.8m
1. Green-field housing requirement (40%):	1.52m
Existing and planned sites @ 25 units/ha:	1.05m
Shortfall on current patterns:	**0.47m**
2. Existing and planned green-field sites @ 40 units/ha:	1.68m
Surplus green-field homes from released sites:	0.16m
3. Current brown-field housing requirement (60%):	2.28m
Potential of same sites @ 40 units/ha:	3.65m
Green-field housing requirement if brown fields @ 40 units/ha:	0.15m
Surplus homes from released green-field sites @ 40 units/ha:	**1.53m**
Green-field land already in pipeline more than covers requirement	

▶ **Chart 6.3b: Green-field and brown-field requirements 1996–2021**
Sources: Royal Town Planning Institute (1999); Revised Planning Guidance for Local Authorities, DETR, March 2000; DETR (1999p)

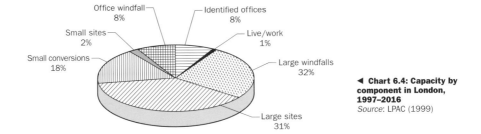

Office windfall
8%

Identified offices
8%

Small sites
2%

Live/work
1%

Small conversions
18%

Large windfalls
32%

Large sites
31%

◄ **Chart 6.4: Capacity by
component in London,
1997–2016**
Source: LPAC (1999)

the existing frame of the city. Imposing the full council tax on all empty property, second homes and pieds à terre would give us an incentive to make better use of what we have. Chart 6.4 shows the potential sources of housing in London.

More than 80 per cent of all additional dwellings in London are already on brown-field sites. A crucial element of these are what are called 'windfall sites', which are not part of the official planning system. They can be large areas, but more often they are small, uncounted pieces of land, usually less than an acre in size, or existing buildings that can be converted to new uses. They turn up because someone somewhere has a sharp eye for small scraps of land and buildings. Windfall sites provide space for between a third and a half of all new development in the country. They offer great potential for making cities work.

If we shift densities to the post-war average of forty dwellings per hectare and maximise windfall sites, then we may only need to put 15 per cent or less of new building on green-field sites. If we reached a density of fifty, our preferred minimum, we have enough brown-field sites, windfalls, empty buildings and capacity within existing buildings to carry us for twenty years. This applies in small towns as well as cities, as we have shown.

◀ A compact urban centre,
Warwick
William Cross/Skyscan Photolibrary

Yet requirements for road width and access, car parking and garages in rural and urban sites play havoc with attempts at compact, 'sustainable' design. So do some of the rules about light, storey heights, attics and semi-basements, density, privacy and overlooking and other arcanely British building regulations.[282] The Great Fire of London of 1666 still influences these rules! We need simple design guidelines that planners and developers can then apply with maximum flexibility.[283]

Zoning for single uses still strangles mixed development near city centres and around the periphery of built-up areas. Local politicians in Newcastle, terrified by job losses, hold on to the idea of industrial and business zones in the heart of the former industrial areas, where jobs are desperately short, thus hampering the regeneration of the worst-hit areas, where new ideas of mixed development might take off. There are many ways of integrating business with leisure and residential development, using modern public transport to support greater density, more services, shops and eating places. This approach is more likely to attract than to deter investment. Glasgow and Birmingham have adopted this mixed-use strategy.[284]

In our crowded and self-interested society, we need to broker our collective interests in the name of protecting our individual gains. Planners are one of the keys to our 'herring fishing' problem. It is their job to protect our common goal: a 'green and pleasant land, with a decent home for all at a price they can afford'. They are the rationers of land, the people who say no. This is because land is not like other commodities. Citizens have a collective right to the use of land, enshrined in our common law. Land is the only way to provide housing, work, transport and food: in other words, survival. To achieve this for all and to protect the land for future generations, we have to adopt a custodial approach. An enforceable green belt around cities helps, but unless all smaller towns have mini-green belts too, the problem simply moves – as Christchurch shows. Increasingly, land is becoming an environmental sink, pooling our waste. Our modern life style impacts on the land in far-reaching, unsustainable ways. The common good requires that we handle land differently from here on.

In the past twenty years, planners have rationed the wrong things in the wrong ways. The density of new development has been pushed too low for urban or rural communities to be self-sustaining. Too much green land has been released, at too low density for there to be room for all who want to use it. The protection of cars and the focus on individual self-interest have been too strong to allow buses or other, more-collective public services to be viable. Planners are caught between developers, politicians, employers, the car lobby and an increasingly affluent consumer. A classic consequence of these conflicting pressures is Preston's new dockside development, which is dissected by dual carriageways, scattered with single-storey business units and giant car parks, too far from the town to walk, of too low a density to support restaurants or shops – with no pavements, no core, no plan. It is widely criticised in Preston owing to the political scandals surrounding its developer deals, and it is an appalling place to try to get around without a car.[285]

The green belt, one of the truly monumental planning achievements of the twentieth century, can tell us something. It is simple, clear, popular, enforceable and fair. Its rules apply to all. Planners can help us to stop the race over the countryside by applying such simple and enforceable rules: brown fields and empty buildings first; mixed uses; sustainable energy; higher density; compact design; minimal environmental impact.[286] The creation of legally enforced green belts around each built-up area, as already happens in the Hertfordshire new town of Hemel Hempstead, would put the clear onus on local authorities to protect land, to recycle and infill, to maximise use of existing spaces and to adopt moderate densities – and would oblige them make an overwhelming case for any exceptions. We could reinstate the positive value of planning while getting rid of the clutter of negative rules that hamper creative solutions to our land problems.

City recycling

City renewal requires a long-term perspective, with specialist developers and builders who can spot hidden opportunities and see their potential. Planners can facilitate this process by being more open to mixtures of use. The complexities of small, hemmed-in sites require such a change of approach. Many 'volume' builders still argue against the new pro-urban, pro-infill approach, and because of their immense clout and financial resources they have been able to persuade planners and politicians to favour big schemes. There have been many scandals arising from the abuse of control over land. Some argue that, because of the problems of dealing with land outside the market, there should be a much freer, more typical market.[287] Britain, with its limited amount of land, its history of land speculation and its comprehensive planning system, regulates too tightly the use of land. The balance between allowing growth and change, preventing abuse and avoiding waste and damage is largely in the hands of local planners, politicians and developers. They can 'stitch it up' unless the system is transparent and simple.[288] For the big developer, all the incentives point in the direction of big sites. This helps to explain why windfall sites are overlooked both by major developers and the official planning system.

Yet these uncounted spaces are vital to the dynamic of cities. We need to maximise the incentives to use spaces that are inconvenient for big developers. Otherwise the scope for city revitalisation will be undermined as growth strategies sweep all in their train, often in the interest, not of urban communities, but of major developers – and possibly local politicians. In Newcastle, the bitter struggle over building on former green belt land is driven by developers' demands and the fear of losing the chance for investment.[289] It is not clear what the city will gain by this.

Cities are like giant pools filled with corks. The many parts of the city – streets, plots, buildings, gaps and other types of land use – jostle, change position and crowd roughly together, some hidden, some conspicuous. They are constantly shifting, so plans for city renewal need a strong vision but also flexibility in implementing that vision.

The dramatic recovery of New York in the 1990s has been about rediscovering every nook and cranny of the city that can brought to life again.

The future for our cities cannot be about carrying out a clean sweep – it can only be about fitting in with the grain of our already-built environment, simply because we have used so much land. When young people were surveyed about moving back into the centre of Birmingham and Leeds, their first choice was a refurbished existing building.[290] Manchester and Glasgow, abandoned as headquarters by some of the largest enterprises in the world, are gradually drawing in many new enterprises, generally small, filling those holes in the city's fabric with new life. We next explore how that revitalisation is happening.

City centres

Over the last twenty years, every major British city, however decayed and depleted, has seen a revival of its historic centre. Until recently, city centres were dominated by blight and emptiness.[291] Since reorganisation and amalgamation in 1974, local authorities were too big to deliver targeted neighbourhood services on the Dutch and Danish model, too constrained by central controls to make city-wide decisions.[292] The economic crash of the 1970s put immense pressure on the British economy, leading to a crisis of confidence in our old-fashioned structures. Quite suddenly, from 1980, city centres became a necessary pivot in any modernisation process. Thus three challenges – emptying city centres, weakened local government and a new economic order – pushed us towards vital changes in our approach to cities. Three strategies began the process of revival: recycling historic city centres, rescuing the old dock areas and freeing up the planning system.

Historic city centres

In 1979 Michael Heseltine, then Secretary of State for the Environment, confirmed the preservation of more than 170 historic listed buildings in Covent Garden. A comprehensive development plan to turn the area into high-rise office blocks, rather like La Défense in Paris, was finally laid to rest. The most flagrant of all 'scorched-earth' demolition plans had been scrapped, changing permanently the approach to city rebirth. This would not have come about if community groups had not fought every inch of the way. The re-use and restoration of Covent Garden turned the tables on fifty years of neglect.

Covent Garden is now a model that is envied all over the world. The idea of linking conservation with enterprise, modern design with traditional streets, public space with popular entertainment, spread like a forest fire. New and old uses were intertwined; history and avant garde inventiveness, art and design were all fêted. All London gained from the ever-expanding traffic-free core that was saved from the bulldozer. Covent Garden influenced the expansion of areas like Camden Lock and Smithfield. Both these had a very different genesis and still operate as more traditional types of markets, but now have some of Covent Garden's flair and dense mingling of people and activity.

Covent Garden inspired other initiatives too. Coin Street, on the south bank of the Thames almost next to the National Theatre, developed co-operative, affordable housing, enterprise and public spaces. The conversion by Coin Street Community Builders of the OXO Tower to apartments with a popular but expensive restaurant and bar at the top shows how affordable housing can be combined with income-generating enterprise.

The transformation of the entire South Bank has gradually followed, creating one of the most dynamic cultural centres in Europe and transforming the poorer, neglected side of the Thames into a lively, mixed-use public area. The riverside walk filled with pedestrians is now linked by a new footbridge to St Paul's Cathedral, helping to join London's newest cluster of arts venues – the Globe Theatre, the Tate Modern, the Design Museum – to the heart of the City. The old power station that has been turned into the Tate Modern, housing sculpture and modern art, had a million visitors from all walks of life in its first two months. And the footbridge's opening troubles have only enhanced its attraction![293]

Derelict dock areas

Virtually every British city has at its heart a river or a canal. The London Docklands Development Corporation was launched in 1981 as a public–private partnership to reclaim and re-use the magnificent abandoned docks of the old Port of London. Today, the resident population of the Isle of Dogs, part of Docklands, has quadrupled from twenty thousand in 1980 to eighty thousand and is still growing, although the lack of an overall plan, the completely *ad hoc* system for approving development and the clumsy government subsidies to help private investors seriously damaged the extraordinary potential of its long river frontage.

The first decade of Docklands was divisive, free-market orientated, office-dominated, expensive and unpopular. Olympia and York, one of the richest developers in the world, created Canary Wharf, the largest office development in the country, but were bankrupted by the government's failure to provide the vital transport infrastructure or a mixture of uses to spread the risk. The development itself is an oppressively gigantesque, single-function workspace, packed in the day, almost dead at night. But after a decade of uncertainty the towering office blocks are lit up with activity, and the Docklands light railway, after many early failures, is extending out both east and south of the river, encouraging the brown-field regeneration of the Thames Gateway. The new fast tube line linking the Millennium Dome and Waterloo with Canary Wharf and the Royal Docks transforms the economic potential of the whole of Docklands. Much now hinges upon whether the local population benefits from the transformation or is displaced by it. Evidence suggests that there is some spin-off in jobs and housing, but the link between the immense wealth and the extreme poverty must constantly be made.[294] The main potential for London's Docklands still lies to the east, around the Royal Docks, and it remains to be seen whether the exuberance of the South Bank can be echoed further eastwards.

In every major city, new development corporations were set up to reclaim valuable abandoned docks and canal areas; there were twelve in all, centred on city 'heartlands'. They sparked off a string of public transport initiatives. High-density, mixed-use developments and conversions along canals and docks have been successful beyond anyone's dreams. New and restored buildings reflected in water entice people back into cities. They offer an escape from traffic. Pedestrian and cycle paths now follow this unique landscape, full of wildlife and unexpected occupants. Parks, old estates, new housing association schemes, converted warehouses, factories, lock keepers' cottages and museums mingle with new enterprises. High-tech media and design companies find new developments in an industrial but green setting particularly attractive. They are densely urban yet have the calm and quiet of the country.

The success of development corporations still provokes bitter arguments – about the cost, the central control, the market orientation. But they did awaken local politicians to the vast potential of the centre of their cities. After ten years of investment they reverted to the local authority domain, and the investments were paid off, mainly after the demise of the corporations. Industrial towns and cities such as Rochdale, Bradford, Crewe, Gateshead, Middlesborough, Wigan, Carlisle and Coventry – deeply problematic places that have lost their earlier *raison d'être* – have produced their own regeneration plans for their centres. No one would have thought it possible before the rescue of the old docks.

New funds for the regions, local government and neighbourhood renewal target resources at urban renewal.[295] They bring together not just public–private partnerships, but different government and local authority services too. Joining up government and attracting private investment through semi-private regeneration companies is now a key local authority strategy. It works if it focuses on a bounded, manageable area and attracts real additional resources as well as government subsidy. Government funding kick-started this new approach, and has levered in far more private money than the initial public investment.[296] Most city hinterlands remain untouched, but almost every older ex-industrial city centre boasts a major success story. This revival is literally a stone's throw away from the catastrophic decline in inner neighbourhoods. The lessons can be applied, as we will show in Chapter 7.

Planning

Local planning powers constrain land use. As we have explained, this is their role. Throughout the post-war period, urban local authorities had acquired huge stocks of brown land, tied up in long-term plans that had become obsolete: road widenings no longer required; urban school and hospital developments; traffic schemes; housing redevelopment; and plans for open spaces. In the early 1980s, local authorities were forced to abandon these blighting, outdated plans and put many of the sites up for sale.[297] Partly because of this release of urban brown land, the shift towards a 50 per cent brown field target became possible in 1995. But the forced release of unused land and buildings in centre cities helped to weaken planning restrictions on green-field development. Non-urban local authorities, including many resistant shire counties, released land to encourage development. This fuelled over-building, as we have shown. The gains in centre cities were thus offset by the costs of low density and green-field sprawl.[298]

Impact

The impact on cities of the relaxation of land controls, the restored infrastructure and the conservation of historic centres has been immense. Cities did not expect the government-created development corporations to work as well as they did, attracting private as well as public resources, new housing, new residents, new amenities and tourists. They have responded with their own dramatic plans: new high-density, mixed-use developments; secure and environmentally attractive experiments in public space and pedestrian priority; adventurous new homes remade within old infrastructure; new integrated transport plans. It was only in the 1990s, ten years after the earliest Docklands initiatives, that these ideas caught hold. The new centre-city developments are popular beyond the dreams of developers, and fetch prices far above their expected value, suggesting that there is a pent-up demand for centre-city living, blocked by years of decline and lack of supply. For the first time in a century, city centres all over the country are gaining residential populations. In Glasgow, Newcastle and Manchester, among the most expensive homes are now those in the very centre of the city. Recently, the first sale in Newcastle's centre to top a million was much publicised. In London too the highest-price properties are in the centre, not on the outskirts.[299] The success of the new high-density developments suggests that people are looking for something different, that a new type of household may be recolonising city centres and that density *per se* is not a problem.

Chart 6.5 sets out the stages in this development.

Inner neighbourhoods

The rescue and renewal of existing buildings and historic areas sets the pace for a revaluation of our dignified and often attractive terraced streets. It has highlighted the thousands of abandoned spaces that suck the life out of cities. The gains in wealth creation and enterprise we have seen in cities have not yet had a positive impact on social cohesion. The freedom to develop and the funds provided by government to help renewal have left many inner neighbourhoods foundering around a revitalising core. Some argue that the success of the centres has been possible only at the expense of the poor inner-city neighbourhoods that ring them. To unleash their huge potential, each run-down neighbourhood needs a focused structure of the kind that go-ahead local authorities have pioneered in places such as Newham and Tower Hamlets in London or that Manchester is developing in Wythenshawe and east Manchester.

City councils are transferring increasingly run-down public housing to more innovative, community-based partnerships such as local housing companies and the urban regeneration companies, releasing energy and innovation. Redesigning the environments and shared spaces of the poorer inner council estates – most of which are close to city centres and to colleges and new universities – could make them more attractive and sought after. Truly crafted redesign, particularly of the public areas, open spaces and ground floors, along with bottom-up community involvement can work wonders. It was on

◄ Well-designed, inner-city, low-cost housing, Paris (architect Renzo Piano Building Workshop)
Michael Denance

▶ **Chart 6.5: Rebirth of cities**

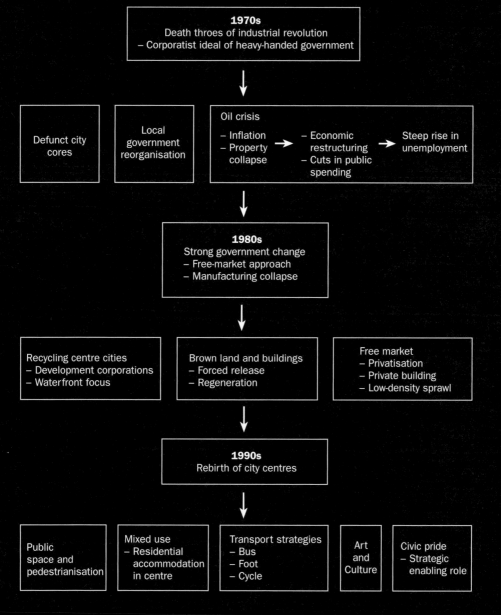

the council estates of the Isle of Dogs that in 1985 we began the joint enterprise of reclaiming cities for their less affluent citizens.[300]

Can we encourage 'urban pioneers' to move into inner-city neighbourhoods while protecting lower-income communities? The revitalisation of such neighbourhoods needs both community involvement and an innovative approach. Barcelona started out from this premise and quickly stimulated popular involvement in renewal. By contrast, our city-centre strategies ignored the inner neighbourhoods only a short walk away. It is not too late to learn from this mistake. Manchester is trying with its eastern and northern regeneration, Newcastle with its 'going for growth', Glasgow with its 'homes for the future'. The Social Exclusion Unit's neighbourhood renewal strategy underlines the urgency of these efforts but, like Barcelona, calls for a simple, bounded set of goals – to increase jobs, to empower communities, to improve public services and to support local leadership – that can be applied everywhere, neighbourhood by neighbourhood. We discuss these goals in Chapter 8.

Remaking city spaces

We like historic cities and vibrant capitals; we enjoy landmarks new and old; the blend of history and modernity; the settled-in feel and the thrill of change; the new activities alongside and within old buildings. We like compact small towns; we like village centres. Our more attractive cities are humming with vitality, a mix of work, home and leisure – a somewhat jumbled and only partially planned assemblage of buildings adapted over time to their environments. A closer look will reveal a dense pattern of land use that would be hard to create from scratch.

Combining physical attraction with the excitement of activity seems the recipe for success. This helps people to connect up in an informal, often random way. A sense of community, of shared interest, grows in functioning public spaces where streets, shops, cafés and public institutions help to weave together our private worlds. The public spaces of the city contrast with the tightly packed density of city buildings, the confinement of cars and buses, the scattered nature of private homes and suburbs.

Architecture had a powerful influence on the history and evolution of cities. It gives form to buildings and the spaces between them. It constantly restores the old and implants the new. It directly affects the well-being of citizens by ordering the places where we spend the most time. Attractive public spaces surrounded by beautiful city buildings encourage the mixing of people and activity, creating community, economy, familiarity and anonymity. The form and layout of cities provide the frame within which cultures and cohesion evolve. Wide central squares, such as the Campo in Siena, act as magnets because the surrounding narrow streets constantly lure people through the shade into the open sunlit public spaces.

Streets are a city's arteries, always converging. The public spaces and central squares can unite or divide the city's people, who are its life blood. Cities all over the world are trying to redress the balance of streets, in favour of people and away from the car, because the vitality of cities stems from the 'life between buildings'. Street fronts broken up with windows and doors provide informal supervision, light and social contact; steps, porches and balconies create meeting points; plant pots, trees, gardens and pocket parks create greenery; floors above shops and offices make unused spaces come alive; small play areas and seats give powerful welcoming signals; street wardens, repair and cleaning make streets safer. Streets make lively cities 'sing'.[301]

Land use is changing rapidly – four times faster than forecast in London[302] – and unpredictably, producing a constant stream of valuable sites. They show how successful cities and communities can unexpectedly generate new forms of building while constantly recreating themselves. Infill and windfall sites are most common in the under-exploited inner areas, as anyone walking around central Glasgow, Manchester, Birmingham or London can see. The same is true in Nottingham, Leeds and Bradford. Rebuilding cities along their 'desire lines', their streets and public spaces, is the 'glue that holds cities together'.

London, Edinburgh, Dublin and Paris have many constantly recycled and lastingly popular neighbourhoods. Recycling poorer, more hard-hit cities such as Manchester is a more difficult and, many think, less attractive proposition. Yet canalside cafés and clubs are fast generating new life. East Manchester, a devastated, half-abandoned area of former industrial housing half a mile from the city centre, could grow again with better transport, more green environments and a concentration rather than scattering of growth. The illustrations on pages 208–9 show the potential for renewal in east Manchester, drawing the city centre regrowth outwards along the 'desire line' of the canals and parks, very much as central London's regrowth has spread outwards along the South Bank and the dock areas.

Cities evolve organically: learning, maturing, adapting. Inventive new developments alongside recycling and re-use give them a creative fusion of continuity and dynamism. Glasgow, Birmingham and Manchester are recreating themselves this way, small area by small area. The idea of organic, compact cities concentrated in the inner core does not stop new activity within existing areas. The many bigger sites of more than ten acres allow new landmark projects to be developed. London alone has several hundred such sites with development potential.[303] Glasgow has nearly 10 per cent of its surface area empty, awaiting new development. It is only at the beginning of its recovery from chronic decline.[304]

The fact that Manchester has some of the lowest house prices in the country may give a negative signal, but it could also be made into a selling point for urban pioneers. To save the vast tracts of now depleted communities, a 70 or even 80 per cent brown target may be necessary. The city desperately needs fast rail links to the rest of the country: under two hours from London in less than five years. It may then persuade major international investors, currently deterred from choosing Manchester by its grimy, industrial environment, to become part of potentially the biggest regeneration project in the country. For with our shortage of land and Manchester's space, it seems certain that the city will regrow.

City virtues

Cities have many advantages. They are more tolerant, more mixed, more anonymous places, where failures and weaknesses are less noticeable and more easily absorbed than in smaller communities. They collect the casualties of harsh competition, family breakdown, school failure, job exclusion – the human debris of modern economic life. But there are limits to what a city can absorb. There is more mental illness, more depression, more aggression and more anti-social behaviour in urban communities. And there are fewer human resources, less community resistance, more risk of breakdown.[305] Cities absorb many of the pressures of change in modern economies, but only a pro-city, anti-exclusion renewal strategy will hold them together.

We all need cities, for all roads do still lead there and all progress is still linked to their health and vitality. The division that now exists between city centres and their inner neighbourhoods makes politicians anxious. They want to attract householders who are, or aspire to be, property owners. Making cities safer and more attractive to investors and home-buyers alike could stop the leaching away of

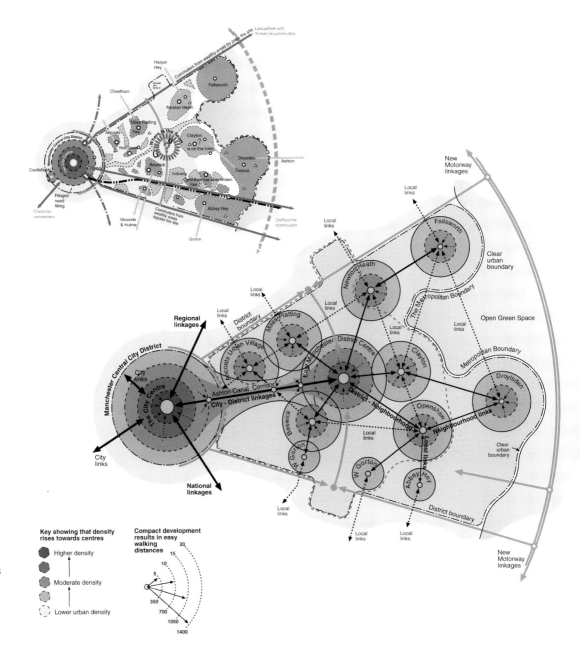

◀ East Manchester as existing:
fragmented urban communities
with potential
*Richard Rogers Partnership with
Andrew Wright Associates*

◀ East Manchester as proposed:
a series of integrated mixed-use
centres drawing the communities
together
*Richard Rogers Partnership with
Andrew Wright Associates*

▼ The Master Plan re-integrates
East Manchester with the City
Centre. New and existing
neighbourhoods are built along
green corridors and canals
*Richard Rogers Partnership with
Andrew Wright Associates*

1 Kilometre

people. Centre cities already show how this can be done. Successful city centres are run by management companies, with uniformed city guides, security staff and concierges. The city funds the company from the savings in insurance premiums accruing from the lower rate of crime and vandalism and the higher incomes. To make inner neighbourhoods work, we need people on the streets, local control, care for public spaces and similar systems for responding directly to problems.

Owning homes in cities would be more attractive if buses were frequent and reliable; if the streets were safe, clean and attractive; if trees were planted and small businesses nurtured. The income the new residents would bring would support new and better city services, greatly improving the quality of life for existing residents. Chart 6.6 shows how sustainable change can happen.

After fifty years of painful decline, inner areas of east London like Clerkenwell, Shoreditch and Stratford are exploding with new life. A few pioneering renovators moved into old property; small new enterprises, workshops and services opened on ground floors; old street markets expanded; cafés and restaurants smartened up and attracted new clientele; the narrow old streets became crowded and lively. The same could happen in Ancoats, on the northern edge of Manchester's pulsing centre; in the old neighbourhoods near Liverpool's Docks, as the Eldonians, a dynamic community co-operative, are showing; and in the Grass Market on the edge of Glasgow's now successful merchant city.

◀ East Manchester: abandoned terraced streets

The population of East Manchester has declined from 86,000 at its peak to less than 20,000 today.

Employment has moved away, and the quality of the urban environment has deteriorated significantly.

Can cities also be made attractive to employers, who currently fight for green-field land almost as greedily as housing developers? Can both low-skill and high-skill jobs grow fast enough to make inner neighbourhoods recover and encourage developers to create new homes there? There are many advantages for employers, particularly for service industries that depend on face-to-face contact and for new

Focus	Action
Brown first – sequential approach to land	**Difficult brown sites** – blanket help for de-contamination
New-style planning – flexible/mixed uses – sustainable design	**Double density** – better use of space – 3, 4, 5 storey building
A different approach to valuing cities – public space in compact settlements	**Good design** – clear, flexible, three-dimentional master plan – makes most of physical surroundings
Government – central, regional, local – neighbourhood	**Local communities** – start with **pioneers**, allow bottom-up initiative
Social Exclusion – primarily an urban problem – neighbourhood renewal	**Council estates and other poor inner areas** attract broader groups – neighbourhood management and local companies
Racial integration – cities thrive on mixture	**Pro-youth** focus – jobs, training, opportunity
Building/housing people – affordable, easy access, flexible tenures – fitting people in	**Save buildings** – support for recycling
Urban environment – green corridors, parks	**Transport** – cut traffic, enforce bus lanes, cycle and foot protection
The need/scope for investment – how much do we need to do to redress the balance?	**In pipeline already** – transport, training, education, health, police, security, regeneration, renovation

▲ **Chart 6.6: Making change happen**

knowledge enterprises, where scale and space are less important than ease and cost of access. Many of the new businesses and new jobs in cities feed off global activity. Many of the most modern production systems are less space-hungry, less energy-intensive and more pro-city. Cities provide the ground-level, integrated, close-proximity back-up that international companies and their mobile workers look for: personal services, security, cleaning, childcare, food and entertainment. Some of the fastest-growing service companies are in these fields.[306] These new jobs feed on revitalised cores and a hinterland of affordable, accessible neighbourhoods for people to live in.

There is one big if: the environmental conditions in cities. This may be where the protagonists of the different arguments can agree. The consequences of sprawl in jobs and homes have already damaged many outer communities. They are becoming harder to expand into. We must apply brown-field targets to rural areas too, so that using small spaces, adding extra storeys, changing uses and densification can make these outlying settlements more compact and more viable. And we can certainly apply urban design principles to suburbs, as Martin Crookston has shown in his work on 'sustainable urban design'.[307] We discuss suburbs, our biggest housing resource, further in Chapter 7. Chart 6.7 shows how we can revive inner cities. Chart 6.8 shows how we could adapt planning to the new environment.

The reversal in the fortunes of outer superstores is a sign of changing attitudes. Green-field development almost always hurts someone. Interestingly, the public reaction to the expansion of airports – the noise, ancillary development and rapid congestion they generate – is clarifying peoples' attitudes and underlining our limits.[308] So far, the objections have eventually been silenced, but it becomes harder to do this as they become more vociferous. As economies

- **The economy needs cities**
- land is finite
- environmental sustainability requires a better ecological balance
- the countryside offers lungs/cleaning/rest/escape – it needs protection
- sprawl is self-defeating – all lose
- social imperatives determine that losers stay behind

- **Redensifying settlements will help cities due to**:
  - shrinkage in household size
  - fitting in more households as they multiply
  - greater wealth and higher demand for better-quality space

- **Cities need:**
  - public transport to support more compact living
  - urban green **open space**
  - more attractive urban environment
  - good public services
  - police, schools, health to satisfy range of incomes

- **Good urban design and architecture makes cities work**
  - better-off people choose attractive places
  - complex activities can work together
  - civic pride generates success
  - reinstating public spaces and prioritising pedestrians creates lively cities

- **Centre city strategies are working**
  - public spaces
  - pedestrian streets
  - intensive public transport
- Success draws people with choice to cities
- Successful ideas apply to inner neighbourhoods
  - to avert demolition and support existing communities
  - to restore conditions and enterprise
  - to rescue services
  - to gain new residents

Could work
- Higher general density
- Flexible zoning
- Easier system for change of use
- Maximum encouragement to conversions and subdivisions
- Limited car space and maximum cycle/pedestrian space
- Transport planning integrated
- Greater use of planning and design experts
- Flexible, evolving development plans

- Support for organic change
- Maximum use of spaces – attics, semi-basements, and cellars

Does not work
- Using low density as quality guarantee
- Restricting mix of uses
- Hampering change of uses
- Zoning – jobs versus homes or leisure

- Over generous road provision

- Over-provision of car parking
- Over wide road junctions
- Numerical rules rigidly applied on density, height, space, conversions etc.
- Failure to adapt to new household shapes
- Outdated development plans

◀ Chart 6.7: Reviving inner
cities

evolve with the use of clean technology and 'virtual' communication, the links between increased production, wealth and the voracious consumption of resources can be broken.[309] We are constantly discovering new ways of reducing pollution and damaging over-use. Cities offer a test-bed for these new ideas. But if the costs of adjustment are to fall evenly, a major environmental commitment and broad agreement across the developed world are needed. Otherwise we in wealthy countries will continue to live off the environmental capital that belongs to the poor as well as the rich.

More compact, more environmentally sensitive development within well-cared for, well-supervised city neighbourhoods would offer a real alternative to our current problems. If the incentives were more fairly allocated to make it more financially attractive, then employers, investors and residents would turn back, like Dick Whittington, towards the city they too-hastily left.

◀ Chart 6.8: Adapting planning
rules

7 Making cities work

Bilbao and Newcastle

City designers and social entrepreneurs

Cities are made by citizens

Re-using urban land

Affordable housing

Suburbs

Economic and social integration

New work and the technological revolution

Social revival of neighbourhoods

Neighbourhood management

Traffic and the transport revolution

Regional identity and urban governance

The environment of cities

City solutions

7   Bilbao and Newcastle

Bilbao is Spain's second industrial city. Situated on the north coast, in the heart of the Basque Country, it was its wealthiest and most modern city in the 1960s under Franco, when Spain was poor, undemocratic and extremely divided. Bilbao was the ugly duckling of Spanish cities owing to its heavy industrial economy, its busy port, its extreme density – mountains lock it in around its commercial centre and harbour.

Bilbao was hard hit by the post-industrial collapse in manufacturing and by terrorism. The Basque separatist movement ETA carried out bombings and assassinations, keeping tourists and investors away. By 1995, Bilbao's port and central areas were chronically decayed; the high-density neighbourhoods clustered around the port had lost any sense of affluence, well-being and even local pride. The population was demoralised. The separatists daubed slogans in Basque on every wall, bridge and hoarding, castigating government, visitors and foreign firms. There was an unnerving resistance both to extremist politics and to outsiders in the local population. The city was at a critical turning point. Its week-long tourist festival in August ended as always with the immolation of a glittering, ornately dressed statue followed by a dramatic drowning of the burning effigy in the inky river – a symbolic ending and beginning.

▲ *previous page*

Car-free Sunday in Rome
AGF–La Verde

Over the following five years a remarkable transformation occurred. ETA, though still active and no longer observing its cease-fire, is compromised by Spain's progress, by the significant autonomy acquired by the Basque regional government, by the restoration of the Basque language and the recognition of Basque rights. The decrease in violence allowed major new investment as Spain's economy grew at record rates. An outstanding mayor galvanised a new tourist-based economy. The most dramatic new landmark, a silver-clad museum funded by the city authorities in partnership with the Guggenheim

Foundation, dominating the old port and the central core of the city, was opened in 1997. A new footbridge across the harbour and the stunning underground stations designed by Norman Foster expand the public space. The rich, if decayed, infrastructure of the dense old city has been given new uses.

The city had a skilled and experienced work force, a determined local and regional government, a strong sense of identity and its own culture and language – the oldest in Europe. These attributes, which had become defensive barriers in the period of steep decline from 1970 to 1990, were converted into a unique resource as the city implemented a revival strategy, linked to international investment, cultural tourism and a lively, dense centre. Bilbao, like Barcelona at the southern end of the Pyrenees, has become the northern gateway to a modern, internationalist Spain.

Bilbao's Guggenheim Museum cost $110 million to build. In 1998 it attracted 1.2 million visitors, in 1999 the same again. In 2000, around three million are expected, four-fifths from outside the Basque Country. This is probably the most important development, for it has opened the city and its region to new ideas and new roles. In the two and half years since it opened the new tourist industry, has generated $400 million in additional spending and $70 million additional revenue to the city council from new businesses and taxes.[310]

▲ *previous page*

Bilbao: regenerating a city through art and culture (architect: Frank O. Gehry & Associates)
David Heald

The Guggenheim Museum is one of the most dramatic buildings of recent years. Its extraordinary curved shape, its startlingly bright metallic cladding and its powerful setting in the harbour make it a landmark and a symbol of openness to new ideas and new people. Bilbao had the assets of density, setting and pent-up energy after years of repression and violence. People have poured in to share this exuberance and enjoy the city's spectacular weaving of new and old, international and local. If Bilbao can achieve this transformation, so can Britain's ex-industrial cities.

In many ways, Newcastle is like Bilbao. It is an industrial port in steep decline; it has a dramatic waterfront setting; its historic centre is compact, challenging and attractive; its inner neighbourhoods are poor, housing a manual workforce with 'old-fashioned' skills and attitudes. Gateshead is Newcastle's sister city on the other side of the Tyne. Together they have formed a new cultural and civic partnership.

▲ Bilbao: Metro designed by Foster Associates
Richard Davies

Newcastle and Gateshead face each other across a quarter of a mile of water, with six dramatically engineered bridges linking them. They have the most appealing river setting in Britain. A new Millennium footbridge will link the great new arts centre on the southern, Gateshead bank with the new museum on the northern, Newcastle bank. Both cities are building expensive new apartments along the Tyne and winning back new populations into the centre as they clamour for growth, for mixed uses and for a recovery of vitality. New flats in the centre of Newcastle sell as soon as they go on the market. Grangertown, climbing up from the city's main station, is possibly the most beautiful and intact Georgian town centre in the country. Newcastle is trying to restore the apartments above the shops and businesses, to mix living and working as the city was originally planned to do.

The city has striking assets: intact and startlingly beautiful Georgian shopping streets; many impressively preserved stone buildings in the centre; an historic theatre and new cultural centres on both banks of the Tyne; excellent rail links and an avant garde metro system to the suburbs; a strong local loyalty to the city; and attractive old industrial buildings inviting new uses, clustered down the deep-cut banks of the Ouseburn, only a short walk from the city centre. But Gateshead's

▲ Newcastle: renaissance of a
great city – two hundred years
ago . . .
Ward Philipson Group

◄ . . . and today
English Partnerships

giant outer superstore and excess green-field building suck the city's vitality away.

You can walk a mile downstream along a new footpath, but as you approach the old industrial riverside, you see the tell-tale signs of abandonment: bare land where council houses stood until recently and boarded-up 'cottage property' that people no longer feel safe in because it is too near the old riverbanks, now unprotected and exposed due to the demolitions. Going westwards, there is a fast road and an industrial zone with corrugated, windowless modern units blocking off the river, destroying a remarkable opportunity to create a new post-industrial mixed-use river front. Many of the old terraces up the steep banks are being abandoned. The city is expecting to demolish six thousand of these potentially attractive homes over the next five to ten years.[311] The central riverside areas of Newcastle have lost around a third of their residents since 1971 and its core is still declining dramatically. Only a stone's throw from the centre, in Benwell and Scotswood, abandoned good-quality homes tell a tale of crime, poor schools, unemployment and depression. People are losing hope after many rounds of effort to rescue these inner areas. Newcastle has become one of the most polarised cities in the country.[312]

Now the city faces some critical choices. Should it, like Bilbao, concentrate its energy on the growth of the city centre, building on the potential of cultural tourism? Or should it, like Barcelona, give each neighbourhood across the city the chance to improve the quality of its environment – the dominant reason, along with schools, why people are leaving the city? Should it pedestrianise the heart of Grangertown, its Georgian shopping streets, creating 'public living rooms' as Copenhagen did, making people want to walk and sit in the centre? For like many former industrial cities, Newcastle has great assets in a captivating setting. It is a walkable, compact city with the infrastructure for double its present population. How can it stop the further dispersal of its most affluent population into the plentiful green-field land that surrounds it – while preventing its poorer communities from sliding into further abandonment? In Chapter 7 we look at how we can make cities beset by such problems work.

In England, we forecast that we will need to house an extra 2.7 million single-person households in the next twenty-five years, most of them in existing cities, many of them in existing buildings. The population may expand by 4.6 million over the next twenty-five years. The social consequences of mishandling this growth could be as serious as the environmental consequences. At least four-fifths of what we will live in thirty years on is already built. So making it more attractive and more adaptable will win strong public support all over the country. We are not arguing for large-scale urban repopulation or high-density cramming to reverse decades of urban decline, as we showed in Chapter 6. We need to entice people into the urban heartlands, where they *de facto* become protagonists in the battle for recovery. We argue for revitalising inner neighbourhoods and suburbs by making better use of the spaces within them. This way, in a world under heavy environmental pressure, we make cities a resource for those who like cities. Suburbs, outskirts and inner neighbourhoods all play a part in what we propose.

City designers and social entrepreneurs

Living and working in a city pushes people to solve city problems. Many of our great urban breakthroughs – in work, housing, public health, transport, government, education, policing and culture – have happened because designers, inventors and entrepreneurs daily face the physical and social problems of cities and have set out to tackle them.[313] By living in the city, they meet and mix with the people who use what they create. Keeping the people with multiple skills to solve urban problems in cities is central to finding solutions that work. Many of our inventors and entrepreneurs have moved away from cities and their pressures. Too much damage in cities is caused from outside; unpopular solutions imposed by the impractical and the unfamiliar. The USA has experienced this acutely: ghettos spread and decline largely because the problem-solvers have left.[314]

New ideas often have unintended consequences. Thus suburbs helped to create inner-city decline. Modern transport dissected inner communities and now strangles most cities with cars. Automation cut the jobs we no longer needed, but now decimates the low-skill jobs we do need. The futuristic, often socially inspired but heavy-handed design that created our most difficult inner-city estates was exacerbated by a delinquent neglect of management and an overbearing disregard for social networks.[315] We live with the results, as city designers and social entrepreneurs battle every day with the pressures of social depletion and physical decay. The Social Exclusion Unit's National Strategy for Neighbourhood Renewal must match the Urban Task Force agenda of making cities work to bring talent and initiative to bear on our urban problems. For physical and social dynamics work together.

We need to attract and hold on to new urban pioneers. These young and energetic doers, whose priorities are to make things work and to find new ways of doing things, are a lifeline for the future because they *want* to live in the city, near work, near friends, near new opportunities. They need homes that appeal to them, often in a very different world from that of the standard suburban dwelling.[316] Their city homes must feel spacious and secure, be near good public transport and shops, and be cheap enough to leave cash to spare for other needs and for pleasures beyond bare survival. At the moment, only the rich and the already established can afford many of the conveniences of urban living. Transport, council taxes and car repairs

Recycle old buildings	Revitalise and redesign obsolete infrastructure	Free-up land uses
↓	↓	↓
organise design competitions for restoring, adapting, converting and reusing older inner neighbourhoods and streets	preserve and extend coherent street pattern – create small manageable open areas as part of street pattern	de-zone and mix uses
↓	↓	
create local 'master or action plans' with residents for renewal of decayed neighbourhoods and estates	support innovative design, new ideas for 'remaking' places	encourage urban pioneers with strong incentives for restoration – urban 'home steading' – urban self-build
↓	↓	↓
encourage new ideas about street activity to enhance attraction of inner neighbourhoods (e.g. home zones, tree planting)	create bus links, cycle lanes, pedestrian routes to link up decaying inner neighbourhoods	support social entrepreneurs with 'community chest' of small grants for innovation
↓	↓	↓
develop new uses for old buildings	protect and restore local landmarks – parks, libraries, churches – re-use for new activities	provide incentives for using small infill sites
↓	↓	↓
maximise infill sites for innovative, blended new buildings	plant trees, create small green spaces	remove blight, clean up land, enforce the sequential approach
↓	↓	↓
give incentives for re-use rather than demolition	re-engage community activists, support voluntary activity, neighbourhood wardens	enforce nuisance orders on empty property and land

▲ **Chart 7.1: The lessons of city centre revival applied to inner neighbourhoods**

are often more expensive in cities. This has to change, so that the mass of city residents feel part of, and benefit from, the huge wealth of cities, so that people will want to come and stay. The residents of poorer urban neighbourhoods deserve to benefit from any improvement – most importantly, the right to stay. Renovation is far more likely to achieve this than demolition.[317]

Attractive renovated homes in popular inner areas are in demand. They are expensive because they are scarce. We need more restored homes near those already thriving. As we restore small corners of cities, we pull in people who will then fight for the next corner to be rescued. Each new urban resident is part of the rescue process. Thus rebuilding our cities happens block by block – for the inhabitants of one area, if they are to stay, will fight for the betterment and inclusion of their immediate surroundings. They will demand cleaner, safer streets and better schools. There is a ripple effect. But change needs a strong vision and the imagination to see places as they can be, as well as how they are now.

Poorly-run communities on the very fringe of city centres could be reborn, leading out to our much larger suburbs. Nothing would more swiftly restore confidence, attract investment and repopulate cities. For these inner neighbourhoods create public attitudes that are hostile to urban living. It is here that neighbourhood renewal and urban renaissance can actually take root, for they have space to enable people to come back to live and work in the city. Chart 7.1 shows how the city-centre renewal we outlined in Chapter 6 can be applied to inner neighbourhoods.

Wider revitalisation grows from pioneering rescue attempts. It should be possible to combine the skills and interests of imaginative urban designers, pioneering new settlers, struggling communities, avant-garde managers and service entrepreneurs into a new pro-city alliance.

Most human activity – in government, business, the arts and the community – requires frequent personal interaction, a clustering of activity. Urban culture and civil society are born of this fusion. Established businesses need cities because they offer large and flexible supplies of services, labour and opportunities. Studies of global cities and the behaviour of high-tech enterprise show how they create new kinds of clustered urban settlements, most often grafted on to or remade from the old – raising density of activity and building in services, shops, workspaces and transport links.[318] The scope for attracting thousands of businesses, big and small, into remade cities is immense. We are already redesigning our cities and their buildings to fit this new world of work.

Cities are made by citizens

Our cities are made by us, so we get what we deserve.[319] Redirecting the huge resources we already pour into our cities can change our image of urban living. We need to *design* what we want and *organise* how we live in a more holistic way. Design is both an art and a science – making places and buildings both more attractive and more efficient.[320] If better design and better organisation draw more people into existing settlements, these new settlers will narrow the extreme divisions in our society. The way we design our streets, open spaces, public buildings and neighbourhoods will give shape to urban society for a long time to come.[321] Can we redesign the places we live in and the systems that run them so that we value more what we have already built in our crowded island?

Throughout history, beautiful cities – their homes and enterprises, their schools and services, their parks and squares, their transport and leisure, their monumental buildings, social networks and connected neighbourhoods – have inspired human creativity. Modern cities need to recapture that gift. For it is vision and inventiveness that restore as well as make cities, as Bilbao illustrates. Innovative design magnetises successful cities. Designing more attractive, more compact, more environmentally sustainable settlements will hold on to urban residents and attract new talent. Good buildings last if we run them properly.

Organising services efficiently will make cities cleaner, safer and more attractive. It is because we care too little about the 'front line', the low-paid jobs that we so grossly undervalue – the wardens, sweepers, keepers, guards, maintenance and care workers – that cities often do not run properly. In Britain, our management record has long been poor. This is why our cities are far down the international league table: only London is among the top forty, whereas seven German cities are.[322] How we manage determines how we live. Since we are hemmed in and constrained by what is already there, it is working with all the elements of complex, living, changing and sometimes dying places that makes for success. That is why design and organisation must go together in rebuilding cities (Chart 7.2).

Designing afresh where we live and inventing new ways to run our communities could make city living the optimal pattern of the future. Cities and settlements are human artefacts, so we will have to live with the consequences of our mistakes. We constantly need to change, renew and add to what we have. So we must find new ways to minimise our impact on the earth. Here are five key issues we identified through the work of the Urban Task Force.

Land is finite. Treating it more responsibly and recycling it more often will become a necessity rather than the desire of a minority. For land is fundamental to survival and in that sense belongs to all. It is our responsibility to protect it for future generations and to share its benefits between rich and poor.[323] Dealing with contamination, dereliction, waste dumping and surplus spaces within built-up areas

What is design?

- Ordering the built environment
- Involving public in design decisions
- Maximising use of streets and public spaces
- Creating continuous frontages to encourage compact vibrant streets
- Creating clearly connected, harmonious forms and patterns
- Creating pleasing and practical spaces around functions and uses
- Solving problems of layout, materials, structure, mass, uses, connections, etc.
- Using desire lines to create flow
- Consciously planning to make spaces work
- Developing skills to fit new buildings within existing frame
- Applying skills to deliver projects from start to finish
- Combining science, art, planning in delivering physical changes
- Using physical change to improve quality of life
- Creating new buildings within landscape, surroundings & existing layouts
- Making physical form respond to social needs
- Facilitating social & economic activity

How do we organise?

- Making things work
- Problem solving
- Creating systems that deliver
- Maintaining what is there
- Creating teams that produce practical outcomes and work to targets
- Monitoring and enforcing agreed standards and outcomes
- Prioritising hands-on approach – supporting ground level jobs
- Involving customers, users, citizens in plans, decisions and delivery
- Organising training so people have skills to deliver
- Ensuring budgets are stuck to and managing spending
- Negotiating funds and wider resources
- Winning and sustaining political involvement and support
- Linking up with partners
- Working to a wider strategic agenda
- Facilitating action from the ground
- Responding to local plans
- Creating small autonomous project teams
- Managing local-scale problems locally

Problems of design

- Weak design skills and poor design education
- Limits of physical design to order society
- Misunderstanding of social networks
- Barriers to lay understanding
- Lack of holistic approach
- Imposed structures and plans
- Lack of public participation

Problems of management

- Top-heavy structures
- Limited vision and poor leadership
- Too little delegation or team work
- Lack of trust
- Bureaucratic procedures
- Waste of resources at top
- Unsupportive structures
- Over-reliance on rules, targets and regulation

has to have top priority. How we re-use vacant land, revalue public spaces and regenerate run-down buildings and neighbourhoods is the key to a future of more compact development.

Economic and social integration makes cities more attractive to people wanting to live in them and employers wanting to locate in them. This needs good architecture. We could link many more of the new jobs with new homes within the city if we tackled the stigmatising social conditions of surviving inner-city communities that fuel physical decay. A new mixed-use, mixed-function type of neighbourhood would introduce the vitality and integration on which our social survival depends. Cities do not have to be the centres of social breakdown. Change helps, not hinders, cities.

Transport already influences many of our decisions. Car use has increased twelvefold in fifty years, supplanting and now blocking alternatives. Traffic and congestion are major inhibitors of city recovery but also of economic expansion.[324] We must design new ways of moving people around in larger numbers by more concentrated methods to make our streets and settlements more people friendly. Denser public transport helps both social and economic regeneration.[325]

◀ **Chart 7.2: Design and organisation**

Urban governance and leadership shape the renaissance of cities. Voters can influence the way we do things, but people in cities are so disillusioned that barely a quarter bother to vote in local elections. In inner neighbourhoods the turnout is even lower – unless it is for a highly local issue that residents can really influence. This is partly the fault of central government for centralising power and responsibility.[326] We need visionary leaders with a commitment to city renewal. Most people despair of influencing large systems and only feel able to change things when they are directly involved and doing something. Success depends on tackling problems in bite-sized chunks, while seeing each problem as part of a bigger picture.

Theme	Issues
Land	Undervalued land and unsustainable use Unequal VAT for repair and new build Hidden subsidy to green-field building Cost of brown-field contamination and reclamation Sprawl, low density and abandonment
Economic and social integration	Poverty/unemployment/job losses/skills gap Area polarisation – alienation/disorder/anti-social behaviour Ethnic disadvantage and concentration Vandalism and environmental degradation Community fragmentation – family breakdown and child-care problems Investment and enterprise gap
Traffic	Overuse of cars and congestion Accidents/pollution Walking and cycle decline and danger Rail overload and disinvestment Buses slowed by traffic
Urban governance	Weak political leadership/weak public participation/sense of powerlessness Loss of urban 'professionals' – hands-off systems Depleted mainstream urban services – education, health, police, etc. Neglect of parks and open spaces Neglect of public realm, urban environment, vandalism, insecurity
Environment	Unmeasured impact and hidden costs of development Inadequate recycling of waste and rubbish Energy inefficiency and overuse – pollution of air/ground/water Greenhouse gas emissions & global warming Loss of greenery, trees and land

▲ Chart 7.3: Five key themes

The key to good governance is therefore grass-roots involvement combined with strategic vision.[327]

Environmental pressures are growing. Our rapid urbanisation and dispersal into the suburban hinterland has broken the traditional link between conserving the land and supporting human development. The threat is growing rapidly. Modern urban living causes far worse environmental damage than more traditional settlements because it consumes more, wastes more and re-uses less. We cannot carry on as we are: accessible land will run out, and pollution of the air, the water and the land will overwhelm progress. It is better to stop before it is too late.

The one hundred linked recommendations the Urban Task Force made[328] address these five main categories of problem that require action. Chart 7.3 sets out the dominant themes and the most feasible actions.

The rest of Chapter 7 applies each of these five themes in turn to city revitalisation.

Re-using urban land

Managing land use without over-regulation, allowing economic growth while limiting environmental damage, encouraging concentrated development without constraining innovation – all these require a delicate juggling act by central and local governments. Cities need to reach a sufficient size to be able to provide the variety of people and activities on which economic growth depends. But city growth and suburban sprawl have their limits. Either they burst at the seams, as is happening all over the developing world today, or they shrink and sprawl simultaneously, as is happening in the USA and to a lesser extent Europe. Compact cities, towns and villages made up of closely-woven neighbourhoods can provide that rich mixture of people and activity that gives places a sense of purpose and identity. Historically, compact cities arose because of constraints on land and transport and the need for defence. Because land is now so constrained, at least in England and many other European countries, the idea of the compact city is once again appealing.

Large cities all over the world have slowed their growth.[329] There are some megacities, but their growth has proved unmanageable.[330] Smaller cities and towns are now growing much faster – which has been the pattern in Britain for a century. This is partly because they are sufficiently manageable to absorb growth. But they also attract growth because people – including businesses – often find smaller, more manageable places more attractive. So we have to make smaller cities and towns work at higher density as part of the urban recovery, if we are to stop them simply sprawling and ultimately joining up across the country. Many of our empty buildings and usable spaces are in the smaller cities where people may be most attracted to living. As we saw in Chapter 6, strong green belts around smaller as well as larger settlements are vital to contain sprawl.

Urban extension has absorbed many smaller communities, as happened with Stockport, Altrincham and Manchester or with Croydon and London. The government can do something far more imaginative than simply allowing one low-density development to merge with the next, as is happening in parts of Hampshire, Essex and Dorset. The best design skills can create compact, integrated, mixed-use cities for the twenty-first century along public transport links, using the dense urban framework that already exists and doubling its utility.[331] Milton Keynes, Ashford, Crawley, Stansted and other growth centres could develop significantly within their existing 'envelope' if infill sites were maximised, if higher densities were introduced and if public transport within these towns was made comprehensive and intensive. The successful new town of Hemel Hempstead shows what can be done. The town's emphasis on the integration of different tenures and different incomes, careful design and layout, sensitive infill within existing patterns and the conversion of existing buildings make it an outstanding model of planned growth.

In order to give people a sense of belonging, and to win them over to new ideas, we need to build on the resonance of 'small is beautiful' while emphasising the connections with bigger, wider communities. Curitiba, Barcelona and London do this. London is a chain of boroughs. Abercrombie, the famous post-war London planner, thought of the inner and outer neighbourhoods of great cities like London and Dublin as 'urban villages', an image that appeals to many.[332] The idea of neighbourhood does *not* work against the bigger and more complex notion of a city. It simply gives people a sense of identity with the place where they live and which they consider their home. For they can feel swamped by the anonymity, confusion and scale of the city.

If we focus on neighbourhood regeneration as one of the essential components of urban renewal, it then becomes possible to break down our large, complex systems into small, manageable areas that people can identify with and will defend, starting with their own homes. It is helpful in this connection to visualise a neighbourhood as an onion: the tight core is the home, the street, the neighbours; the looser layers around it include local shops, buses, schools and doctors; and the wider outer skin reaches across neighbourhood boundaries for work, entertainment, friend and relatives.[333]

Across inner London throughout the last thirty years, inner neighbourhoods have gained new value, a process that is causing house prices to escalate after a decade of stagnation. Renovation, tree planting, lively streets, better public transport, a booming service sector, street markets and pedestrian priority have all played their part. In most boroughs, the population is increasing after eighty years of shrinkage,[334] thanks to a new pace-setting image of city living that appeals to the young, the mobile – some of the new households we have to accommodate. This proves that inner neighbourhoods can be recycled, revalued and repopulated. Although London, as the capital, has special advantages, many of its problems of long-term inner depopulation, job loss, poverty and physical decay are common to all cities.

In 1972, low-income residents in potentially attractive Georgian slum clearance areas of Barnsbury fought for the right to stay in their improved homes.[335] This greatly strengthened the survival and recovery of Islington as a mixed neighbourhood. Through the 1970s, when Margaret Hodge was chair of housing, the local council, so tardy in the slum clearance era, became a pioneer in the early shift to rehabilitation. It brought large-scale demolition and estate-building to a decisive end, guaranteed renovated housing for displaced tenants, supported the formation of the earliest housing co-operatives of the period and organised the biggest rehabilitation programme in Inner London under the Housing Action Area legislation of 1974. Much of Islington's success today as a mixed and thriving inner neighbourhood stems from a council with citizen participation and respect for traditionally-popular street patterns.

A very different kind of reversal and renewal comes from the reclamation of contaminated land. The Greenwich peninsula, with the Dome and Ralph Erskine's millennium village, demonstrates the cost, complexity and urgency of tackling the 'badlands' near the heart of our cities. The whole Thames Gateway project is based on this idea. At sustainable urban densities, the areas to the east of London could accommodate much of the expanding population. The new transport links make higher density possible.[336] Well-planned new settlements on brown land help cities under pressure: Florence is planning a new neighbourhood of twenty thousand people on a wedge of brown land beyond the historic city and towards the airport, preserving green land for parks and integrating new homes, new jobs and leisure.

Affordable housing

Over-pricing, competition and polarisation are likely consequences of economic growth, but there are many ways of protecting residents within existing urban communities while at the same time encouraging newcomers and new activities. New York City Council is the largest landlord in the USA, with 150,000 homes run by the City Housing Authority. In a city of intense land shortage and extreme poverty, the combination of a huge private rented market providing 65 per cent of homes and significant public and non-profit housing helps low-income workers to survive.[337]

In cities and countryside under pressure we need to adopt a range of strategies to protect cheaper homes. Maintaining and upgrading existing housing rather than demolishing it and replacing it is one important way. Old Georgian terraces can often be subdivided two or three times. And small Victorian terraces can be knocked through to make bigger homes. Unpopular council properties can be transformed by enhanced security, improved environments, on site maintenance and open access.[338]

Council estates are rarely demolished for structural reasons. Woodberry Down in Hackney – dense, seventy-year-old balcony blocks containing a thousand flats – is a typical example of a potentially, well located, solid estate that could provide affordable housing far into the future if the council *wants* to save it. The Peabody model of estate management with on-site resident super-caretaking, close supervision of conditions and constant renewal and upgrading of the physical fabric sustains the value of older balcony and flatted estates like Woodberry Down.[339]

Florence: a new, compact, sustainable neighbourhood for 20,000 people on brown land to the west of the historic city

▼ An environmentally responsive design harnesses wind, sun and water to halve the energy used
Richard Rogers Partnership

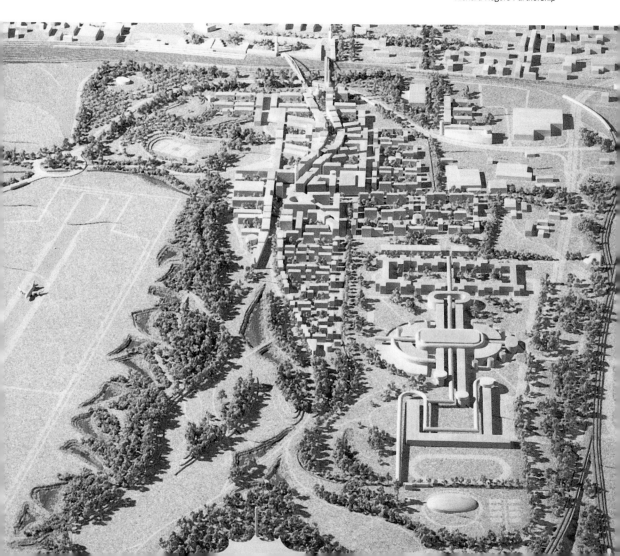

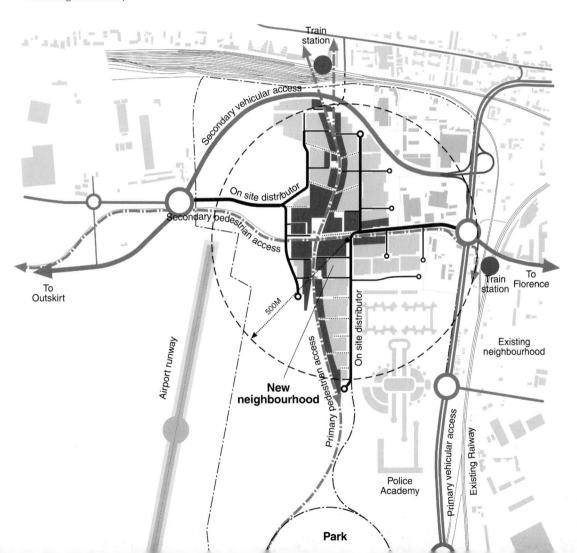

▼ A mixed community: the central
pedestrian route is lined by public
buildings and linked to public
transport
Richard Rogers Partnership

Train
station

Secondary vehicular access

On site distributor

Secondary pedestrian access

To
Outskirt

500M

Airport runway

Primary pedestrian access

On site distributor

**New
neighbourhood**

Train
station

To
Florence

Existing
neighbourhood

Police
Academy

Primary vehicular access

Existing Railway

Park

An essential element is to manage lettings to attract a broader social mixture of people. Across Europe, this has proved vital to renewal.[340] Letting subsidised council housing to higher income groups raises two questions. Should they pay unsubsidised, market rents? Probably yes, since this would still provide relatively cheap and therefore attractive housing, usually close to city centres. Should 'market tenants' have the right to buy their council home, just like other tenants? No. In fact, there should be no right to buy in popular, high demand areas, so as to ensure an affordable supply for key workers and to retain a social mixture as city centres become more valuable again. This should also apply in national parks, preserved villages and other areas of particular pressure. Tenants deprived of the right to buy could receive purchase grants or shared ownership options, as has already been tried.[341]

There are more fundamental problems with the ownership and management of urban council estates. One is the lack of serious and systematic investment. The other is weak front-line services. If we want to preserve the existing stock of more than four million council homes, we shall have to alter radically its condition, style, mixture of occupants and level of supervision. Nothing would more quickly restore its popularity as affordable housing. People who need affordable homes may make up half the population of cities. A mixture of owning and renting, of lower and middle incomes, of rent levels and uses would give new value to a supply of housing that in major cities all over the country is fast running out of takers.

The transfer of council housing to non-profit local housing companies is partly driven by the desire to break out of historic patterns. With residents on the governing body, there is a chance to involve existing communities in new ways of running estates. So far, nearly half a million homes have been transferred and another three hundred thousand are in the pipeline. These local housing companies are introducing a far more hands-on style of management, in close alliance with the tenants. Glasgow and Birmingham are proposing to transfer their entire council stock of one hundred thousand homes each to independent, non-profit companies. This greatly increases the likelihood of more mixed, more varied patterns, with more renovation, more participation and more rescue of existing communities – as long as these big cities allow a genuine devolution to local communities and to resident-orientated housing associations.

Cost-rent schemes and shared lettings by housing associations and private landlords offer young key workers affordable rented homes. The CASPAR projects in Birmingham and Leeds – market rent, low cost, privately financed homes – show that it is possible to build attractive, affordable, high-density flats for single and two-person households on windfall sites in centre-city locations.[342] So does the Homes for the Future experiment in Glasgow. These schemes are affordable by averagely paid workers as long as the buildings are carefully maintained and managed – the small, continuous investment and upgrading that keeps dense flats functioning.[343] We shall briefly describe these two projects because they demonstrate the need for a bolder approach.

Right by Birmingham's central canal, only ten minutes walk from the city centre, the Joseph Rowntree Foundation, a housing charity, has built two five-storey blocks of forty-six flats on a tiny half-acre site, at a density of 230 homes to the hectare, nine times higher than the average for new developments. The architecture is consciously urban and modern, with high energy and environmental standards, and with internal wood and metal stairs and suspended footways, giving each flat its own entrance. Joining the two buildings is a stone-paved inner courtyard covered with a glass roof where residents meet. The style is reminiscent of early industrial dwellings in France and Belgium, yet it appeals to young couples and single people wanting a modern city life style. Each of the comfortable, well equipped and spacious one-bedroom flats has its own outdoor balcony. They are 'affordable' for workers who can pay £107 a week in rent, who want to live in the city centre and who want to rent rather than buy. The scheme was fully let before it opened and is being copied in Leeds. It relies on bank loans and pays for itself, providing a competitive return on investment. Many investors are now pursuing this model. Market testing showed that people's favourite option was renovated old property, but the CASPAR scheme has its own modern charm, with its strong inner-city style and its views over the centre: old sites waiting to be reclaimed, old canal paths turning into new cycle and foot ways, old bridges restored, new bridges built, people everywhere – a new sense of place.

Glasgow has even more adventurous experiments in affordable housing. It boasts around sixty co-operatives and community-based housing associations, a unique Scottish creation to help restore old inner tenements in the wake of massive slum clearance; twenty tenant-managed co-operatives created to break up council estates into smaller, resident-controlled communities; and an almost outlandish affordable housing experiment, supported by Scottish Homes, right in the centre.

▶ Glasgow: drawing people back into 'Homes for the Future' (architects: Ushida Findlay, Elder & Cannon, Rick Mather, City of Architecture 1999)
David Churchill

The Homes for the Future project, on the edge of Glasgow Green running along the river Clyde, provides a hundred new mixed-income homes for rent and purchase in a triangle of derelict land.[344] Only ten minutes from the city centre and opposite the Gorbals, the new homes, mostly flats, took only eight months to build, sold immediately for far in excess of the asking price and attracted working tenants into one of the poorest and most run down inner neighbourhoods. The buildings are ultra-modern and full of light and brightness, an attempt to escape the 'neo-Georgian' terraces and 'neo-modern' tenements

of many city regeneration projects. Some have criticised their 'chameleon-like, chaos-based geometry'. The wood-clad blocks, low terraces and semi-circular cascading balconies are deliberately attention-seeking – 'like competing species in an architectural zoo'. But like the CASPAR project in Birmingham, they challenge preconceived ideas about city living and they tap into an enthusiastic new market.

To provide more houses, we can take advantage of less-conventional opportunities: by converting redundant offices, warehouses, unused shops and the upper floors above shops; by supporting urban pioneers who are willing to reclaim empty council or private property with improvement loans, a form of homesteading; by building flats over new commercial developments, supermarkets and garages; by giving owner-occupiers incentives to create flats for rent within existing homes, like the Germans do.[345] We must ensure that there are affordable homes in all new schemes and prevent developers from buying their way out of the obligation. Using sustainable design principles, we can triple average density in the most-popular areas from 27 to 75 homes per hectare. We should also minimise car parking requirements: it is horribly common to see double parking spaces, almost all empty, outside sheltered homes.

We need to recognise that there is a ready and often under-used supply of affordable homes within the existing stock.[346] Housing associations can go back to doing what they do best and what many of them were formed to do – buying and repairing existing properties to ensure the survival of mixed communities.[347] We should recognise the smaller space requirements of young single people by supporting alternatives to self-contained flats. We should make it easier for single-person households to share and recognise they form partnerships quickly. We need equivalents of student halls of residence for young people who are not at college, but in training or gaining work experience. The Foyers, which combine simple rooms, training and eating facilities in cities, are a model we can replicate.[348]

The need to provide special help for the small minority of people who cannot support themselves should not be confused with the need to help people at turning points in their lives who are temporarily having trouble finding the right accommodation at the right price. Flexibility is the key. The London Planning Advisory Committee has shown that, over the coming generation, we could accommodate up to two hundred thousand more households than official estimates suggest within the Greater London boundary if we followed new planning guidance.[349]

Suburbs

Suburbs are where most people live and where many families want to be. They provide half our urban housing and cover perhaps two-thirds of urban land. Suburbs are also an under-recognised resource in need of revaluation.[350] Their potential is on a different scale from that of inner cities.

Suburbs are basically popular and spacious low-density housing areas with significant gardens and road space, connected to the city but built beyond its dense core in a simpler, more uniform, more spread out pattern. Older suburbs have often become incorporated into the city proper. More recent suburbs often have too few people and too many cars. They could become much more attractive if they had more amenities, better public transport, more shops and more diverse activity. Most suburbs are based on the increasingly outmoded norm of the nuclear family, but if they were adapted to accommodate new types of household, they could appeal to a wider range of people, attract re-investment and accommodate more small households while maintaining the same population as they were built

Suburban assets

- Popular housing form
- Affordable for middle-income families
- Large supply
- Ample space
- Resilient lasting form
- Easy maintenance
- Homogenous population
- Transport links – potential for improvement
- Safe and secure atmosphere
- Spacious gardens
- Safe investment for home buyers
- Space for children and belongings
- Potential for additional homes and jobs

Suburban liabilities

- Poor energy use – over-reliant on cars
- Poor land use – spare spaces
- Poor layout – over-expanse of tarmac
- Some declining older suburbs
- Limited facilities
- Limited range of styles and activity
- Little gradation between streets and centres
- Dull, monotonous form
- Dormitories for commuters
- Low-income suburban estates can decline rapidly
- Hard to adapt
- Little mixed use
- Too much road space

▲ **Chart 7.4: Suburban assets, liabilities and potential**
Source: Llewellyn Davies (2000); Gwilliam, M et al. (1998)

for. Regenerating suburbs could significantly expand urban housing capacity.[351]

Suburbs offer many of the spare corners, under-used buildings and patches of land that cry out for small additions. Renovating, managing, diversifying and densifying suburbs so that they become neighbourhood centres in their own right and more integrated into urban patterns should be part of the renewal strategy of towns and cities. Chart 7.4 sets out the assets and liabilities of suburbs.

The potential for change in the suburbs is largely unexploited. Owners can add rooms and even flats over garages, in roofs and in bare spaces; they can subdivide houses to provide an additional unit. Hertfordshire County Council is doing this.[352] Shopping parades can be redesigned to incorporate accommodation; higher densities of people can support better bus services; clustering activity can create lively hubs; councils can create local centres with additional services and leisure; parish council-type structures can encourage civic involvement; voluntary organisations can contribute to local development. Large outer council estates, often the suburbs with the most problems, can accommodate a greater social mixture and become more integrated with owner-occupied suburbs. The right to buy has already helped to achieve this in many places. Non-profit housing associations with residents on their board can facilitate a more-mixed development. The standard suburban design can be adapted to increase the number of homes, improve the use of space and create a more attractive street pattern in suburbs.

▲ Suburbs are land hungry – do we have room for more?
Martin Bond/Environmental Images

Suburbs are part of cities, but to remain popular they need to enhance their city qualities while preserving their green and open feel. Curitiba's revolution was driven by the core idea of transport links to the furthest suburbs. For we like to be in touch with wider communities – communities of learning, such as universities, and communities of interest in things like music or sport. So connecting suburbs to centres in ways other than by car is essential. A higher concentration of people would make this possible. By revaluing inner urban communities and by expanding the potential of existing suburbs, we can almost certainly meet the need to house additional households and at the same time make already built-up areas more compact, more lively, more cared for. The land we have already taken and used has immense but under-exploited potential.

Economic and social integration

New work and the technological revolution

There are many conflicting ideas about what makes the economy of cities flourish or fail and about how they will fare in the twenty-first century. There is talk of telecottages and home working, of ever growing leisure, mobility and retirement time. Some people believe that these changes might make cities redundant. Newcastle, Manchester, Glasgow and Birmingham are considering the large-scale demolition of unpopular neighbourhoods; others propose laying turf or planting trees over abandoned inner areas, creating new green environments in the place of unloved communities. But reforesting the inner cities will do nothing to alleviate the intense poverty of their communities, any more than it will make good the damage we are causing to green fields. At the same time, it is clear that cities cannot be replaced by the wired-up economy. For all its immense flexibility, high-tech activity relies heavily on proximity, and all the evidence so far suggests that centre cities are becoming more, not less, important, even though outer job growth is still far faster than inner recovery, both here and in the USA.[353] City centres are becoming more important for the concentrations of research and development skills in universities, for the administration, services and cultural activities that will support the new patterns of economic activity.[354]

The IT revolution on which most new work now depends has in its sights a youthful urban generation that employers were discounting only five years ago as insufficiently skilled. These 'poorly qualified' young people jump at the chance of computer training.[355] Their energy, their city-slicker style and their press-button ease make them attractive to the newer, smaller, more flexible service businesses. So we may be seeing the beginning of a work revolution in cities, involving both services and information technology. New high-tech clusters are forming around redbrick universities: Manchester's growing biotech industry is pushing development in the south of the city.

All over our city centres, pioneering enterprises are creating new service jobs. These new businesses behave much like the new settlers. They are looking for secure, attractive, spacious offices, shop fronts and workshops. They too find the new urban environment exciting. Their knowledge-based skills thrive on the dense interaction of cities, even though they often recruit their workers from outside and give them travel incentives – cars, petrol, season ticket loans – to bring them in. Job creation in cities may influence inner neighbourhood revival, but the converse is also true. Islington's now thriving Upper Street and Angel were blighted areas until the 1980s, when the new residents created demand for new services.

Job expansion is already happening faster than expected. Many of London's inner streets – desolate only five or ten years ago – are bursting with new enterprises. The new homes appear alongside the new jobs, as the fashion for lofts, warehouses and converted terraces in deeply-decayed areas like Hoxton and Spitalfields show. Even more encouragingly, the same is happening in Glasgow, which has expanded its service sector faster than other cities – though admittedly from a very low base.

Hulme, a mile south of Manchester's city centre, provides another dramatic demonstration of this new pro-urban trend: property and land prices there went up fifty-fold between 1997 and 1999, though again from a low base.[356] When the supermarket chain Asda opened a large store in the area, they trained local people for the many new jobs, creating new confidence. A Foyer offering training and links to employment has also opened. The areas next to Hulme are now beginning to regenerate.

Many of these new jobs are part-time and require flexible working, new technology skills and considerable personal aptitude. Women seem to adapt more easily to these requirements, but young men are increasingly going for the new-style jobs too.[357] The urban work force, often considered inadequately qualified for the new high-tech or service jobs, can find 'spin-off' employment in building, bars, buses and security. In Britain, there is belated recognition of how indispensable this 'hand care' work is. Glasgow has uniformed street guides throughout its centre. Interpersonal skills such as caring, communication and humour are increasingly required in previously 'manual' jobs to prevent the abuse of public areas and anti-social aggression. If we manage our urban environment as it deserves, we will need many more street workers and front-line human faces to make the public realm secure.

Other new jobs are in the offing: project development and project delivery are urban skills in short supply. Both physical regeneration and new enterprises depend upon universities training more highly skilled organisers – 'symbolic analysts' as they are called in the USA.

Social revival of neighbourhoods

The greatest challenge will be to create urban residential environments and amenities that appeal to people who are wealthy enough to have choice. The new city style must be magnetic enough to make entrepreneurs want to work there.

Manchester illustrates both the problems and the potential. Its beautifully-restored centre is a magnet around which inner neighbourhoods can begin to revive. South of the city, in the direction of Ringway International Airport, renewal is already working. The Wythenshawe estate, originally an enviable model of suburban council housing at its best, lost population and popularity rapidly when Manchester's industrial base collapsed in the 1980s. But today it is fast recovering as growth spreads out from the centre and as residents actively organise the restoration of seven thousand homes through an independent, community based company. In March 2000 the government announced help for a rapid-transit extension through Wythenshawe to Ringway Airport, maximising the estate's chances of recovery.[358]

We must link the centres where new growth is happening with the inner and outer areas where there is still decline. These are wide open – but still not appealing enough to people with enterprise, environmental commitment and new ideas. The residents of these depleted areas can be part of their transformation, as Wythenshawe shows. They have been left behind by brutal changes in employment patterns. Usually they are written off as demoralised and insufficiently skilled to take new jobs. But they often have strong local loyalties, are desperate for new opportunities and oppose the uprooting of their communities. These are assets that can be used. Local people can become key workers alongside teachers, doctors and shopkeepers, offering the 'hand care' that would make such areas viable. These are not 'dead-end' people, but the people by whom our wealth was built and by whom cities can be rebuilt.

Neighbourhood management

One major contributor towards this change is neighbourhood management, an idea embraced by both the Urban Task Force report and the Social Exclusion Unit's new strategy.[359] It combines new-style jobs with social and economic integration. The aim is to restore neighbourhoods and prevent disorder by providing street wardens, community links, care and repair with a local manager in charge.

Neighbourhood management can be applied to town and city centres as well as to residential neighbourhoods. Coventry paved the way by setting up a company to stop the mounting crime and vandalism and consequent loss of trade in its shopping centre. It employed security, cleaning and car-parking staff, funded by a partnership between the city council and the main retailers based in the shopping centre. Vandalism and crime have virtually disappeared, the shops are doing more business, people are returning to the city centre and the Town Centre Management Company is being copied all over the country.[360] Chart 7.5 shows how neighbourhood management works, based on the seven experiments we visited.

For many of the hands-on tasks of running city streets and neighbourhoods, economies of scale are not possible. So we should always be clear about what has to be done by people in the front line and what can be run through centralised, machine-based systems or call centres, given that our task is to restore neighbourhoods within cities as well as rebuilding cities as a whole. Chart 7.6 shows the core local services. We need local co-ordination and hands-on control to give them real impact. These services would provide about three hundred and fifty jobs for every thousand homes.[361]

▶ **Chart 7.5: The essential components of neighbourhood management**
Source:
Poplar HARCA
Broadwater Farm Estate
Waltham Forest Community Based Housing Association
Coventry Town Centre Company
Monsall Estate, Manchester
Bloomsbury Tenant Management Organisation
Clapton Community Housing Trust
1999

The government, local councils and residents are developing neighbourhood management in many experimental forms to help the four thousand run-down inner neighbourhoods of our town and cities. The great strength of neighbourhood management is that, although designed for inner-urban problems, it can apply to all sizes and types of community.[362] All built-up communities, including villages and scattered settlements, need a local focus to keep things working.

How neighbourhood management works	What neighbourhood management can deliver
Neighbourhood manager • high status • budget • control over neighbourhood conditions • co-ordination of services • community liaison • hands-on responsibility	**Core services** • housing management (where renting from social landlords) • repair and street conditions • super-caretaking and environmental services • warden, concierge and security services • nuisance control
Neighbourhood office • organisational base • delivery of core services • information and access point for local and external liaison	**Co-operation with other public service** • police • health • education • training and job links • community provision

Neighbourhood team
• dedicated to defined local area
• prioritising security
• tackling basic conditions
• building community support and involvement
• organising local staff to cover basic services
• providing core, multiple links
• hands-on street presence
	Community representation
	• local agreements
	• local boards
	• arm's-length models
	  – community-based housing association
	  – local housing company
	  – tenant management organisation
	  – community trust
	  – town-centre company

	Retail management • security • environment • insurance • customer liaison • public transport links

CORE LOCALLY ORGANISED SERVICES

- **Major public welfare services**
  School/higher and further education
  Policing
  Social Services
  Elderly/community care/mental health
  Warden services
  Childcare/nurseries/family centres
  Health
  Social Security/Income Support
  Job centres/employment

- **Housing**
  Rent account and investment and housing benefit
  Access, allocation, advice, homelessness
  Repair and maintenance
  Tenancy liaison
  Enforcement of basic conditions

- **Environmental**
  Street cleaning
  Refuse collection
  Nuisance control
  Repair and maintenance of public spaces
  Parks, playgrounds and planting

- **Special responsibilities**
  Crime prevention
  Partnerships
  Business liaison
  General well-being of area
  Promotion of local interests
  Neighbourhood/community/youth development
  Training

- **Security**
  Direct police role
  Warden/concierge/super-caretaking
  Private/security contracts

- **Leisure and amenities**
  Libraries
  Youth service
  Sports facilities
  Community centres

SPECIAL/AREA FOCUSED NATIONAL PROGRAMMES

- **Regeneration Programmes – single regeneration budget**
- **Zone initiatives**
- **Additional funding – National Lottery**
- **Targeted area initiatives – Sure Start, New Deal for Communities**

The government's National Strategy for Neighbourhood Renewal, launched in April 2000, is a brave attempt to pull together all the solutions needed to make poor neighbourhoods work: economic development, community empowerment, mainstream services and local leadership. The emphasis on jobs, residents and core public services fits exactly with our vision for inner neighbourhoods. One of the biggest challenges is to bring together the different urban communities. Ethnic minorities are playing a strong entrepreneurial role. Their contribution to social vitality is immeasurable.

Startling in their absence from the National Strategy are any proposals about upgrading physical conditions. The urban environment which, as Chapters 2 and 3 of this book show, so directly affects people's attitudes and behaviour is hardly mentioned. We need to marry the Urban Task Force's proposals for physical renewal with the strong social agenda of the National Strategy for Neighbourhood Renewal with its six hundred recommendations. We believe that social and economic integration – the second of our five key themes – is fundamental to cities, but also that cities are physical entities within which we work. We must keep physical and social conditions in harness if we are to persuade people and jobs to stay in cities.

◀ **Chart 7.6: Layers of neighbourhood services and tasks from local to national**

Traffic and the transport revolution

Information technology transfers vastly more information by wire or through the air than human mobility can. But if cities are to act as the employment centres of this new world of knowledge-based enterprise, then we need better public transport, more people-friendly city environments and an end to over-reliance on cars. Businesses like locating in attractive, well-connected and well-serviced environments. There may be a new trade-off in favour of cities: cleaner, more high-tech enterprise; more concentrated personal contact and less car movement within city centres; better public transport.

An essential element in reviving built-up areas is to provide new transport options within and, most importantly, between neighbourhoods. The most obvious way is to focus on pedestrians, cyclists and buses. People should be able to walk into the centre of their neighbourhood to find shops, schools, doctors and buses. From every neighbourhood it should be possible to travel quickly, cheaply and comfortably to places of employment and evening entertainment. But people will only resort to public transport if car travel becomes too inconvenient or too expensive and if new methods are introduced. Sophisticated design and engineering are vital. Curitiba scoured the globe to find the right chassis to make their city buses smooth, fast and fuel efficient.[363]

Cities can begin to shift the balance away from cars by restricting parking spaces and subsidising public transport with the money. This is a win-win situation as long as the shift is visible and wins public support. Strasbourg has revolutionised its image by laying twelve kilometres of innovative tramlines and giving bicycles, pedestrians and buses priority alongside the trams.[364] It also transformed its canals into transport routes. The impressive mayor of Strasbourg, Katherine Trautman, has generated a real enthusiasm for a people-centred rather than car-dominated city. Strasbourg, Copenhagen and Curitiba show that by reducing car use in the centre in favour of buses, trams and cycle and pedestrian ways, the whole city begins to transform its transit system.

Vehicles must be able to move around a city, but many journeys are neither necessary nor good for the city. Essential access can be organised, and most streets should remain open, but speed-controlled, for this purpose. Other ways to make public transport more attractive include: directing a much higher proportion of transport spending towards it; integrated local transport plans – bus, light rail, main-line trains, coaches, roads, walking and cycling – that cut across local authority boundaries; strict enforcement of bus lanes, with prohibitive fines for cars and vans that transgress (the fines can fund the enforcers); pedestrian streets and squares, with cycle paths wherever possible; city-wide flat fares on the buses, with integrated ticketing and transfer points; barring cars on Sundays from central areas and the streets lining parks; better-designed buses, railway carriages and stations; clear information at stations and bus stops about services and arrival times; good lighting and staff to make vulnerable passengers feel safe; accessibility for people with mobility problems; tree planting to make walking and cycling routes as attractive as possible. There are infinite possibilities: special family tickets for buses would end many a nightmare car journey with bored, bottled up children; special fast lanes for cars with more than one passenger; speeding up ticket queues; extending all-in transport passes.

Manchester, Edinburgh, Newcastle, Oxford, York and London have all enticed people out of their cars and onto the bus or the metro. Oxford is outstanding because it combines a comprehensive park and ride scheme with bus- and bike-only streets, cycle lanes and bike racks all over the city and fast trains and buses to London. Some inner London buses are to have cameras fixed at front and back to detect transgressors in bus lanes. Something similar is needed for cycle lanes in London too.

Urban metro systems need to be integrated with bus routes. Buses are by far the most adaptable system of mass transit, at a twentieth of the cost of underground systems.[365] Trams come somewhere between the two in cost, but offer the great advantage of reserved tracks. Brussels, Zurich and Amsterdam all have impressive tram systems. However, buses have the advantage that they can move between neighbourhoods, into city centres and out into the country. Along densely used routes in Paris and Brussels, new double-length articulated express buses and trams are sweeping up passengers. Dedicated, enforceable bus priority enables buses to offer the advantages of trams at about a tenth of the cost.[366]

Plans for bus lanes can also include cycle paths and wide pavements for pedestrians. If made safe, cycling confers incredible freedom and releases new enthusiasm for cities. Physically separate cycle tracks can run alongside every road and be part of every street. The need for cars is then hugely reduced, as Strasbourg, Gothenburg, Copenhagen and Amsterdam show. Cycling is taking off in every city where traffic is at strangulation point and where even minimal protection is offered: the little green shoots of cycle ways in Paris and New York now have a few brave cyclists.

A pioneering idea for residential streets widely adopted in Germany, Holland and Denmark is the Home Zone. Pedestrians have absolute priority on a street-long pedestrian crossing. Traffic is reduced to walking pace, five or ten miles an hour, within the designated area. Home Zones rely on the involvement of residents, as they only work with community support; the impact on street life and social contact of restricting traffic is dramatic.[367] Zones are being piloted in London, Leeds, Manchester, Monmouth, Nottingham, Peterborough, Plymouth and Sittingbourne. Many local authorities, particularly in cities, are keen to join the experiment. So are residents' groups all over the country.

▶ Reclaiming the streets – regenerated quayside, Newcastle
Leslie Garland/Environmental Images

The advantages of reclaiming the streets and public spaces for people have been demonstrated in Copenhagen. A detailed study of the city found that as pedestrian areas have increased sevenfold since 1968, pedestrian usage has multiplied four-fold. Charts 7.7a–c show this.

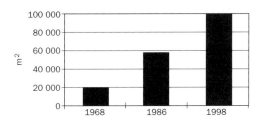

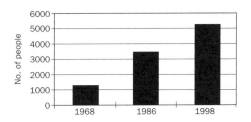

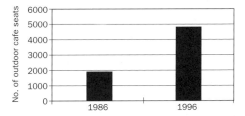

▲ **Chart 7.7a: Pedestrian street space in Copenhagen**
Source: Gehl (1996b)

▶ **Chart 7.7b: People standing or sitting in pedestrian streets**
Source: Gehl (1996b)

▶ **Chart 7.7c: Outdoor cafes in central area of Copenhagen**
Source: Gehl (1996b)

Among the most important transport developments in Europe are its new high-speed railways. Not only do they have far less environmental impact – they use the least energy per passenger mile, while aircraft use the most – but they are becoming the fastest mode of travel from city centre to city centre. Britain's cities will certainly gain from the new railway boom.[368] The planned high-speed rail links that will shift movement around Europe from road and air to railways will also shift economic opportunity beyond south-east England towards the north. The positive impact on cities of a well-run railway network, building upon on our existing track system, could transform the pattern of investment. Until the TGVs (*trains à grande vitesse*) were introduced in France, most people travelled to Lyon by air or road. The journey took a long time, and investment was sluggish. Since the TGV, Lyon's mayor Raymond Barre has been able to revolutionise conditions in the centre and spread growth out towards the poorer *banlieues*, where large social-housing estates are in great difficulty.[369] High-tech invention and precision engineering can help us solve transport problems.

Regional identity and urban governance

Every city is rooted in a regional culture, as for example Barcelona is rooted in the proud traditions of Catalonia. Regions have a strong identity, a loyalty to their regional capitals and smaller towns and a common frame of reference that can be invaluable to visionary city leaders such as Pascal Maragall or Jaime Lerner. Central government can encourage rather than neutralise this regional identity, thus giving impetus to city revival. Spain and Italy have been particularly successful in introducing regional governments based on traditional kingdoms.[370] Common dialects, artistic and musical traditions, folklore and landscape are all used to bolster regional pride and development. This creates the need for regional capitals like

Barcelona, Bilbao, Naples, Milan and Turin, where new political and social movements grow out of rooted traditions, producing a dynamism that attracts talent.

By devolving responsibility to regional governments in Scotland and Wales, we have already inspired creative, if expensive, projects in the regional capitals. Glasgow, Swansea and other cities will benefit from the new regional pride created by devolved decision-making as they search for an identity that marks them out. England, with its large conurbations and more dense land use, may follow a different approach, more strongly based on cities within regions.

The intense competition between regional cities can produce a creative tension. But twin cities like Newcastle and Gateshead, Manchester and Salford, Liverpool and Birkenhead, Birmingham and Wolverhampton, Leeds and Bradford need to work together within a 'city region'. The depletion of cities is often exacerbated by lack of co-operation between adjacent local authorities that should be working together. Can the cities of Greater Manchester or the Midlands make their city region an asset, rather than each component city draining energy from the others? The cities of the Tyne have formed a partnership with a shared cultural focus that is pulling in resources to one of the most beautiful riverside settings in the country. There is a great deal more scope for this kind of cross-city partnership, although they seem harder to achieve here than in continental European regions. The French have recently set up fifty experimental inter-communal, conurbation-wide councils to pull decision-making together.[371]

The climate in this country has been so hostile to local government for so long that only the bravest would stick their heads above the parapet. Yet cities offer a fantastic opportunity. For this reason mayors may yet flourish in Britain as they do in so many other countries. If we create more powerful city regions and give more responsibility to local authorities to tackle their problems, we will certainly see new leadership emerging. Rewarding cities for innovations that benefit the wider community seems obvious. It would give local government a new legitimacy.

Civic leadership depends on local pride, active democracy, citizen involvement and the development of many small-scale local projects to stand alongside the visions and strategies of the leaders. Barcelona and Curitiba both epitomise this approach. People will see some point in fighting locally to make things happen within their city, their region – the place where they belong – if they see their actions matched by local vision, local pride and local progress. One of the most noticeable characteristics of Glasgow is the real sense of achievement in many of the community-based initiatives we visited. The idea of logging every neighbourhood initiative, no matter how small, as part of a city-wide regeneration barometer would show people how small but essential actions can add up to real change: a brown site re-used, an empty building converted, a new job created, a community warden introduced, a shop opened, a new bus lane demarcated, so much rubbish recycled or so many trees planted. In economic depressions, we count the number of job losses. In cities, we need a regeneration count. Newham council in east London, at the entrance to the Thames Gateway, would score highly. From involving communities in identifying local eyesores to winning the Eurotunnel link to the north for Stratford, this impoverished borough is suddenly on the map as it persuades the city to lean eastwards.

Revitalising local government is a cornerstone of city recovery. But it needs to be done from the bottom up: from neighbourhoods, where people know what is going on, to the city, where politicians, businesses and civic bodies link up. Rotterdam illustrates this linkage. Community warden schemes employ young local people to care for the streets, linking them directly into their neighbourhoods, cutting crime, improving street conditions, enhancing pride. This increases support for wider changes in the city. In Spanish cities, the residents of each block of flats are required by law to form a community association that collectively takes responsibility for the condition of that block. Each resident pays into a common fund to cover basic maintenance, cleaning and supervision. Spanish cities, made up of dense neighbourhoods with blocks of flats at four hundred to the hectare, maintain incredibly clean and attractive conditions. Residents of all incomes are expected to be members of these associations, and it is practically impossible for the foreign visitor to define any area of a Spanish city as 'poor' – because it is clean, lively, cared for and full of small family businesses. As a result, neighbourhoods are bustling, mixed communities, with shops, transport and well maintained, busy, people-filled streets.

In Britain we lag far behind other European countries in caring for our public realm. Even many of our town parks, a legacy of earlier civic vision, are less frequented today for lack of wardens, gardeners, keepers or adequate security.[372] Five thousand public parks could be reinstated in our cities and towns through local participation and front line jobs to replace cut-throat contracts. In the 1990s, it took New York City less than a decade to rescue Central Park from crime and misuse. Now it is full of families, cyclists, roller-bladers, horse riders and baseball teams – the Sunday ban on cars through the park has turned it into a cascade of people.

New York's streets mirror Central Park in microcosm, with their pocket parks, sometimes only twenty feet square, sometimes a small triangle of newly planted trees and bushes where before a traffic sign stood. New York's Green Streets initiative organised small community-based planting schemes throughout the city. The city will plant the parks if local groups will care for them. The 34th Street Association, amid the giant skyscrapers by the Empire State Building,

From the strategic centre to the local neighbourhood

Strong sense of regional and local identity

↓

Co-operation with adjacent cities and surrounding towns

↓

Vision for city

↓

Integrated transport plans with cheap fares – in partnership with surrounding authorities

↓

Open public debate of ideas

↓

Detailed, applied, flexible plan for renewal – developed with maximum involvement of public

↓

Cultural centres and landmark events

↓

Participation by local people of all kinds and ages in action plans for the city and neighbourhoods

↓

Bottom-up action plans for neighbourhood renewal and neighbourhood management

↓

Local community and voluntary organisation – self-help

↓

Local referenda and ballots for major decisions, e.g. creation of local housing companies

↓

Strong front-line services – street wardens, super-caretakers

↓

Commitment to public realm – people **share** all spaces in the city

cares for hyacinths and tulips in giant planters all along the busy street. Walking up Broadway towards Harlem, you might suddenly find yourself in a tiny railed garden in the middle of the street, with two benches, some shrubs and a little path where three toddlers play safely while their mothers chat. A 'zero tolerance' approach to litter, graffiti, vandalism and anti-social behaviour of all kinds has helped to protect these tiny green plots.

City governments need to revive civic loyalty and ambition, tap community resources, generate care and attract sufficient investment to make cities into magnets again. Local leaders have to make things work to stay in power. But they could make small things stand out, like the green streets of New York do. Chart 7.8 shows the role of civic leadership in restoring cities.

The environment of cities

City spaces can be beautiful. The people make them come alive in a melting pot of ages, races and backgrounds. On Easter Sunday in Rome, when there are a million people in St Peter's square and the surrounding streets, the atmosphere of that giant gathering is electric. When the main thoroughfare of Central Park is jammed with joggers, not cars, there is magic in the leafy pathways. When the streets of Notting Hill become a carnival for three days, people forget class, colour and creed.

◀ **Chart 7.8: Role of civic leadership in urban renaissance**

In public spaces, the harshness of city life can melt away in an awesome re-ordering of the built and social environment. But noise, buildings and dirt often press in on city residents. Tests on children in Los Angeles showed that their sleep was disturbed, their concentration reduced and their nervous tension increased by traffic and aircraft noise. People find concrete, tarmac and the hard, unbroken surfaces of buildings oppressive. The lack of greenery can make people depressed and want to leave. There is something calming about wide open spaces, green fields and trees, away from the hubbub of modern life.

We can learn much from successful New Towns and suburbs about what people search for. They like their gardens, their parks and their access to open country. So if we can provide these things for city dwellers, they will be more likely to want to stay. Since noise and traffic are a major pressure on urban residents, taming them in the green spaces we create is crucial.

If greening becomes a priority, developers can green the tiniest spaces, thanks to the sophistication of modern landscape design. Greening the city is as important as making it safe. In fact, the two activities are part of the same process of care. New York's hundreds of community and street associations guard metre-square plant pots and young trees, watering them, keeping away litter and dogs.

There are many ways of providing green spaces. If we are to build at higher densities for smaller households, a majority of whom are childless, we must provide enclosed, secure, tree-planted squares, gardens and courtyards that everyone living around them can enjoy – the kind of square made famous in the film *Notting Hill*. Higher densities work better if each household has some outdoor space: a balcony, a patio, a roof or access to a garden. It must be big enough for the family or a few friends to relax and eat in. Many people are happy with the smallest of outdoor areas, so long as they feel it is theirs. Everyone in the new Peabody environmental flats in Hackney has a balcony or patio and the thirty flats share a small communal garden.[373] People can turn the tiniest spaces green with creepers, climbers, window boxes, pots and tubs. If a city as dense, huge and ungreen as New York can do it, then certainly Manchester can. Where are its trees?

▶ Barcelona: integration of good design, materials and landscape

Trees perform a vital function in cities: absorbing carbon dioxide, releasing oxygen, casting shade in summer, screening traffic noise, and above all softening and framing buildings, streets and open spaces. Many of the most attractive and sought-after city neighbourhoods are tree-lined. Large mature trees are part of the charm of Paris, London, Bonn, Zurich, Copenhagen and Madrid. Barcelona and Manchester seem to like trees less.[374]

Islington's 'tree for a tree' scheme, organised in the 1970s by a remarkable council employee named Peter Bonsell, has transformed Islington from one of the least-green to one of the most-green boroughs. In this, the inner London borough with the least open space, the council wrote to residents asking them if they wanted to share the cost of a tree in front of their house or block. Residents chose the species from a selected range of proven urban survivors. The council then planted it outside their house, with full protective supports. The streets that benefited most were the less-wealthy, more racially-mixed streets of Holloway and Archway. Here, the poorer families were not expected to pay, but their involvement in the scheme was critical. The vast majority of these trees survived and Islington's streets are now green and graceful.

The 'backyard project' developed in Preston's Asian community greens the small back yards of nineteenth-century terraces with hanging baskets, tomato plants and small pots of herbs. The old Victorian terraces of Manchester, with their front doors on to the street, are being greened by enclosing the alleys and turning the back yards into gardens that back on to each other. At a stroke, this opens the way for tree-planting, lawns and flowerbeds. It improves security by doing away with the unsupervised back alleys. In Germany, tower blocks are often covered at lower levels with creepers to soften their hard concrete surfaces.

Adding trees around car parks and school playgrounds can have a similarly magical effect, enclosing and softening the ugly, angular spaces, helping to screen out pollution and introduce nature into nurture. Every urban school needs a green challenge. There is a movement to create green playgrounds by planting children's gardens, involving them in tree nurseries, putting grass and benches around the kick-about areas, growing creepers up the walls.

Urban housing estates also cry out for greenery. But first there must be a plan agreed between residents, especially the younger ones, and the council – which is why the Islington 'tree for a tree' scheme and the New York Green Streets scheme work. Imposing green landscaping on an existing community without its consent and involvement will not work. Estates can only be greened if the local kids help with the planting. Some estates have created nature gardens with wild buddleia, willows, spring bulbs, ponds and butterflies. Some have developed enclosed communal gardens, some allotments, some organic market gardens.

Green corridors through cities are beginning to link one urban park with another through tree-lined, traffic-calmed streets. The Ramblers' Association, normally associated with the Right to Roam the countryside, is helping to create a green ring right around inner London. Sometimes these green corridors follow a disused railway line, like Finsbury Park's Parkland Walk in north London. Sometimes they are narrow threads of park created specially to link bigger spaces. Rivers and canals can help, as they are often natural green ways within cities. These projects can be organised in every small community. But they usually flourish within a wider environment of city regeneration.

Also urgently needed is a new vision for our historic parks, most of them beautifully planted and until the 1980s lovingly maintained. It is expensive in labour to care for urban parks. There are many human predators. And if they are not properly cared for, they become littered, damaged and insecure. By not tending them carefully, we are doing the equivalent to our cities of cutting down trees on the rim of the Sahara – allowing the desert to spread even wider. Our parks harbour birds and insects, they entice children and young people. They help us to breathe. They give cities the light, air and greenness they need. They provide pathways and cycle routes through cities. We can make them work in that inspiring, unifying, energising way that all successful public spaces do – for parents and children, for the elderly who cannot go far, and for the youthful single and sharing households who are not yet interested in gardening for themselves but who need somewhere to be in the open, to walk and run, to let off steam, and picnic with friends. Urban parks are one of Britain's great green creations. If they are cared for and peopled, we can use them to attract new residents.

Protecting established parks and creating 'pocket parks', making streets easier to walk along by reducing traffic, organising better street cleaning and repair, more security and participation – all these make citizens feel that they can add their contribution. Barcelona, Strasbourg, Copenhagen and New York all have strong mayors who over the years have pushed these ideas. They have all worked to involve neighbourhood organisations. Will mayors – an untried innovation in our cities – be able do the same in Britain?

As discussed in Chapter 5, if we are to make cities truly green we must make them consume less energy and create less rubbish. By designing a building – home, office or factory – well, we can cut its energy use by 50 per cent, simply by obeying the basic laws of energy efficiency.[375] Increasingly we can use renewable, non-polluting energy. The tonnes of waste a city like London produces every day could mostly be re-used. The current alternatives are to burn it or

▲ Portland, USA: a successful city
with strong public transport and
anti-sprawl 'smart growth' policy
C. Bruce Forster/Viewfinders

ISSUES	DESIGN	ORGANISATION
Land	• Master plan for city renewal • Create, enhance public space • Design compact, mixed-use development • Use brown land first, maximise recycling • Beautify urban environment • Design in more, smaller households	• Restrict green-field land releases • Adopt sequential, brown-first approach • Equalise VAT for repair and improvement with new build • Subsidise decontamination, minimise risk • Regenerate from centre outwards
Social and economic integration	• Apply people-friendly social vision • Win urban pioneers through design • Prioritise mixed-use patterns • Attract investors and businesses through imaginative design • Upgrade and integrate poor neighbourhoods	• Organise neighbourhood renewal • Encourage and empower local organisations • Foster pro-youth attitudes • Encourage more diverse landlords and investors • Support and enhance affordable housing • Support public-private initiatives
Traffic	• Design and engineer integrated transport • Design buses, trams, trains to encourage riders • Design pavement, cycle and bus ways to minimise traffic • Design park and ride and light rail • Design Home Zones with residents • Design inter-city high-speed rail	• Organise fast, reliable buses, trams etc. • Encourage and protect walking, cycle, bus lanes • Organise Home Zones • Impose parking and congestion charges • Prioritise elderly, families, disabled • Prioritise links to poor neighbourhoods • Shift bias from roads and cars
Governance	• Create master plans for inner neighbourhoods and estates • Maximise informal contact and control through people-focused design • Involve public in design decisions • Create landmark buildings and spaces • Redesign streets and open spaces • Develop new regeneration skills • Focus on quality	• Link with designers on long-term maintenance • Support regional and city wide structures • Experiment with town centre and neighbourhood management • Institute warden and super-caretaking schemes • Establish urban regeneration and housing companies • Reduce area polarisation and racial separation
Environment	• Enhance open space, pocket parks, greenery • Create green corridors and plant trees • Design balconies, patios, gardens, squares • Reclaim canal and riverside pathways • Engineer lightest environmental impact • Design with minimum energy waste • Design recycling systems • Redesign old buildings and old infrastructure	• Protect environment at micro and macro level • Reprioritise and protect green area and parks • Care for streets and open spaces – human presence • Plant along streets and in small spaces • Recycle waste – at least 50 per cent • Control pollution and air quality • Encourage small-scale action

dump it – both heavily polluting unless the incinerator turns waste back into energy. There is a massive outcry about incinerators: for example, allotments near the Byker estate in Newcastle have been poisoned by ash from the adjacent incinerator. It is more trouble but in the end more useful to recycle waste. This can be done by using combined heat and power generators, which recycle waste into energy and are more than twice as efficient as conventional generators. Helsinki heats 90 per cent of its homes this way – in Britain it is under 1 per cent.[376] In fact, in Britain we recycle less than 10 per cent of our waste, whereas cities in Europe and the USA recycle 50 per cent. During the 1990s, New York quadrupled its household waste recycling in five years.[377] Cities need more people. But more people will mean more waste unless we change the way we design and run our cities – the resources they consume and the rubbish they produce.

City solutions

◀ Chart 7.9: City solutions

Making cities work involves land and environment, good governance and economic progress, public transport and social integration. Above all, it requires an environment that people like, one that is peaceful and prosperous, fair and fun. To do this, we need to run cities, their buildings and public spaces for the citizens. We need to adopt a custodial approach to the physical and social environment of cities – they are our collective responsibility and hold our collective future. Carelessly, many cities have lost their appeal. We can achieve the opposite: to hand on to future generations a better cared for, more sustainable, fairer urban environment than we inherited. Chart 7.9 summarises the main ideas of this chapter around the five themes we identified at the beginning. It shows how both design and organisation shape cities. It confirms that the future is in our hands.

8 Cities need citizens

Compact cities

Cohesive cities

Recreating neighbourhoods

Future of cities

8

It is impossible to imagine a world without cities. For thousands of years they have been the magnet for trade, learning, culture, politics and experiment. In today's more crowded, more materially advanced world, we need cities for all the same reasons. But far more importantly, they offer a way out of the deep social cleavages that have opened up as a result of economic development. The gaps are still widening. But cities can bring people, ideas and experience together in a new dynamic that can help to solve some of the problems of over-development.

Citizenship means different groups of people coming together for a common, civic purpose. So cities need a centre where people can gather; where services thrive and multiply; where different activities intermingle; where public spaces draw people in; where public transport minimises the impact of the car and maximises street space and social contact. In a successful city centre, people dominate the streets.

Thirty years ago, Birmingham had the 'ugliest city centre in the country'. Its 1960s Bull Ring shopping arcade and its concrete inner motorway acted as giant barriers between people and street life. It had the greatest concentration of concrete tower blocks in Europe, over three hundred in all. It was a utilitarian, arrogant and repelling city. People fled the centre and inner neighbourhoods if they could. Birmingham now has one of the largest ethnic-minority communities in Britain, with some of the deepest inequalities.

Glasgow has broadly similar legacies. It is Britain's poorest city, with the highest concentration of unemployment and the most violent crime in the country. Glasgow built hundreds of tower blocks too, but it dispersed much of its dense population miles from jobs, shops, pubs, churches and social networks into giant peripheral council estates. The inner city shrivelled – the East End alone lost 70 per cent of its population between 1960 and 1975.

▲ *previous page*

Notting Hill: high density with squares and gardens
Martin Jones/Arcaid

Both city centres look dramatically different today. They are re-inventing a compact, walkable core full of cultural attractions, new and renovated shops, cafés and people. They have opened up public squares and restored their traditional civic architecture. They are winning residents back into the centre by creating new styles of home within the old city, mixing income groups and uses.

Glasgow is now pedestrianising its main shopping streets and has become an arts centre for tourists from all over the world. It is restoring over-hastily condemned and newly popular tenements in an attempt to hold on to traditional urban communities and recapture a dense, enterprising atmosphere. Birmingham has created grand new car-free public squares enclosed by arcades, civic buildings, new residences, new enterprises and pedestrian streets, opening up to new life the densest network of city-centre canals in the country.

These two cities once had the worst of reputations. With their youthful and dynamic new image, they can now compete with London and Edinburgh. They mingle work with leisure in their central areas; home and enterprise share the same streets; old buildings and new fit into a strong traditional street pattern. Above all, they have consciously recreated over the last two decades the idea of public space – cities for citizens. People are moving back to live near the centre because of the sense of action, the new jobs, the feeling of being where it's at and of playing a part in a new kind of city, a new kind of future.

▲ Modern Dutch housing: enjoying your own space (architect: MRVD)
Richard Burdett

Rebuilding the core of the city is the obvious first step. Will the dynamism of these two city centres spill over into their impoverished inner neighbourhoods, where decay still threatens to cause total disintegration? Will the large deprived communities that ring these centres become part of the new city, or will their exclusion just get worse? We first look briefly at how we can recreate more compact, more sustainable cities. Then we outline our idea of a more cohesive, more integrated city. The one hinges on the other.

Compact cities

Citizens gravitate towards a compact city because they like its energy, opportunity, diversity and excitement, all of which are the results of close proximity. But attractive, integrated urban environments do not just happen. They are the product of choice and good design. We can make them come about if we want to, although obviously no one individual or group can do it. Cities require both collective action and a host of individual efforts.

To make cities work in all their parts, at both the widest and the most local level, to fit together the hundreds of elements needed, is not a simple task. It requires not just vision, but architecture, engineering, social and communication skills, organisation and leadership. Flexible spaces and buildings within existing streets and neighbour-hoods can meet changing needs. They require, in addition to careful design itself, high-quality craftsmanship, attention to detail, tight control and long-term management.

▲ Glasgow: a tight grid pattern now being regenerated
Ranald MacInnes/Homes for the Future catalogue

Cities are about sharing spaces for a collective purpose. Good architecture helps us to order these shared spaces, to manage them in partnership with the people who use them. Compact cities are at the opposite pole from urban sprawl, where new homes are scattered on open land away from the connecting points of society. To succeed, we need many groups to work together, to reinforce the collective role of cities. It is this role that was lost through the dispersal of populations into scattered suburbs and through the break-up of compact city patterns by planned, single-function estates and by fast roads.

It is the rediscovery of the compact city, of the value of proximity and interchange, of the potential for reintegrating our fragmented society that makes older, uglier cities and their central neighbourhoods suddenly more desirable. Birmingham and Glasgow epitomise this

▲ Living between buildings, Leeds
Bipinchandra/Photofusion

shift of attitude. But it needs a strong social vision as well as careful design to pull the different communities together and encourage a sense of shared citizenship. Architects, developers and community representatives can work together to integrate the different social and income groups. As Chapter 7 showed, this is what is happening in Glasgow's Homes for the Future and Birmingham's CASPAR project.

Architecture has played a crucial role in the creation and recreation of great cities. It has contributed structures that symbolise civic purpose and order, beautiful and solid enough to have lasted for centuries, and civic spaces that encourage participation in cultural and social life. The free exchange of ideas, the interaction of people from different backgrounds – these vital activities rely on the settings that buildings and spaces provide. Architecture has immense power to damage or delight. Therefore the voice of the citizen is crucial to regenerating cities. People roundly rejected the old, over-dense, disease-ridden, filthy, impoverished industrial cities and fled if they could. But planners, largely without community consent, then decided to dismember the traditional compact urban patterns. Now people are beginning to come back, seeking a new kind of density – of services, leisure, social contact and support.

A reviving city centre lies cheek by jowl with the city's inner neighbourhoods. The new bridge from St Paul's Cathedral, in the City of London, crosses the Thames to the reclaimed South Bank, only a few yards from some of London's poorest inner-city estates, worst schools and most serious crime. These run-down areas need the people who use the centre, or they will empty and die. If city councils support local effort and devolve some resources and decisions to the community, the next layer of inner neighbourhoods can build up compact local centres and their own identity – this is the secret of Barcelona's success. These neighbourhoods then start to attract residents working in the city who can contribute to their regeneration. At the same time they hold on to their traditional communities. As congestion and parking restrictions make driving into the centre of cities less and less attractive, inner neighbourhoods and suburbs need new public transport links, such as express bus routes and better suburban train lines. In this way, rebuilding compact, mixed use, well-designed city centres generates a more integrated, more densely peopled, more desirable whole city. Sprawl loses its attraction.

We need to work from the centre outwards, layer by layer, starting by reconnecting the innermost neighbourhoods, which are only minutes on foot from vibrant centres. Pedestrian, cycle and bus routes can displace other vehicles from the same space, reducing the barrier previously represented by traffic. Fast one-way road systems around city centres become obsolete and destructive when inner neighbourhoods are closely linked to the centre and begin to recover. Needless through traffic can be pushed out and decayed inner rings of homes, shops and services can become potential growth areas. The environmental potential of city centres and inner neighbourhoods then becomes visible. As we limit traffic and restore public spaces, buildings and neighbourhoods, we clamour for more greenery. With support and very small incentives, public bodies, residents and businesses will make streets greener, cleaner, safer.

A compact city therefore works on four axes:

Creating a vibrant, dense centre;
Revitalising inner neighbourhoods;
Organising accessible public transport across the city;
Protecting and enhancing the environment.

Who is in charge of this web of activities? Cities draw together many voices. As a result, they can edge forward or slide backwards in unexpected ways. The prospect for cities is improving, allowing us to do more to build cohesion between areas, people, organisations and interests.

Cohesive cities

Cities are places of extremes, and recovery could make them more so: the very wealthy and the very poor often live as near neighbours, with walls, visible or invisible, in between. The success of city centres has pushed up property prices far beyond expectations, making them unaffordable to all but a lucky few. Their density, their night life, their busy streets and original spaces make them highly attractive to some but unsuitable for others. The people who cannot afford or do not want luxury centre city apartments or warehouse and canal-side flats have largely abandoned the inner neighbourhoods as too insecure and decayed; they prefer the quieter, safer, greener suburbs. But as land becomes scarcer and smaller households multiply, such people and their offspring are the most likely resettlers of the still depopulating but potentially attractive inner neighbourhoods. These large, unexploited and uncared for areas hold the key to affordable housing. They have capacity, they have surviving but struggling communities, they offer proximity, mixed uses and amenities crying out for reuse. They have too often lost their compact form, but can regain it if we recycle brown land carefully.

Is it possible to reconcile the interests of low-income inner-city communities that do not want to be displaced and those of the majority of households, neither rich nor poor, who want good-quality, spacious homes in a pleasant, safe environment, close to work, good schools, shops and transport? Cities have deep inequalities in education, income, housing standards and environments, making poorer neighbourhoods deeply unattractive. It is impossible, many would argue, to do away with these inequalities. But unless cities work constantly to prevent social, racial, physical and economic divisions, their communities will fall apart and the city will not work. A major cause of slum clearance in twentieth-century Britain was the almost complete neglect of inner-urban neighbourhoods over half a century. We must not repeat that mistake today.

Upgrading poorer neighbourhoods implies sharing resources. Within cities, the availability of resources depends upon wealth-creating enterprise and citizens with buying power, skills and commitment staying in the city. Therefore we need to stop the leaching away of ordinary working people, the neither rich nor poor. The original welfare state was built on this compact – all gain if all contribute. Public services still have strong public support because the rich pay in and gain alongside the poor, and both benefit. Cities are also built on this compact. All too often the poor suffer the worst of the city but are trapped while the rich escape. To overcome the long legacy of social exclusion, cities must hold on to both richer and poorer communities and recreate them together. Skills and resources must be shared so that neighbourhoods are upgraded for everyone.

Inner neighbourhoods have lost their ambitious people and their poverty has intensified. But they survive: many amenities still function; residents struggle to make things work again. The fight for survival offers new opportunities. Workers who commute into the city centre may find the proximity, vibrancy and social mix of inner neighbourhoods more attractive than the distant, dull suburbs. Inner areas offer empty homes and spaces crying out for new uses.

Neighbourhood renewal begins small but can grow if the city as a whole supports these embryonic communities. Every city has to take many simple steps, block by block, street by street. Key workers need to feel confident enough to stay in the inner city, valued enough to fight against deprivation and close enough to the communities they serve to identify with their problems and prospects. A fairer distribution of teachers, doctors, police and transport would encourage them. Existing residents will then stay and new residents will want to come.

How can we redesign these inner areas so that they start to become appealing? First, we need a plan of action based on existing communities and clusters of activity, so that the neighbourhood starts to renew itself immediately. The voice of the residents, so seldom heard, is vital here. Second, we need to build intensively on this core of neighbourhood vitality. We can broker local priorities such as safer, cleaner streets and better schools and jobs with the wider interests of the city. Third, we need to create a secure, cared for environment. CCTV cameras on towers are no substitute for a human presence on the streets – a warden, a policeman, a super-caretaker. This new feeling of security will help the schools, shops, bus routes, health centres and other facilities that make an area come alive. Finally, we need to link the city centre to the inner neighbourhoods. We need to create a denser, closer texture in these neighbourhoods to make up for the earlier demolitions and population loss. Many smaller households want to be near friends and amenities. The new pressure to re-use brown spaces gives us a chance to revive troubled inner neighbourhoods and conserve suburbs as well as revitalise city cores.

The four axes of cohesive cities are therefore:

Stimulating the local economy by improving skills and jobs – this requires links to the centre;
A strong voice for residents and control over local conditions;
Equal public services for all, including neighbourhood management;
Physical and environmental care, giving confidence to potential *and* existing residents.

Recreating neighbourhoods

Restoring seriously run-down communities is far harder than arresting their decline – which is why many cities and towns simply prefer to knock down their worst neighbourhoods. The decay of inner areas, where many people could afford to live but most will not, leads to a shortage of affordable housing. As standards rise, the problem gets worse. Yet older inner-city housing often has more space, more originality, more 'curb appeal' than many modern developments. It is simply being abandoned because of the combination of social exclusion and urban dereliction. The unused or under-used is always abused. Conversely, activity spawns activity. Brown-field development creates urban jobs – in building repair, renovation, environmental maintenance, transport and services.

Work is the key to overcoming poverty and exclusion. So we need a more blended approach to cities, attracting people and enterprise, designing and managing space, working out from compact centres into compact neighbourhoods. With growing density and restoration, urban services of all kinds expand: local shops, eating places, child care, cleaning, security and care work. Every new job is a step forward. Education, networking, support and enterprise all help these left-behind communities to reconnect. Otherwise demolition and further dispersal become the only answer. Newcastle is currently advocating large-scale inner-city demolition for the third time in as many generations.

We love cities at their best and hate them at their worst. We can revalue the empty spaces that pock-mark our cities by prioritising brown over green building. We can persuade citizens to support simple changes that will combine to transform urban conditions – security, green streets, clean environments, priority for pedestrians and buses, better schools and recycling waste. Many aspects of city living are too artificial, imposing heavy costs on human society as well as the natural environment. But cities are also living organisms, dependent on their surrounding environments, shaped by the capacity of the people living and working in them to sustain, replenish and remake them.

The physical form of cities and the social conditions within them are intimately connected, and are both the product of human endeavour. Unless we work on both together, cities will founder. When neighbourhoods become troubled, cities lose some of their vibrancy. But the often invisible links between people and places help cities to work over generations. It is this continuity that can fuel the rebirth of urban neighbourhoods.

Future of cities

All settlements, from the smallest village to the largest cities, work better if they have compact, cohesive patterns. At the same time, we need to reduce waste and conserve energy, resources and land. So we must make our built up areas work. This does not mean allowing them to deteriorate. If neighbourhoods are safer and cleaner, then more mixed communities will develop, skills will be shared and standards will rise – as literacy and numeracy in city schools already have. It does not mean less space either, but less wasted space, thanks to better design – converted flats and houses are often more spacious than new ones. It does not mean less greenery, but more: window boxes, tubs, trees, gardens, parks and squares can appear everywhere if enough people are involved in making it happen. It does not mean no cars at all, but fewer pointless, frustrating journeys and more efficient, economic and pleasant public transport. It does not mean forcing people into unsafe neighbourhoods and surrounding them with ugly buildings. It means carefully bringing buildings back into use to create better-designed, better-cared for and more-secure homes and neighbourhoods. It does not mean no demolition at all, but a bias in favour of retaining and reinstating communities rather than flattening them. It does not mean no new building. It means planning compact, connected, textured new developments that minimise environmental impact and maximise cohesion.

By the end of the next generation, most of the population of the world will be living in cities. They can be run efficiently, inclusively, compactly and sustainably, as Curitiba, a Third-World city with explosive growth, shows. Making cities sustainable means making them more compact, more cohesive and more alluring than today – less damaging to the globe's pressured environment, healing the stark divisions that characterise today's cities. Helping people to feel that they have a voice in making their cities work will relieve the sense of powerlessness that often makes city dwellers seek simpler, more peaceful environments.

On our crowded planet, in our green island, most of us depend on cities. We can only make them work if we counter the fragmentation of the post-industrial age. Noise, congestion and aggression make people fear cities. Design, management, education, support and leadership are the counterweights in a populous, competitive, multi-racial and highly-developed world. The changes sweeping across societies in the developed and developing world are played out most powerfully in cities. For cities not only concentrate problems but also solutions – the vital role of citizens. Because of this, cities hold the key to our common future.

▶ Notting Hill Carnival, London
Katherine Miles/Environmental Images

Notes

1 Esteban, J (1999)
2 Glasgow City Council (1999)
3 Esteban, J (1999)
4 City of Barcelona (1999) Crime survey
5 Esteban, J (1999)
6 Power, A, and Mumford, K (1999)
7 Power, A (2000) RSA lecture
8 Interview with senior manager in international electronics firm wanting to relocate, August 1999
9 North Manchester Regeneration Panel (1999)
10 Perlman, J, Mega-cities project, quoted in Girardet, H (1996)
11 Gehl, J (1996a; 1996b; 1999)
12 *Times Atlas of the World* (1997)
13 Urban Task Force (1999)
14 Sassen, S (1994)
15 Hall, P (2000a)
16 Cullingworth, JB (1979)
17 Turok, I, and Edge, N (1999); British Business Parks (1999)
18 Jargowsky, PA (1996); Wilson, WJ (1996)
19 *The Economist* (2000c)
20 SEU (1998a)
21 DETR (1999p)
22 Arendt, H, in Rowe, P (1999)
23 Rowe, P (1999)
24 Halsey, AH (1988); UNEP (2000)
25 London Borough of Islington (1968)
26 Burrows, R, and Rhodes, D (1998)
27 IPPR (2000)
28 Briggs, A (1983)
29 Briggs, A (1968)
30 The People's Panel (1999)
31 Travers, T (1998)
32 UTF (1999b)
33 SEU (1998a)
34 Burnett, J (1991)
35 Crookston, M (1999)
36 Halsey, AH (1988)
37 ONS 1951–1991 census data
38 Abercrombie, P (1945)
39 Power, A (1987)
40 DoE (1968)
41 DETR (1999n)
42 Holman, B (1999a)
43 SEU (2000a)
44 Bramley, G, et al (1999)
45 Power, A, and Mumford, K (1999)
46 Turok, I, and Edge, N (1999)
47 DfEE (1999c)
48 Hills, J (1998)
49 Turok, I, and Edge, N (1999)
50 Lupton, R (forthcoming)
51 Rose, J (1969)
52 SEU (2000b)
53 Rose, J (1969)
54 DoE (1974–1997)
55 Peach, C (1998a; 1998b); Modood, T, et al (1997)
56 Modood, T, et al (1997)
57 HUD (1999)
58 Commission for Racial Equality (1998a; 1998b)
59 ONS (2000); Halsey, AH (1988)
60 Ibid
61 Glennerster, H, and Hills, J (1998); Modood, T, et al (1997)
62 Power, A, and Mumford, K (1999)
63 Power, A, and Tunstall, R (1995)
64 Hills, J, et al (1999)
65 Davies, N (1999)
66 SEU (2000b)
67 DfEE (1999b)
68 OFSTED (2000)
69 City of Newcastle, Department of Education, 1999
70 Estate agents' evidence
71 Blunkett, D (1999)
72 Home Office (2000)
73 Ibid
74 Hall, P (1998)
75 Power, A, and Mumford, K (1999)
76 SEU (2000b)
77 DETR (1999n)
78 DETR (1999l)
79 Ibid
80 *The Economist* (2000d)
81 DETR (1999l)
82 Turok, I, and Edge, N (1999)
83 Giddens, A (1990)
84 Kontinnen, S (1983)
85 Ibid
86 Henderson, T (1999)
87 House of Commons Select Committee on Environment, Transport and Regional Affairs (1999)
88 Howard, E (1898)
89 Jacobs, J (1990)
90 Gwilliam, M, et al (1998)
91 Gehl, J (1996b)
92 DoE (1991)
93 Halsey, AH (1988)
94 Thomson, F.ML (1990)
95 Burnett, J (1991)
96 Hill, O (1883)
97 Burnett, J (1991)
98 GLC Housing Committee minutes 1976
99 Hall, P, and Ward, C (1998)
100 Hall, P (1990)
101 Swenarton, M (1981)
102 Experience in the North Islington Housing Rights Project 1974–1980 showed that inner London residents were screened for their work record to ensure that the New Towns would be 'economically viable'; Glasgow City Council (1999); DoE (1974–1977)
103 Gwilliam, M, et al (1998)
104 Holmans, A (1987)
105 Saunders, P (1990)
106 Donnison, D (1967)
107 Ministry of Housing and Local Government (1969)
108 Lockwood, C (1999); HUD (1999)
109 Katz, B, and Bradley, J (1999)
110 Crookston, M (2000)
111 Burdett, R (2000)
112 Thomson, FML (1990)
113 Ibid
114 House of Commons Committee on Housing in Greater London (1965)
115 Thomson, FML (1990)
116 Author's visit to Federal Department of Housing and Urban Development (2000)
117 Simmins, M (1999)
118 UTF (1999b); DETR (2000a)
119 DoE (1974–1977)
120 Power, A (1987)

121 Dunleavy, P (1981)
122 Ibid
123 Power, A (1993)
124 Hamilton, R (ed) (1976)
125 Macey, J, and Baker, CV (1964); the GLC closed its waiting lists in the 1960s because of the problem of rehousing from slums
126 Ministry of Housing and Local Government (1969)
127 Crossman, RHS (1977)
128 Priority Estates Project (1982; 1984)
129 Power, A (1987)
130 London Borough of Islington (1968)
131 Power, A (1987)
132 Harloe, M (1995); Dunleavy, P (1981)
133 DoE (1987)
134 Power, A (1999)
135 DoE (1974–1977)
136 McLennan, D (1997)
137 DoE (1974)
138 Power, A, and Tunstall, R (1995)
139 Ratcliffe, P (2000)
140 BBC (1995)
141 Power, A, and Mumford, K (1999)
142 Rudlin, D (1998)
143 DETR (1999n; 2000a)
144 Bramley, G, et al (1999)
145 London Borough of Hackney (1999)
146 Power, A (1999); HTA (1998)
147 Ibid (Trellick Tower, Kensington and Chelsea)
148 SEU (1998a; 2000b)
149 Gehl, J (1999)
150 DETR (1998c)
151 DETR (1999j)
152 Millennium Dome, Transport Zone (2000)
153 The Economist (2000c)
154 Jowell, R, et al (1999)
155 DETR (1999i)
156 DETR (1999f); Audit Commission (1999a)
157 Ibid
158 HUD (1999)
159 DETR (2000f)
160 DETR (199f); Audit Commission (1999a)
161 AA (2000a; 2000b)
162 UN (1997)
163 Gehl, J (1996b); Appleyard, D (1981)
164 British Medical Journal (1999)
165 Power, A, and Tunstall, R (1997)
166 Ibid
167 HUD (1999)
168 Lockwood, C (1999)
169 Fialka, J (2000); HUD (1999)
170 Atkinson, M, and Ellliott, L (1999)
171 Power, A, and Wilson, WJ (2000); Jargowsky, P (1997); HUD (1999)
172 Massey, DS, and Denton, NA (1993); HUD (1998)
173 HUD (1999)
174 Centre for Architecture and the Built Environment, author's personal communication
175 Castells, M (1999)
176 Sassen, S (1994)
177 Jowell, R, et al (1999)
178 Grayling, S, and Glaister, S (2000); Curitiba Municipal Secretariat for the Environment (1992)
179 DETR (1999f)
180 DETR (1999f)
181 Statement by the Chief Executive, Railtrack, after the Paddington rail crash, 5 October 1999
182 BBC Panorama (1999a)
183 The Economist (2000b)
184 Millennium Dome, Transport Zone (2000)
185 Virgin Trains (2000)
186 BBC Panorama (2000a)
187 Ibid
188 Walters, J (2000)
189 AA (2000a)
190 Gehl, J (1996a; 1999)
191 City of Strasbourg (1999)
192 DETR (1999e)
193 DoT (1996)
194 Sustrans (2000)
195 DETR (1999i)
196 HUD (1998; 1999)
197 Satterthwaite, D (ed) (1999)
198 UNEP (2000)
199 Parliamentry Office of Science and Technology (1998)
200 DETR (1998i)
201 Author's visit to World Bank, Washington, May 2000
202 House of Commons Select Committee on Environment, Transport and Regional Affairs (2000a)
203 DETR (2000g)
204 Rees, W, in Satterthwaite, D (ed) (1999)
205 UNEP (2000)
206 Rees, W, in Satterthwaite, D (ed) (1999)
207 National House Builders Council (1998)
208 Power, A, and Mumford, K (1999); Power, A (2000)
209 Giddens, A (1999)
210 Power, A (1999)
211 The Economist (2000d)
212 Ibid
213 Nivola, PS (1999)
214 Girardet, H (1996)
215 UNCHS (1996)
216 UN (1997)
217 Girardet, H (1996); Satterthwaite, D (ed) (1999
218 Brown, P (1999)
219 Watanabe, N (2000); Girardet, H (1996)
220 UNEP (2000)
221 Ibid
222 Katz, B, and Bradley, J (1999)
223 Freedland, J (1999)
224 Meadows, D H, et al (1972)
225 May, R (2000)
226 World Bank (2000); DETR (1999q)
227 Rees, W, in Satterthwaite, D (ed) (1999)
228 Nivola, P S (1999)
229 National Parks (1999)
230 Danish National Urban Renewal Company (1989); information received by the author
231 Manchester City Council, Regeneration Panel, comparative property values from Grimley Eve Surveyors, 1999
232 LPAC (1999)
233 DETR (1999n)
234 LPAC (1999)
235 Halifax Building Society (1999)
236 Holmans, A, and Simpson, M (1999)
237 Power, A, and Tunstall, R (1997); DETR (1999n)
238 Murphy, M (2000)
239 DETR (1999p)

240 Cherry, A (1999)
241 DoE (1992)
242 Holmans, A (1995)
243 Pfeiffer, U (1999)
244 KPMG (1998; 1999)
245 DETR (2000c)
246 Kent Thames-Side (1999)
247 DoE (1995)
248 Hall, P (2000b)
249 Urban Splash (1998a; 1998b); Freedman, C (1996)
250 School Spending Allowance
251 DoH (1998; 1999)
252 SEU (2000b)
253 UTF (1999b)
254 Weaver, M (2000)
255 JRF (2000)
256 HTA (1998)
257 UTF (1999b)
258 Thamesmead Annual Reports 1983–1999
259 DETR (2000g)
260 Walker, L (2000); Kirby, P (2000)
261 Richard Rogers Partnership (1998); Latham, I, and Swenarton, M (1999)
262 British Business Parks (1999)
263 Gavron, N (2000)
264 Crime Concern (2000)
265 Webster, D (1999d)
266 British Airports Authority (1998); meeting at the London School of Economics
267 Power, A, and Bergin, E (1999); The Economist (2000d)
268 Best, R (2000)
269 British Business Parks (1999)
270 Cheshire, P, and Shepherd, S (1999); Pennington, M (1999)
271 Hall, P, and Ward, C (1998)
272 DoE (1992)
273 Thomson, D (2000)
274 'The people – where are they coming from? The housing consequences of migration' (1999) Joseph Rowntree Foundation seminar, September 20
275 Blair, T (1999a)
276 LGA (2000)
277 Llewellyn Davies (2000); Urbanisme (1999)
278 Power, A (1999)
279 Rudlin, D, and Falk, N (1999); Latham, I, and Swenarton, M (1999)
280 KPMG (1998; 1999); UTF (1999b); Royal Town Planning Institute (1999)
281 Rudlin, D (1998b)
282 UTF (1999b)
283 Llewellyn Davies (2000)
284 Latham, I, and Swenarton, M (1999)
285 See Hall, P (2000) Work and the places to be for the experience of Skipol
286 Llewellyn Davies (2000)
287 Pennington, M (1999)
288 BBC (1995); Patten, C (2000)
289 Power, A, and Mumford, K (1999)
290 JRF (1998)
291 DoE Urban Development Corporation reports 1981–1998
292 Henney, A (1982)
293 Millennium Footbridge closure, 12 June 2000
294 DETR (1998l)
295 HM Treasury (2000)
296 DETR (1998l)
297 Land Planning Act 1981
298 KPMG (1999); UTF (1999b)
299 Savills, FDP Survey of Residential Property (1998)
300 Power, A (1995)
301 LPAC (1999)
302 Glasgow City Council (1999)
303 Hebbert, M (2000)
304 LPAC (1999)
305 Power, A, and Tunstall, R (1993); James, O (1995)
306 Newman, K (1999)
307 Llewellyn Davies (2000)
308 British Airports Authority report to author (1998)
309 Rees, W, in Satterthwaite, D (ed) (1999)
310 Guggenheim Museum, New York
311 Newcastle City Council (1999)
312 Ibid; Power, A, and Mumford, K (1999)
313 Jacobs, J (1996)
314 Wilson, WJ (1987)
315 Burbridge, M, et al (1981)
316 JRF (1998)
317 Power, A (1999)
318 Llewellyn Davies, UCL Bartlett School of Planning and COMEDIA (1996)
319 Briggs, A (1983)
320 Rogers, R (1997)
321 Gehl, J (1996b)
322 Mercer, W M (2000b)
323 Patten, C (2000)
324 Atkinson, M, and Elliott, L (1999)
325 DoE (1993a)
326 Patten, C (2000)
327 Curitiba, Municipal Secretariat for the Environment (1992)
328 UTF (1999a)
329 UNCHS (1996)
330 Ibid
331 DETR (2000c)
332 Bannon, M, (1985)
333 Power, A (2000)
334 ONS (2000)
335 Power, A (1974)
336 DETR (2000b)
337 New York City Council Information (2000)
338 Power, A, and Bergin, E (1999)
339 PEP (2000)
340 Power, A (1999)
341 Hills, J (1998)
342 JRF (2000)
343 Ibid
344 Glasgow City Council (1999)
345 Power, A (1993)
346 Bramley, G, et al (1999)
347 National Federation of Housing Associations (1986)
348 Foyer Federation (1999)
349 LPAC (1999)
350 Crookston, M (1999; 2000); SEU (1998a)
351 Pitt, J (1999)
352 Ibid
353 HUD (1999); Turok, I, and Edge, N (1999)
354 Castells, M (1999)
355 Power, A, and Bergin, E (1999)
356 Hume Regeneration Company (1999); evidence from author's visit
357 Power, A, and Bergin, E (1999)
358 DETR (2000d)

359 UTF (1999b); SEU (2000b)
360 Association of Town Centre Managers report to the UTF (1999)
361 Power, A (1992)
362 Power, A, and Bergin, E (1999)
363 Curitiba, Municipal Secretariat for the Environment (1992)
364 City of Strasbourg (1999)
365 Grayling, T, and Glaister, S (2000); Curitiba, Municipal Secretariat for the Environment (1992)
366 Ibid
367 DETR (1999g)
368 *The Economist* (1998)

369 *The Economist* (2000b); Caisse des Dépôts et Consignations Comité d'Evaluation (2000)
370 Putnam, R D (1993)
371 Caisse des Dépôts et Consignations Comité d'Evaluation (2000)
372 Greenhalgh, L, and Worpole, K
373 Opening of Murray Grove, Peabody Trust, 10 November 1999
374 Estebán, J (1999)
375 Borer, P, and Harris, C (1998); Girardet, H (1998)
376 Girardet, H (1998)
377 Girardet, H (1998)

References

AA (2000a), Great British Motorist 2000 survey

AA (2000b), 'UK motorists get Europe's raw deal', *AA Members' Magazine*

Abercrombie, P (1945), *Greater London Plan 1944*, London: HMSO

Appleyard, D (1981), *Liveable Streets*, Berkeley: University of California Press

Asbury, P (1999), Bowes Park Action Group, letter to author (7 December)

ASDA (1999), 'ASDA plans to roll out 50 new ASDA fresh stores in five years', press release (15 November)

Atkinson, M, and Elliott, L (1999), 'He means business', interview with Digby Jones, Director General of CBI, *Guardian* (20 November)

Audit Commission (1996), *Misspent youth . . . young people and crime*, London: Audit Commission

Audit Commission (1998), *Home alone: the role of housing in community care*, London: Audit Commission

Audit Commission (1999a), *All aboard: a review of local transport and travel in urban areas outside London*, London: Audit Commission

Audit Commission (1999b), *A life's work: local authorities, economic development and economic regeneration*, London: Audit Commission

Bailey, N, Turok, I, and Docherty, I (1999), *Edinburgh and Glasgow: contrasts in competitiveness and cohesion*, Interim report of the Central Scotland Integrative Case Study, Glasgow: University of Glasgow, Dept of Urban Studies

Baldwin, P (1999), 'Postcodes chart growing income divide', *Guardian* (25 October)

Ball, M (1998), *School inclusion: the school, the family and the community*, York: Joseph Rowntree Foundation

Bannon, M J (1984), *A hundred years of Irish planning: the emergence of Irish planning 1880–1920*, Dublin: Turoe Press

Barcelona, City of (1999), *Delinquency in Barcelona City*, Barcelona: PSC-Secretaria

Bartlett, S, et al. (1999), *Cities for children: children's rights, poverty and urban management*, London: Earthscan

BBC (1995), *The New Jerusalem*

BBC News (1999), Summary of the rail survey by Tim James (29 November)

BBC Panorama (1999a), 'The great train jam' (29 November)

BBC Panorama (1999b), 'The house price lottery' (28 June)

BBC Track Record (1999), Key issues: a guide to the main issues by BBC transport correspondent Tom Heap (29 November–4 December)

Best, R (1999), Director, Joseph Rowntree Foundation, letter to Julian Pitt, Hertfordshire CC (21 December)

Best, R (2000), Chartered Institute of Housing plenary speech (13 June)

Blair, T (1999a), Annual Beveridge Lecture (18 March)

Blair, T (1999b), Prime Minister's New Year Message, Sedgefield (29 December)

Blayey, S (2000), 'Urban shambles', *Observer* (23 January)

Blunkett, D (1999), *Social exclusion and the politics of opportunity: a mid term progress check*, Speech by the secretary of state for education and employment (3 November), London: DfEE

Borer, P, and Harris, C (1998), *The whole house book: ecological building design and materials*, Powys: Centre for Alternative Technology

Boseley, S, et al. (2000), 'Incinerator cancer threat revealed', *Guardian* (18 May)

Boylan, E (2000), Speech at Chartered Institute of Housing annual conference (June)

Bramley, G (1998), *Housing surpluses and housing need*, paper presented to the Capital's Housing Action Conference, University of York

Bramley, G, et al. (1999), *Low demand housing and unpopular neighbourhoods. Second draft report to the DETR*, Edinburgh: School of Planning and Housing, Edinburgh College of Art/Herriot-Watt University

Braunstone New Deal Task Force (1999), *New Deal for Braunstone: delivery plan*, Leicester

Briggs, A (1968), *Victorian cities*, Harmondsworth: Penguin Books

Briggs, A (1983), *A social history of England*, Harmondsworth: Penguin Books

Brindle, D (1999), 'Potted history', *Guardian* (27 October)

British Business Parks (1999), *Briefing paper on British Business Parks*, Walsall: British Business Parks

British Medical Journal (1999), 'Preventing Osteoporosis, falls and fractures among elderly people', *British Medical Journal*, vol. 318, pages 205–206 (23 January)

Brown, P (1999), 'Washed up', *Guardian* (27 October)

Burbridge, M, et al. (1981), *An investigation of difficult to let housing*, London: Department of the Environment

Burdett, R (2000), *Density and quality of life in cities*, LSE London Lecture (10 May)

Burnett, J (1991), *A social history of housing 1815–1985*, London: Routledge

Burrows, R (1997), *Contemporary patterns of residential mobility in relation to social housing in England. Research report*, University of York: Centre for Housing Policy

Burrows, R, and Rhodes, D (1998), *Unpopular places? Area disadvantage and the geography of misery in England*, Bristol: Policy Press

Cabinet Office (1999), *Sharing the nation's prosperity: variations in economic and social conditions across the UK. A report to the prime minister* (December)

Carvel, J (1999), 'University drop-out rates reflect class roots', *Guardian* (3 December)

Castells, M (1999), *The Information Age: economy, society and culture*, London: Blackwell

Centre for Regional Economic and Social Research (1999), *Landlords*, Sheffield: Sheffield Hallam University, in association with the Housing Corporation

Cherry, A (1999), Evidence presented to the UTF

Cheshire, P, and Sheppard, S (1997), *Welfare economics of land use regulation*, Research Papers in Environmental and Spatial Analysis No 42, London: London School of Economics, Dept of Geography

Cheshire, P, and Sheppard, S (2000), *The political economy of containing urban sprawl: sustainability or asset values?* Paper presented at the World Congress of Regional Science, Lugano, Switzerland (May)

Cheshire, P (1990), 'Explaining the recent performance of the European Community's major urban Regions', *Urban Studies*, vol 27, no 3, pages 311–333

Cheshire, P (1999), 'Cities in competition: articulating the gains from integration', *Urban Studies*, vol 36, nos 4–6, pages 843–864

Cheshire, P, and Carbonaro, G (1996), 'Urban economic growth in Europe: testing theory and policy prescriptions', *Urban Studies*, vol 33, no 7, pages 1111–1128

Cheshire, P, and Sheppard, S (1999), 'Land strapped – constrained land supply skews prices', *ROOF*, Winter

Cheshire, P, and Sheppard, S (2000), 'Building on brown fields: The long term price we pay', *Planning in London*, 33, April/June, pages 34–36

CLES (1999), *Homes with jobs: delivering New Deal through social landlords*, Manchester: CLES, Building Positive Action

Cole, I, Kane, S and Robinson, D (1999), *Changing demand, changing neighbourhoods: the response of social landlords*, Sheffield: CRESR, Sheffield Hallam University/London: Housing Corporation

Commission for Racial Equality (1998a), *Reform of the Race Relations Act, 1976*, proposals for change, submitted to the Secretary of State for the Home Department (30 April)

Commission for Racial Equality (1998b), *Stereotyping and racism*, report of two attitude surveys carried out by the CRE into identities, stereotypes and experiences of racism among South Asians, African Caribbeans and white people, London: CRE

CPRE (1996), *Housing with hindsight. Household growth, housing need and housing development in the 1980s*, London: CPRE

CPRE (1999a), Housing and the Environment, London: CPRE

   Housing types and tenure

   Plan, monitor and manage

   Spatial distribution of additional development and impact on urban areas and sustainability

   Urban renaissance and countryside protection

CPRE (1999b), *The Crow Report: a CPRE critique of housing proposals in the report of the Public Examination of Regional Planning Guidance for the South East*, London: CPRE

Crime Concern (1998a), *Reducing neighbourhood crime: a manual for action*, report prepared by Crime Concern for the Crime Prevention Agency at the Home Office, London: CPA

Crime Concern (1998b), *Safe as houses: a community safety guide for registered social landlords*, published by Crime Concern for the Housing Corporation, Swindon: Crime Concern

Crime Concern (2000), President's Council Meeting (11 May)

Crookston, M (1999), Evidence presented to the UTF

Crookston, M (2000), *Calling suburbia: Richard Rogers has a plan for you . . .*, London: Llewelyn Davies

Crossman, R H S (1977), *The diaries of a cabinet minister. Secretary of State for Social Services, 1968–70*, London: Hamish Hamilton/Cape

Cullingworth, J B (1979), *Essays on housing policy: the British scene*, London: Allen and Unwin

Curitiba Municipal Secretariat for the Environment (1992), *Curitiba. The ecological revolution*, Curitiba: Municipal Secretariat for the Environment

Davies, N (1999), 'Schools in crisis', series of articles, *Guardian* (14–16 September)

DETR (1998a), *A New Deal for transport: better for everyone*, London: Stationery Office

DETR (1998b), *Housing Investment Programme: Housing Annual Plan*, London: DETR

DETR (1998c), *Road accidents in Great Britain 1998: the casualty report*, London: Stationery Office

DETR (1998d), *The impact of large foodstores on market towns and district centres: executive summary*, London: HMSO

DETR (1998e), *The impact of urban development corporations in Leeds, Bristol and Central Manchester*, Regeneration Research Summary No 18, London: DETR

DETR (1998f), *Government Statistical Service Information Bulletin: land use change in England*, London: DETR

DETR (1998g), *New Deal for Communities*, London: DETR

DETR (1998h), *Planning for sustainable development: towards better practice*, London: DETR

DETR (1998i), *Planning for the communities of the future*, London: DETR

DETR (1998j), *The Government's Response to the Environment, Transport and Regional Affairs Committee. Session 1997–8, Housing*, London: Stationery Office

DETR (1998k), *Transport Statistics Report: walking in Great Britain*, London: Stationery Office

DETR (1998l), *Urban development corporations: performance and good practice*, Regeneration Research Summary No 17, London: DETR

DETR (1998m), *Walking in Great Britain*, London: Stationery Office

DETR (1999a), *Annual Report 1999: The Government's Expenditure Plans 1999–2000 to 2001–02*, London: DETR

DETR (1999c), *Quarterly bulletin of rail statistics*, Transport Statistics Division (TSA) (December 12)

DETR (1999d), *Cross-cutting issues affecting local government*, London: DETR

DETR (1999e), *Cycling in Great Britain*, Personal Travel Factsheet 5 (December), London: DETR

DETR (1999f), *From workhorse to thoroughbred: a better role for bus travel*, London: Stationery Office

DETR (1999g), 'Lord Whitty Announces nine Home Zone sites', press release no 788 (4 August)

DETR (1999h), *National land use database: provisional results for previously developed land in England*, Government Statistical Service Information Bulletin no 500 (20 May)

DETR (1999i), *National Travel Survey: update 1996/98*, London: DETR

DETR (1999j), *Travel to school*, Personal Travel Factsheet 2 (June), London: DETR

DETR (1999k), *Where does public spending go? Pilot study to analyse the flows of public expenditure into local areas*, London: DETR

DETR (1999l), *1998 Index of Local Deprivation: a summary of results*, London: DETR

DETR (1999m), *Land use change in England*, No 14, London: DETR

DETR (1999n), *National Strategy for Neighbourhood Renewal: unpopular housing*, Report of Policy Action Team 7, London: DETR

DETR (1999o), 'Household growth down – John Prescott', press release (29 March)

DETR (1999p), *Projections of households in England to 2021*, London: DETR

DETR (1999q), *Quality of life counts: indicators for a strategy for sustainable development for the United Kingdom. Baseline assessment*, London: DETR

DETR (1999r), *Interim evaluation of English Partnerships*, Regeneration Research Summary no 24, London: DETR

DETR (2000a), *Housing Green Paper*, London: DETR

DETR (2000b), *Housing*, Planning Policy Guidance Note no 3, London: DETR

DETR (2000c), 'Prescott announces more responsive approach to meeting South East's housing needs', press release (7 March)

DETR (2000d), '£280 million budget bonus for transport – public transport and pensioners gain', press release 225 (23 March)

DETR (2000e), *Quality and choice*, London: DETR

DETR (2000f), *Tomorrow's roads: safer for everyone. The Government's road safety strategy and casualty reduction targets for 2010*, London: DETR

DETR (2000g), *Waste Strategy 2000 England and Wales, Parts 1 and 2*, London: Stationery Office

DfEE (1999a), *Excellence in cities,* London: DfEE Publications

DfEE (1999b), *School performance league tables*, London: HMSO

DfEE (1999c), *A fresh start: improving literacy and numeracy*, report of the working group chaired by Sir Claus Moser, London: DfEE Publications

DfEE (1999d), *Jobs for all: National Strategy for Neighbourhood Renewal*, report of the Policy Action Team on Jobs, London: DfEE Publications

DoE (1968), *Old houses into new homes*, London: HMSO

DoE (1974), *Difficult to let*, unpublished report of postal survey

DoE (1974–77), *Inner areas studies*, London: HMSO

DoE (1987), *PEP guide to local housing management, vols 1, 2, 3*, DoE for the Priority Estate Project

DoE (1991), 'City Challenge', press release

DoE (1992), *The relationship between house prices and land supply*, London: HMSO

DoE (1993a), *East Thames Corridor: a study of development capacity and potential*, London: HMSO

DoE (1993b), *The use of density in land use planning*, Planning Research Programme, London: HMSO

DoE (1995), *The Thames Gateway planning framework*, London: HMSO

DoE (1996), *Urban trends in England: latest evidence from the 1991 Census*, London: HMSO

DoH (1998, 1999), Statistics, London: DoH

Donnison, DV (1967), *The government of housing*, Harmondsworth: Penguin Books

Donnison, D, and Middleton, A (eds) (1987), *Regenerating the inner city: Glasgow's experience*, London: Routledge & Kegan Paul

DoT (1996), *The National Cycling Strategy*, London: DoT

DSS (1999), *Opportunity for all: tackling poverty and social exclusion. First annual report*, London: Stationery Office

Dunleavy, P (1981), *The politics of mass housing in Britain, 1945–1975: a study of corporate power and professional influence in the welfare state*, Oxford: Clarendon Press

Dwelly, T (ed) (1999), *Community investment: the growing role for housing associations*, York: Joseph Rowntree Foundation

Economist, The (1998)

'Britain's provincial cities. In London's shadow' (1 August)

'Birmingham. From workshop to melting pot' (8 August)

'Cities. The leaving of Liverpool' (15 August)

'Glasgow. Refitting on the Clyde' (22 August)

'Leeds. Streets paved with brass' (29 August)

'Middlesborough. Rejuvenating Hercules' (5 September)

Economist, The (1999a)

'Urban sprawl: to traffic hell and back' (8 May)

'Urban sprawl: a hydra in the desert' (17 July)

'Urban sprawl: wired in the woods' (31 July)

'Urban sprawl: right in the governor's back yard' (24 July)

'Urban sprawl: people want a place of their own' (7 August)

'Urban sprawl: aren't city centres great?'(14 August)

'Urban sprawl: not quite the monster they call it' (21 August)

Economist, The (1999b), 'Poverty' (23 October)

Economist, The (1999c), 'Poor students' (30 October)

Economist, The (1999d), 'How rich is London?' (18 December)

Economist, The (1999e), 'Blair's baby' (18 December)

Economist, The (2000a), 'Fewer and wrinklier Europeans' (15 January)

Economist, The (2000b), 'France – a city revived' (26 February)

Economist, The (2000c), 'Oxera study on rail and road investment and costs' (22 April)

Economist, The (2000d), 'A continent on the move' (6 May)

Empty Homes Agency (1999a), Letter from the Chief Executive to the Urban Task Force (7 August)

Empty Homes Agency (1999b), 'England's empty homes', press release (3 March)

Environment and Urbanisation (1996), vol 8, no 1, April, London: IIED

Environment and Urbanisation (1999), Sustainable cities revisited II, vol 11, no 2, October, London: IIED

Esteban, J (1999), *El Projecte Urbanistic – valorar la periferia I recuperar el centre.* Barcelona: Aula

Fialka, J (2000), 'Campaign against sprawl overruns a county in Virginia and soon perhaps much of nation', *Wall Street Journal* (4 January)

Finch, J (1999), 'House prices to jump again', *Guardian* (30 December)

Fischel, W (1999), *Sprawl and the federal government*, Cato Policy Report, September/October

Foyer Federation (1999), *Annual report*, London: Foyer Federation

Freedland, J (1999), 'Powerless people', Guardian (1 December)

Freedman, C (1996), 'Northern exposure', *Estates Gazette* (3 June)

Gavron, N (2000), Report to the Urban Task Force on London's capacity for housing

Gehl, J (1996a), *City quality – the Copenhagen way. Public spaces and public life in the city centre 1962–1996*, paper for Car-free Cities conference, Copenhagen, 6–7 May 1996

Gehl, J (1996b), *Life between buildings: using public space*, Copenhagen: Arkitektens Forlag

Gehl, J (1999), *Creating a human quality in the city*, paper for Living and Walking in Cities conference, Brescia, 14–15 June

Gehl, J, and Gemzoe, L (1996), *Public spaces public life*, Copenhagen: Architectural Press

Geitner, P (1999), *Germans find happiness without autos*, Associated Press

Giddens, A (1990), *The consequences of modernity*, Cambridge: Polity in association with Blackwell

Giddens, A (1999), *Runaway world: how globalisation is reshaping our lives*, 1999 Reith Lectures, London: Profile

Girardet, H (1996), *Gaia atlas of cities: new directions for sustainable urban living*, Stroud: Gaia

Girardet, H (1998), Report to the UTF

Glasgow City Council (1999), *Homes for the future*, Glasgow: Glasgow City Council

*Glennerster, H, and Hills, J (1998) Ed. The state of welfare II: the economics of social spending/Martin Evans et al. Oxford, New York: Oxford University Press

Glennerster, H, Lupton, R, Noden, P, and Power, A (1999), *Poverty, social exclusion and neighbourhood: studying the area bases of social exclusion*, London: CASEpaper 22

Government Office for the East of England (1999), *Draft regional planning guidance for East Anglia*, report of the Public Examination Panel (June)

Government Office for the North West, *Town centre management in the North West of England*, Manchester: GONW

Government Office for the South East (1999), *Regional planning guidance for the South East of England*, report of the Public Examination Panel (September)

Grayling, T (2000), 'Fairer fares', *Guardian* (9 January)

Grayling, T, and Glaister, S (2000), *A new fares contract for London*, London: IPPR

Greenhalgh, L, and Worpole, K (1995), *Park life: urban parks and social renewal*, London: DEMOS/Comedia

Groom, B (1999), 'Inspectors recommend 1m new homes for south-east', *Financial Times* (9–10 October)

Guardian, The (2000), 'A new century, a new resolution', supplement with WWF (1 January)

Gwilliam, M, et al (1998), *Sustainable renewal of suburban areas*, London: Joseph Rowntree Foundation

Halifax Building Society (1999), Index of average house prices, fourth quarter

Hall, P (1990), *Cities of tomorrow: an intellectual history of urban planning and design in the twentieth century*, Oxford: Blackwell

Hall, P (1996), *Building a new Britain*, London: Town and Country Planning Association

Hall, P (1998), Evidence presented to the Urban Task Force (November)

Hall, P (1999a), 'Growing sense of emptiness', *Guardian* (15 September)

Hall, P (1999b), 'Sirens sound over the countryside', *Financial Times* (2 November)

Hall, P (1999c), *Sustainable cities or town cramming?* London: Town and Country Planning Association

Hall, P (2000a), Work and the places to be, *Town and Country Planning Magazine*

Hall, P (2000b), Evidence presented to the UTF

Hall, P, and Pfeiffer, U (1999), *The urban future 21*, Bonn: Empirica

Hall, P, and Ward, C (1998), *Sociable cities: the legacy of Ebenezer Howard*, Chichester: Wiley

Halpern, D (1995), *More than bricks and mortar? Mental health and the built environment*, London: Taylor & Francis

Halsey, A H (1988), *British social trends since 1900: a guide to the changing social structure of Britain*, Basingstoke: Macmillan

Hamilton, R (ed) (1976), *Street by street*, London: Shelter

Harloe, M (1995), *The people's home? Social rented housing in Europe and America*, Oxford: Blackwell

Hebbert, M (2000), *Singing streets of London,* Third Eila Campbell Memorial Lecture, Birkbeck College, London, 1 March 2000

Hencke, D (2000), 'Children at risk from poisoned ash on paths', *Guardian* (8 May)

Henderson, T (1999), 'Byker Wall homes saved by heritage housing plan', *The Journal* (23 December)

Henney, A (1982), *Inside local government*, London: Sinclair Browne

Hetherington, P (1999a), 'Alarm over targets for south-east homes', *Guardian* (8 October)

Hetherington, P (1999b), 'Fat south, thin north', *Guardian* (14 October)

Hetherington, P (1999c), 'Plan to rebuild Newcastle is biggest since war', *Guardian* (1 December)

Hetherington, P (1999d), 'Rebirth of bombed city centre', *Guardian* (22 November)

Hill, O (1883), *Homes of the London poor*, London

Hills, J (1998), *Income and wealth: the latest evidence*, York: Joseph Rowntree Foundation

Hills, J (2000), *Reinventing social housing finance*, London: IPPR

Hills, J, et al (1999), *Persistent poverty and lifetime inequality: the evidence*, proceedings of a workshop held at H M Treasury, chaired by Professor John Hills, 17–18 November 1998, CASEreport 5, London: CASE

HM Treasury (2000), *Comprehensive Spending Review*, London: HM Treasury

Holman, B (1997), *FARE dealing: neighbourhood involvement in a housing scheme*, London: Community Development Foundation

Holman, B (1999a), *Faith in the poor*, Oxford: Lion Publishing

Holman, B (1999b), 'Limited imagination', *Guardian* (31 March)

Holmans, A, Morrison, N, and Whitehead, C (1998), *How many homes will we need? The need for affordable housing in England*, London: Shelter

Holmans, A (1987), *Housing policy in Britain: a history*, London: Croom Helm

Holmans, A (1995), *Housing demand and need in England 1999–2011*, London: Joseph Rowntree Foundation

Holmans, A (2000), Letter to author on population growth and housing demand

Holmans, A, and Simpson, M (1999), *Low demand: separating fact from fiction*, York: Joseph Rowntree Foundation

Home Office (1998), *Concern about crime: findings from the 1998 British Crime Survey*, Research Findings no 83, London: Home Office Research Development and Statistics Directorate

Home Office (2000), *Recorded crime statistics: England and Wales, October 1998 to September 1999*, Issue 1/00 (January), London: Home Office Research Development and Statistics Directorate

House of Commons Committee on Housing in Greater London (1965), Report of the committee on housing in Greater London, chairman Sir Milner Holland, presented to parliament by the minister of housing and local government, London: HMSO

House of Commons Select Committee on Environment, Transport and Regional Affairs (1999), *Twentieth report: town and country parks*, London: Stationery Office

House of Commons Select Committee on Environment, Transport and Regional Affairs (2000a), *Sixth report: Environment Agency*, London: Stationery Office

House of Commons Select Committee on Environment, Transport and Regional Affairs (2000b), Proposed White paper. Vol 1, Report and proceedings of the committee. Eleventh Report, London: Stationery Office

Howard, E (1898), *Tomorrow: a peaceful path to real reform*, London

HTA (1998), Project profiles on Waltham Forest tower blocks

HUD (1997, 1998, 1999), *The state of the cities*, Washington: US Department of Housing and Urban Development

IIED (1999), *Addressing environment and development in urban areas: the work of IIED's Urban Group*, London: IIED

IPPR (2000), Results of survey conducted for the IPPR Review of Housing, London: IPPR

Jacobs, J (1990), *The economy of cities*, New York: Random House

James, O (1995), *Juvenile violence in a winner-loser culture*, London: Free Association Books

Jargowsky, PA (1997), *Poverty and place: ghettos, barrios and the American city*, New York: Russell Sage Foundation

Jencks, C, and Peterson, P E (1991), *The urban underclass*, Washington: Brookings Institution

Jenkins, S (1999), 'The lure of lucre is robbing England of its countryside', *Sunday Times* (24 October)

Joseph Rowntree Foundation (1998), CASPAR market research

Joseph Rowntree Foundation (2000), *The secrets of CASPAR*, York: Joseph Rowntree Foundation

Jowell, R, et al (1999), *British Social Attitudes: the sixteenth report*, Aldershot: Ashgate

Jupp, B (1999), *Living together: community life on mixed tenure estates*, London: Demos

Katz, B, and Bradley, J (1999) *Divided we sprawl*. Atlantic monthly (December) Boulder USA

Kent Thames-side (1999), *Looking to an integrated future: land use and transport planning in Kent Thames-side*, Gravesend: Kent Thames-side

Kirby, P (2000), Evidence presented to the UTF on land reclaim

Kleinman, M (1999), *A more normal housing market? The housing role of the London Docklands Development Corporation 1981–1998*, Discussion paper no 3, London: LSE

Konttinen, S (1983), *Byker*, London: Jonathan Cape

KPMG (1998), *Fiscal incentives for brownfield sites*, report to the Urban Task Force (November)

KPMG (1999), *Brownfield housing projections: model assumptions*, report for the Urban Task Force, London: KPMG

Latham, I, and Swenarton, M (1999), *Brindley Place: a model for urban regeneration*, London: Right Angle Publishing.

Laurin, Y (nd), *The tram: a new concept of urban life*, Strasbourg: Transports et Stationnenment

*Llewelyn Davies (2000), *Sustainable residential quality: exploring the housing potential of large sites*, London: LPAC in association with Urban Investment and Metropolitan Transport Research Unit

Llewelyn Davies, UCL Bartlett School of Planning and COMEDIA (1996), *Four world cities: a comparative study of London, Paris, New York and Tokyo*, London: Stationery Office for DoE and Government Office for London

Local Government Association (2000), Annual Housing Conference (February 24)

Lockwood, C (1999), *Urban sprawl: creating sprawl*, three-part series, Environmental News Network (October 28)

London Borough of Hackney (1999a), *Comprehensive Estates Initiative: laying foundations for a sustainable future. CEI Review 1992–1998*, London: London Borough of Hackney

London Borough of Hackney (1999b), Consultation over proposed regeneration plans involving demolition (unpublished)

London Borough of Islington (1968), Medical officer of health's report, 1961 and 1968 census

LPAC (1999), *London housing capacity guidelines 1992–2016: supplementary advice*, London: LPAC

Lupton, R (forthcoming), Report on the first stage of the Areas Study for the CASE, London: LSE

Lyons, M (1999), *Some reflections on the government of towns and cities*, inaugural lecture, Birmingham University (26 November)

MacCormack, R (date unknown), Urban Task Force, Working Group One: Residential densities on brown field sites

Macey, J, and Baker, C V (1965, 1978 & 1982), *Housing management*, London: The Estates Gazette

Maclennan, D (1997), *Britain's cities: a more positive future*, Lunar Society Lecture (November)

Manson, F (1998), *Urban living*, report to UTF (23 October)

Massey, D S, and Denton, N A (1993), *American apartheid: segregation and the making of the underclass*, Cambridge, Massachusetts: Harvard University Press

Mathiason, N (2000), 'Tesco Metros close as high rents bite', *Observer* (21 May)

May, R (2000), Millennium Supplement, *Observer* (January 2)

McSmith, A (1999), 'Hague to jobless: get off your bikes', *Observer* (31 October)

Meadows, D H, et al (1972), *The limits to growth: a report for the Club of Rome's project on the predicament of mankind*, New York: New American Library

Meek, J (1999), 'Muslim neighbourhoods proposed to revive rundown city suburbs', *Guardian* (12 November)

Mercer, W M (2000a), World city rankings, *Guardian* (13 January)

Mercer, W M (2000b), Cost of living survey, http://www.wmmercer.com

Ministry of Housing and Local Government (1969), *Council housing purposes, procedures and priorities*, ninth report of the Housing Management Sub-Committee of the Central Housing Advisory Committee (the 'Cullingworth Report'), London: HMSO

Modood, T, et al (1997), *Ethnic minorities in Britain: diversity and disadvantage*, London: Policy Studies Institute

Moser, C (1996), *Confronting crisis: a comparative study of household responses to poverty and vulnerability of four poor urban communities*, ESD Studies and Monographs Series no 8, Washington DC: World Bank

Mumford, K (2000), *Talking to families in East London*, London: CASE

Murphy, M (2000), Evidence on demographic trends, London School of Economics

National Federation of Housing Associations (1986), *NFHA Jubilee 1935–1985*, Peter Jones, produced by Liverpool Housing Trust Information Services, London: NFHA

National House-Builders Council Conference (1998), *Sustainable housing – meeting the challenge* (11 September)

National Parks (1999), *Lake District National Park: annual report*

New Internationalist, The (1999), 'Green cities', issue 313, June

Newcastle City Council (1999), *Going for growth: a citywide vision for Newcastle 2020*, Newcastle: Newcastle City Council

Newman, K (1999), *Falling from grace: downward mobility in the age of affluence*, University of California Press

NHF (1999), *Special report: planning for affordable homes in London*, London: National Housing Federation

NHF (South East) (1999), *Who needs housing?* London: NHF

Nivola, P S (1999), *Laws of the landscape: how policies shape cities in Europe and America*, Washington DC: Brookings Institution

North Manchester Regeneration Panel (1999), North Manchester Regeneration Report, Manchester: Manchester City Council

Nutall, N (1998), 'Five reasons why official housing figures may be wrong', *The Times* (28 January)

OECD (1998), *Territorial development: integrating distressed urban areas*, Paris: OECD Publications

Office for National Statistics (1991), 1991 Census

Office for National Statistics (1998), *Statistics press release: focus on London 98 1* (April)

Office for National Statistics (1999a), General Household Survey

Office for National Statistics (1999b), Labour Force Survey

Office for National Statistics (1999c), *Social trends, 29th edition*, London: Stationery Office

Office for National Statistics (2000), *Social trends, 30th edition*, London: Stationery Office

Office for Standards in Education (2000), Inspection of Bradford Local Education Authority, May 2000, Office of Her Majesty's Chief Inspector of Schools in conjunction with the Audit Commission

Pacione, M (ed) (1997), *Britain's cities: geographies of division in urban Britain*, London: Routledge

Parliamentary Office of Science and Technology (1998), *A brown and pleasant land: accommodating household growth in England on brownfield sites*, London: Parliamentary Office of Science and Technology

Patten, C (2000), *Reith Lectures: Respect for the earth*, Lecture 1: Governance, BBC Radio 4

Pawley, M (1998), *Terminal architecture*, London: Reaktion

Peach, C (1996a), 'Does Britain have ghettos?' *Transactions of the Institute of British Geographers*, NS 21, pages 216–235, London: Royal Geographical Society

Peach, C (ed) (1996b), *Ethnicity in the 1991 census. Vol 2: The ethnic minority populations of Great Britain*, London: HMSO

Peckham Partnership (1994), *Peckham Partnership: a bid for single regeneration budget funding*, London: London Borough of Southwark/Peckham Partnership (September)

Pennington, M (1999), 'Free market environmentalism and the limits of land use planning', *Journal of Environmental Policy Planning*, 1, pages 43–59

People's Panel, The (1999), Issue 2: January, London: Service First Unit, Cabinet Office.

Pfeiffer, U (1999), Study of elderly housing choices, Bonn: Empirica

Phillips, E M (1999), *Growing old gracefully*, London: William Sutton Trust

Pitt, J (1999), *Conversions could provide the answer*, Forward Planning Unit, Hertfordshire County Council

Plunz, R (1990), *A history of housing in New York City: dwelling type and social change in the American metropolis*, New York: Columbia University Press

Power, A, and Bergin, E (1999), *Neighbourhood management*, CASEpaper 31, London: LSE

Power, A, and Mumford, K (1999), *The slow death of great cities? Urban abandonment or urban renaissance*, York: Joseph Rowntree Foundation

Power, A, and Tunstall, R (1995), *Swimming against the tide: polarisation or progress on 20 unpopular council estates 1980–1995*, York: Joseph Rowntree Foundation

Power, A, and Tunstall, R (1997), *Dangerous disorder: riots and violent disturbances on 13 areas of Britain 1991–92*, York: Joseph Rowntree Foundation

Power, A, and Wilson, WJ (2000), *Social exclusion and the future of cities*, CASEpaper 35, London: CASE

Power, A (1974), *David and Goliath*, London: Shelter

Power, A (1987), *Property before people: the management of twentieth-century council housing*, London: Allen and Unwin

Power, A (1992), *Empowering residents*, London: LSE

Power, A (1993), *Hovels to high rise: state housing in Europe since 1850*, London: Routledge

Power, A (1995), *Trafford Hall: a brief history of the National Tenants Resource Centre 1987–1995*, Chester: Trafford Hall

Power, A (1996), *Perspectives on Europe: unpopular estates in Europe and what can we learn from Europe?* London: Housing Corporation

Power, A (1999), *Estates on the edge: the social consequences of mass housing in Northern Europe*, London: Macmillan

Power, A (2000), 'Social exclusion', *RSA Journal*, no 5493, 2/4, pages 46–51

Pratty, J (2000), 'Cardboard cities', in *Hotline London*, Spring, Virgin Trains

Prescott, J (1998), 'The Green Belt is safe with us', *The Times* (28 January)

Priority Estates Project (1982; 1984), Reports to DoE and DoE Welsh Office (unpublished)

Priority Estates Project (2000), Caretaking Plus London: PEP

Putnam, R D (1993), *Making democracy work: civic traditions in modern Italy* (with Robert Leonardi and Raffaella Y Nanetti), Princeton NJ: Princeton University Press

Rabobank (1998), *Sustainability: choices and challenges for future development*, Leiden: Rabobank International

Railtrack (1999a), *Railtalk*, April

Railtrack (1999b), *Railtalk*, October

*Raoul, JC (1997), 'How high speed trains make tracks', *Scientific American*

Ratcliffe, P (2000), *Improving South Asian access to social rented housing in Bradford*, Bradford: Bradford City Council

Rayner, J. (1999), 'Our five challenges to the Mayor of London', *Observer* (24 October)

Richard Rogers Partnership (1998), Greenwich Peninsula Master Plan

RICS Research Foundation (1999), *2020: visions of the future*, London: RICS Research Foundation

Rogers, R (1997), *Cities for a small planet*, London: Faber and Faber

Rose, E J (1969), *Colour and citizenship: a report on British race relations*, London: Oxford University Press for the Institute of Race Relations

Rowe, P (1999), *Civic realism*, London: MIT Press

Royal Commission on Environmental Pollution (2000), *Energy: the changing climate, 22nd report*, London: Stationery Office

Royal Town Planning Institute (1999), Report to the Urban Task Force

Rudlin, D (1998a), Evidence presented to the Urban Task Force

Rudlin, D (1998b), *Tomorrow: a peaceful path to urban reform*, Friends of the Earth/URBED

Rudlin, D, and Falk, N (1999), *Building the 21st century home: the sustainable urban neighbourhood*, Oxford: Architectural Press

Sassen, S (1994), *Cities in a world economy*, California: Pine Forge Press

Satterthwaite, D (ed) (1999), *The Earthscan reader in sustainable cities*, London: Earthscan

Saunders, P (1990), *Owner occupation*, London: Unwin Hyman

Savills, FPD Savills International Property Consultants (1998), *Land use in cities*. Summer edition.

SEEDA (1999), *Building a world class region: an economic strategy for the South East of England*, Guildford: South East England Development Agency

SERPLAN (1999), Regional Planning Guidance for the South East: Report of the Public Examination Panel, draft SERPLAN response (conference, 18 November)

Shiva, V (2000), *Reith Lectures: Respect for the earth*, Lecture 5: Poverty and globalisation, BBC Radio 4.

Simmons, M (2000), *Housing capacity in Greater London*, paper presented at Housing in London conference (27 January)

Smart Growth Library (1999), 'Clinton-Gore livability agenda: building livable communities for the 21st century', press release (8 September)

Social Exclusion Unit (1998a), *Bringing Britain together: a national strategy for neighbourhood renewal*, London: Stationery Office

Social Exclusion Unit (1998b), *Truancy and school exclusion*, London: Stationery Office

Social Exclusion Unit (1999), *Bridging the gap: new opportunities for 16–18 year olds not in education, employment or training*, London: Stationery Office

Social Exclusion Unit (2000a), *National Strategy for Neighbourhood Renewal: Policy Action Team report summaries – a compendium*, London: SEU

Social Exclusion Unit (2000b), *National Strategy for Neighbourhood Renewal: a framework for consultation*, London: Cabinet Office

Sparkes, J (1999), *Schools, education and social exclusion*, CASEpaper 29, London: CASE

Strasbourg, City of (1999), *Trams*, Strasbourg: Mayor's Office

Summers, A, Cheshire, P, and Senn, L (1999), *Urban change in the United States and Western Europe: comparative analysis and policy*, Washington DC: Urban Institute Press

SUSTRANS (2000), *National Cycle Network*, Bristol: SUSTRANS

Swenarton, M (1981), *Homes fit for heroes: the politics and architecture of early state housing in Britain*, London: Heinemann Educational

Taplin, M (1999), *The history of tramways and evolution of light rail*, http://www.lrta.org/mrthistory.html

Teitz, M (1999), 'Urban sprawl: the debate continues', *Inside America*, November

Thomson, D (2000), interview in *Housing*, June

Thomson, F M L (1990), *Cambridge social history of Britain 1750–1950*, Cambridge: Cambridge University Press

Times Atlas of the World (1997), London: HarperCollins

Town and Country Planning (1999), *Town and Country Planning*, vol 68, no 8/9

Travers, T (1998), 'High hopes', *Guardian* (17 June)

Turok, I, and Edge, N (1999), *The jobs gap in Britain's cities: employment loss and labour market consequences*, Bristol: Policy Press

UCAS (1999), Annual Statistical Tables:1998 Entry, Cheltenham: UCAS

UN (1997), Kyoto Protocol to the United Nations Framework Convention on Climate Change (December 11)

UNCHS (1996), *An urbanising world: global report on human settlements*, Oxford: Oxford University Press

UNEP (2000), *Global environment outlook*, London: Earthscan

Urban Splash (1998a), *Lofts: the hard sell*, Smithfield Buildings, Manchester: Urban Splash

Urban Splash (1998b), *No two lofts are the same*, Manchester: Urban Splash

Urban Task Force (1998), Working Group One: Urban attitudes

Urban Task Force (1999a), *Towards an urban renaissance*, executive summary, London: DETR

Urban Task Force (1999b), *Towards an urban renaissance: final report of the Urban Task Force*, London: Stationery Office

Urban Task Force (2000), *Paying for an urban renaissance: The Urban Task Force's submission to the Government's Spending Review*, London: Stationery Office

Urbanisme (1999), 'Le XXe siècle: de la ville a l'urbain – chronique urbanistique et architecturale de 1900', B, 1999

*Virgin Trains (2000), 'Frontline', in *Hotline*, London: Virgin Trains

Walker, J (1999), 'Green walks', *Rambling Today*, Summer, London: Rambler's Association

Walker, L (2000), Evidence presented to the UTF on land reclaimation

Walters, J (2000), 'Safety casts a shadow over rail summit', *Observer* (21 May)

Watanabe, N (2000), *Why Japanese housing does not last*, thesis for MSc Housing (International), London School of Economics

Weaver, M (2000), 'Island wins right to cut VAT on repairs', *Housing Today* (30 March)

Webster, D (1999a), *Employability and jobs: IS there a jobs gap?* Memorandum of evidence submitted to the House of Commons Employment Sub-Committee (October 11)

Webster, D (1999b), 'Targeted local jobs', *New Economy*, vol 6, issue 4, December

Webster, D (1999c), *Unemployment convergence in 1990s Britain: how real?*, forthcoming in Employment Audit (EPI)

Webster, D (1999d), *Corrected ONS unemployment rates for July 1999, unemployment change 1998–1999 and employment change 1997–1998*, Glasgow City Housing (October 5)

Weinstock, M, and Woodgate, S (ed) (2000), *Living in the city*, London: The Architecture Foundation

Wenban-Smith (1999), *Plan, monitor and manage: making it work*, London: CPRE

Wighton, D, and Tucker, E (1999), 'Brussels ruling may hit land regeneration scheme', *Financial Times* (7 October)

Wilcox, S (1999), *Housing finance review*, York: Joseph Rowntree Foundation

Willmot, P (ed) (1994), *Urban trends 2: a decade in Britain's deprived urban areas*, London: Policy Studies Institute

Wilson, WJ (1987), *The truly disadvantaged: the inner city, the underclass, and public policy*, Chicago: University of Chicago Press

Wilson, WJ (1997), *When work disappears: the world of the new urban poor*, New York: Alfred A Knopf

World Bank (2000), *Entering the 21st century: world developments report 1999–2000*, New York: Oxford University Press

Worpole, K (1999), *The value of architecture*, London: RIBA

Wright, P (1992), *A journey through ruins*, London: Flamingo

Zogolovitch, R (1998), Urban Task Force, Working Group One: The density issue (October 23)

Index

Biographies

Richard Rogers

Richard Rogers was born in Florence, Italy in 1933 and studied architecture at the Architectural Association, London and Yale University. One of the foremost living architects, he is best known for such pioneering buildings as the Centre Georges Pompidou, Paris; Lloyds of London; the European Court of Human Rights in Strasbourg; and the Millennium Dome, as well as for large-scale master planning projects such as the Thames Strategy, London; Piana di Castello, Florence; Parc BIT Mallorca; and Shanghai's business district.

A previous Chair of the Tate trustees and Vice-Chair of the Arts Council of England, he is currently Chair of the National Tenants Resource Centre and the Architecture Foundation, London. He is also a member of the United Nations World Commission on 21st Century Urbanisation and of the Urban Strategies Advisory Council in Barcelona. In 1995 he gave the prestigious BBC Reith Lectures, 'Cities For a Small Planet'. In 1998 he was appointed by the Deputy Prime Minister to chair the Governmentís Urban Task Force for the revitalisation of English cities and towns. Most recently he was appointed City Architect by the Mayor of London.

In 1985 he received the RIBA Gold Medal, in 1999 the Thomas Jefferson Memorial Foundation Medal and in 2000 he was awarded the Praemium Imperiale Prize for Architecture.

Richard Rogers was awarded the Legion d'honneur in 1986, he was knighted in 1991 and made a life peer in 1996.

Professor Anne Power

Anne Power is Professor of Social Policy at the London School of Economics. Since 1965 she has been involved in European and American housing and urban problems. In 1966 she worked with Martin Luther King's 'End Slums' campaign in Chicago, and on her return to Britain organised community-based projects in Islington. From 1979 to 1989 she helped set up the Priority Estates Project and helped local authorities in England and

Wales to rescue run-down estates. In 1991 she became founding Director of the National Tenants Resource Centre at Trafford Hall in Chester, which provides residential training for people living and working in low-income communities. She was awarded a CBE in June 2000 for services to regeneration and promotion of resident participation.

Anne Power is a member of the Urban Task Force and the Government's Housing Sounding Board. She is the author of *Estates on the Edge* (1999); *The Slow Death of Great Cities?* (1999), with Katharine Mumford; *Dangerous Disorder* (1997) and *Swimming against the Tide* (1995), with Rebecca Tunstall; *Hovels to High Rise* (1993); and *Property Before People* (1987).